Lyotard and Critical Practice

Also Available from Bloomsbury

Jean-Francois Lyotard: The Interviews and Debates, Jean-Francois Lyotard, ed. Kiff Bamford

Traversals of Affect: On Jean-François Lyotard, ed. Julie Gaillard, Claire Nouvet, and Mark Stoholski

Lyotard and the 'figural' in Performance, Art and Writing, Kiff Bamford

Whale Song, Margret Grebowicz

Lyotard and Critical Practice

Edited by Kiff Bamford and Margret Grebowicz

BLOOMSBURY ACADEMIC
Bloomsbury Publishing Plc
50 Bedford Square, London, WC1B 3DP, UK
1385 Broadway, New York, NY 10018, USA
29 Earlsfort Terrace, Dublin 2, Ireland

BLOOMSBURY, BLOOMSBURY ACADEMIC and the Diana logo are trademarks of
Bloomsbury Publishing Plc

First published in Great Britain 2023
This paperback edition published 2024

Copyright © Kiff Bamford, Margret Grebowicz, and Contributors, 2023

Kiff Bamford and Margret Grebowicz have asserted their right under the Copyright,
Designs and Patents Act, 1988, to be identified as Editors of this work.

For legal purposes the Acknowledgements on p. vii constitute an extension of this
copyright page.

Cover design by Ben Anslow
Cover image: Harold Offeh "Covers: After the Rolling Stones,
Exile on Main Street, 1972" 2013 (© Harold Offeh)

All rights reserved. No part of this publication may be reproduced or transmitted
in any form or by any means, electronic or mechanical, including photocopying,
recording, or any information storage or retrieval system, without prior permission
in writing from the publishers.

Bloomsbury Publishing Plc does not have any control over, or responsibility for,
any third-party websites referred to or in this book. All internet addresses given in
this book were correct at the time of going to press. The author and publisher regret
any inconvenience caused if addresses have changed or sites have ceased to exist,
but can accept no responsibility for any such changes.

A catalogue record for this book is available from the British Library.

A catalog record for this book is available from the Library of Congress.

ISBN: HB: 978-1-3501-9202-7
PB: 978-1-3502-0190-3
ePDF: 978-1-3501-9203-4
eBook: 978-1-3501-9204-1

Typeset by RefineCatch Limited, Bungay, Suffolk

To find out more about our authors and books visit www.bloomsbury.com
and sign up for our newsletters.

Contents

List of Figures vii
Acknowledgments viii

    Introduction   *Kiff Bamford and Margret Grebowicz* 1

Part 1 What Resists Thinking

1 Listening to the Mute Voices of Words: Errant Pedagogy in the Zone
    Derek R. Ford 15
2 Animal Testimony: Cetaceans Between the Interspecies and the
    Inhuman *Margret Grebowicz and Marina Zurkow* 27
3 Under Threat: Rights and the "Thing" *Claire Nouvet* 39
4 A Matter of Time: Color, Affect, and the Suffering of Thought
    Georges Van Den Abbeele 51

Lyotard Supplement I

5 The Affect-phrase (from a Supplement to *The Differend*)
    Jean-François Lyotard, translated by Keith Crome 67
6 The Other's Rights *Jean-François Lyotard, translated by Chris Miller
    and Robert Smith* 75

Part 2 Long Views and Distances

7 Citing and Siting the Postmodern: Lyotard and the Black Atlantic
    John E. Drabinski 85
8 Jean-François Lyotard's Marxism, in *Socialisme ou Barbarie* and the
    Algerian War *Claire Pagès* 99
9 Lyotard and the Inhuman Mode of Production *Bartosz Kuźniarz* 111
10 Lyotard, After Us *Yuk Hui* 125

Lyotard Supplement II

11 Apathy in Theory *Jean-François Lyotard, translated by Roger McKeon* 141
12 "What we cannot reach flying we must reach limping…" *Art Présent*: Interview with Jean-François Lyotard *Alain Pomarède, translated by Kiff Bamford and Roger McKeon* 151

Part 3 Why Art Practice?

13 Mute Communication: Drawing the Military-Industrial Complex
    Jill Gibbon 169
14 Critical Practice and Affirmative Aesthetics *Ashley Woodward* 177
15 "hang on tight and spit on me": Lyotard and Contemporary Art
    Stephen Zepke 191
16 Uncertain? For sure. Limping? Certainly: Limp Thoughts on
    Performance Practice *Kiff Bamford* 205
"Afterward": Lyotard's Prescience *Peter Gratton* 219

Bibliography 225
Notes on Contributors 231
Index 235

Figures

2.1 Marina Zurkow, *A Swarm is My Bonnet* (2018). Nylon banners, 84" x 42" each. Installation view, Cape Cod Modern House Trust. Image: Dylan Gauthier 27

2.2 Right whale callosity. Image: Iain Kerr Ocean Alliance 28

2.3 Image of Stumpy (#1004) from the North Atlantic Right Whale Catalog. Image: Anderson Cabot Center, New England Aquarium / rwcatalog.neaq.org 31

2.4 Marina Zurkow, *A Swarm is My Bonnet* (2018). Digital drawing. 32

2.5 Marina Zurkow, *A Swarm is My Bonnet* (2018). Digital drawing. 35

2.6 North Atlantic right whale breaching. Image: Anderson Cabot Center, New England Aquarium 36

2.7 Aerial photograph of a North Atlantic right whale. Image: Northeast Fisheries Science Center, taken under MMPA Permit #17355 36

4.1 Diagram showing temporal positions, adapted by the author from a sketch by Jean-François Lyotard, after Edmund Husserl. 53

13.1 Jill Gibbon, Eurosatory, Paris, 2018, ink on paper, 140 mm x 192 mm. 167

13.2 Jill Gibbon, DSEI, London, 2017, ink on paper, 140 mm x 192 mm. 167

13.3 Jill Gibbon, Milipol, Paris, 2019, ink on paper, 140 mm x 180 mm. 168

13.4 Jill Gibbon, DSEI, London, 2017, ink on paper, 140 mm x 180 mm. 168

13.5 Jill Gibbon, Eurosatory, Paris, 2018, ink on paper, 140 mm x 192 mm 175

13.6 Jill Gibbon, Eurosatory, Paris, 2018, ink on paper, 140 mm x 180 mm 175

13.7 Jill Gibbon, Milipol, Paris, 2019, ink on paper, 140 mm x 180 mm. 176

13.8 Jill Gibbon, Milipol, Paris, 2019, ink on paper, 140 mm x 180 mm. 176

Acknowledgments

The editors would like to extend thanks to the following:
Dolorès Lyotard for permission to include the interview from *Art Présent* and her support of the project.

Roger McKeon for his offer of the "Apathy in Theory" translation and generous contributions to the translation of the *Art Présent* interview.

Johannes Türk and Estela Vieira of the the Center for Theoretical Inquiry in the Humanities at Indiana University, whose symposium on Lyotard's *The Differend* brought Kiff Bamford, Margret Grebowicz, and Claire Nouvet together, igniting further collaboration.

All the contributors for their generous response to invitations, requests, and queries.

Leeds School of Arts at Leeds Beckett University, for covering permissions costs.

Center for Philosophical Technologies, Arizona State University, where Margret Grebowicz was a visiting scholar in 2020–1, while working on this book.

For permission to include citations as epigraphs: University of Minnesota Press, Stanford University Press, Polity Books, Semiotext(e), Éditions Galilée, Éditions Klincksieck, Amnesty International.

Liza Thompson and Lucy Russell at Bloomsbury, and the contributions of the anonymous reviewers.

Introduction

Kiff Bamford and Margret Grebowicz

A New York sideshow photographed in the 1930s. The mouth stuffed, the speech muted. Chosen for, but later lost in the collaged cover of The Rolling Stones' *Exile on Main Street*.[1] Presented anew by the artist Harold Offeh through live performance and still photography: the mouth stuffed but speaking this time, excavating the buried image, confronting its historical silencing, and thus the structures of silencing in general.

This is a critical practice, one that asks questions and demands a response. In the live version the artist inserts large gobstoppers into his mouth in visual acknowledgment of "Three Ball Charlie," forcing their—his and Charlie's—mouths to mimic an exaggerated smile. Offeh then stands there, for the duration of a track from that album *Exile on Main Street*, played as the sugar in the spheres of candy dissolves into sticky saliva and dribbles from the aperture, the site of speech. Silenced into a smile. The silence speaking volumes.

For better or for worse, Lyotard remains tied to *The Postmodern Condition*, especially within an anglophone context. The postmodern condition he analyzed in the post-industrial societies of the later twentieth century remains the context for many of the crises which face the twenty-first: a distrust of all-embracing systems—the "metanarratives" which have become his catchphrase—whilst accepting the dominance of consumer capitalism, free market economics and a global trade based on exploitation and expansion. But the postmodern condition is not singular, and the contributions to this volume are proof of that. And whilst the expansion of global capital appears simply to roll out a monoculture, its flex and adaptability are proven. Arms sales to Saudi Arabia, or how about a football club?[2]

Lyotard did not accept the limitations of the discipline of philosophy. He avoided the arid genres produced by academic specialization and collaborated across disciplines long before it was fashionable. He courted confrontation. Questions of technology, politics, ethics, and communication were among the arenas in which he participated because of their contemporary urgency. His writings repeatedly ask us to listen, to think again about that we believe we already know. Sometimes he mercilessly mocks our failed attempts at critique: your objections are only heard within the sphere of the recipients' desired frame of reference, their genre of discourse. The critique is never really heard at all. This is why we need critical practices.

It was his attention to the crises in the humanities, politics, and the arts, which began decades before academics made them their explicit focus, that pushed Lyotard to explore the relationship between critique and creativity. In 1983 Lyotard was asked to help in the planning of an exhibition at the Centre Georges Pompidou, Paris. The title of the exhibition was to be *Nouveau Matériaux et Création* (New Materials and Creativity). This presented some difficulties for him: in an interview, he recalls, "I said to myself, 'Creativity? What is that supposed to mean?' And again, 'What is "new" supposed to mean?'"[3]

The resulting exhibition—described as a dramaturgy, a work of art—adopted a neologism as its title: *Les Immatériaux* (The Immaterials or non-materials). Drawing on art, science, and technology, it filled the whole fifth floor of the Pompidou for sixteen weeks in 1985, bewildering many as it created a "feeling of incertitude."[4]

The present collection encountered obstacles in its planning that echoed Lyotard's *what is "new" supposed to mean?* It was initially titled *A New Lyotard: Thinking in Crisis*, but the inherent proposition that it was obvious what would constitute "new" in relation to Lyotard was rightly questioned by the anonymous reviewers. At the same time, Lyotard's question resonated with us and the reviewers indicated its prescience: it was a question for "our times." Thus, we aim to retain the spirit and ambition of this troubled original title and the problems it poses. And whilst not everything within these pages will be unfamiliar or new to all readers, we have collected fresh looks at what we presume to know of Lyotard's work. All of this is grounded in the larger goal of exploring and articulating the capacity of his thinking to meaningfully address current global concerns and crises.

Lyotard himself was the last person to think the world needed another book about Lyotard. This is why our goal here has been to develop an idea inspired by his work, but specific to our times and our common project: the idea of critical practice. Some of the chapters here elucidate the aspects of Lyotard's thinking that continue to provoke us—the Thing, the intractable, the inhuman, infancy, debt—to position them in relation to themes that are emerging as ever-more central to contemporary thinking and life: sexuality, animals, militarism, economic growth. Others actually attempt to *perform* critical practice, to present new possibilities for what counts as critique. And all of it is couched in what is perhaps the most important aspect of Lyotard's diagnosis above: its assault on the presumptions that carry with them a sense of superiority over, and wilful ignorance about, the so-called "developing world"—now sometimes the "Global South"—on which what in Lyotard's day was called "the West" still relies and feasts. What are critical practices that can undermine this self-styled position of cultural dominance?

Our response is not fueled by a desire to "export" Lyotard scholarship geographically and culturally. As John E. Drabinski writes in his chapter, for example, the Afro-Caribbean cultural legacy does not need Lyotard's lexicon to voice its concerns: "It is an intellectual tradition comprised of its own vocabulary and conceptual innovations, so needs no such enhancement or elevation."[5] No more did those living in Colombia need a foreign philosopher to "think through the drama of your country," as Lyotard wrote to Amparo Vega in 1997 amidst the ongoing social and political turmoil: "You diagnose an extreme case tearing civil society apart, so violent that the differends themselves [*les différends même*] are stifled."⁶ But "the West," in contrast, does need to be made aware of that which it has forgotten and continues to forget in its ongoing commitment to logics of cultural and economic imperialism.

We decided to take on this task by exploring the potential of the "feeling of incertitude" in which Lyotard so ardently believed. Who is "speaking," where they are doing it, to whom they are addressing it, and how this is undertaken will determine the extent to which a certain newness—and indeed this "incertitude"—presents itself. Our explicit intention is to breach the silos of academic specialization in a manner that takes its cue from *Les Immatériaux*, whose reach went beyond the usual confines and expectations of either a grand expo, art exhibition, or show of industrial design, and whose potential as an approach, we believe, has yet to be fully explored. The exhibition works well as a cipher for what is both overlooked and prescient in Lyotard's work in general. It is a unique and powerful example of a philosopher refusing to be restricted by the conventional confines of philosophy as a discipline, acknowledging rather the opportunities that emerge from collaboration with specialists in diverse fields, and by experimenting with other media and forms of experience and presenting such experimentation as the motor of philosophical inquiry and "production." The experimental soundtrack that accompanied the visitor to the exhibition compiled sounds, music, philosophy, literature, and poetry as an intrinsic part of the visitor's experience, but one over which they had no simple control. Unseen signals altered the tracks played depending on the position of the visitor's body in space.

The exhibition itself is slowly gaining recognition as a landmark event in the history of exhibitions, but the multifarious forms of its reach seem even more appropriate to today's philosophical landscape. This signals a shift from philosophy as traditionally understood to what we are calling "critical practice"—an important but often overlooked aspect of Lyotard's thought and one we have tried our best to animate, perform, and trouble here, insofar as that is possible in a modest book.

Having—perhaps—avoided the potential pitfalls of "the new," the title on which we have settled, *Lyotard and Critical Practice,* invites further comment: *what is "critical" supposed to mean?* As several of the contributors make clear, this is not only "critical" in the sense of critique, but critical as urgent: a tipping point where change is about to occur. It is also a reminder of the pressing nature of the many issues engaged with here and the demand for critical practices. In his drift from Marx in the 1970s, Lyotard laughed at critique, seeing it as ineffectively enmeshed within the unchanging discourses of the system. As Stephen Zepke reminds us, Lyotard urged us to "laugh at critique" as itself "deeply rational, deeply consistent with the system. Deeply reformist: the critic remains in the sphere of the criticized, he belongs to it, he goes beyond one term of the position but doesn't alter the position of terms." Lyotard turned instead to the critical function of the *work* of art.⁷ It is, then, with the lightness and laughter of critical practice that this collection seeks to continue to trouble critique or criticism.

One related challenge is to figure out what counts as critique anymore, given Lyotard's (1993) assessment that "The ideals of Western civilization issuing from the ancient, Christian, and modern traditions are bankrupt ... It makes itself the world's museum. It thereby ceases to be a civilization. It becomes a culture."⁸ For Lyotard, this is a dead culture obsessed with its own aestheticization, and his diagnosis is an intentional affront to the Eurocentric assumptions from which many continue to think, practice, and practice critique. What happens to critique, as Europe becomes a taxidermied version of itself, on ever-more calcified display in the halls of the university?

The affective aspects of uncertainty have animated much of Lyotard's work since his decisive political awakening in Algeria. The current critical landscape has just recently become equipped to deal with them, however. The bankruptcy of Western civilization quoted above from the "Crypts" section of Lyotard's *Postmodern Fables* evokes echoes of Sigmund Freud's *Civilization and its Discontents*, written under the shadow of both the First World War and the rise of European fascism in the late 1920s. Whilst aspects of Freud's evaluation are implicit in Lyotard's undermining of the West's cultural assumptions, it is perhaps the prevalence of feeling that draws Lyotard's attention to Freud's most speculative writing. This is most clearly apparent in the many references made to *Beyond the Pleasure Principle*, the later sections of which provoke Lyotard's own speculations in the essay "Apathy in Theory," included here in English translation for the first time. Lyotard is concerned with the hesitancy with which Freud proceeds: mid-section, Freud writes of the need for a "breaking off," displaying a lack of certainty about the paths down which he is to venture. Yet Freud continued to write. And so of course did Lyotard.

This collection has one shared entry point into the affective aspects of uncertainty: the forgotten "Thing." It runs through Claire Nouvet's chapter, wherein psychoanalytic concerns emerge not only from Lyotard's reading of Freud and Jacques Lacan but also from the infancy of the other's voice, that which is not given voice but remains. The Thing haunts the supposedly voiceless animals in Margret Grebowicz and Marina Zurkow's discussion of the right whale, whose very nomination ironically articulates its fate at the hands of human hunters, in its "rightness" as prey. Today the species is rendered "right" to survey through the whales' distinctive callosities. These markings are made visually present by the cyamids they host on their bodies, which in turn act as indicators of environmental damage, interpreted by humans via satellite imagery. Hidden forms of communication—mute, in the terms of Lyotard's "affect-phrase"—are the signs picked up through the act of drawing as reportage by Jill Gibbon. Drawing undercover in the largest arms fair in the world, where the West sells its technologies of annihilation and repression through an aesthetics of awe, the body is left to speak its unease: responding to the Thing it witnesses.

The Thing, the intractable, the inhuman, infancy, debt—these are all attempts to name that which drives the affect of uncertainty. In Claire Pagès's account of Lyotard's involvement with the militant group Socialisme ou Barbarie, it is his shifting attitude and approach to Marx which reveals an ebbing away of an initial conviction. Writing about his experience of Algeria in the early 1950s, Lyotard identifies not only the radical injustices that motivated a militant political awakening, but also the intractable differend between the aims and desires of the parties involved in the struggle for independence he chronicled and the mire of postcoloniality. The belief that one struggle, such as national liberation, would lead "to a process of total liberation"[9] was where he felt Frantz Fanon and many others were mistaken. The unexpected emergence, or reemergence, of the intractable Thing destabilizes even liberatory political plans, as Van Den Abbeele writes in his contribution—pointing to the popular Algerian uprising in 1960-1 and its quick suppression through a veneer of liberation. The complex mess of interwoven, long-standing multiple injustices might temporarily coalesce under the metanarrative of promised emancipation, but its superficial unity cannot cover over the unpayable debt which refuses the ordered temporality of articulable phrases.

In the four texts by Lyotard included here, these themes of uncertainty, infancy, the inarticulate "affect-phrase" surface and resurface in differing ways. In "Apathy in Theory" we see Lyotard's careful negotiation with Freud's thinking: he attends to the hesitancy within the development of the thinking itself, to a Freud challenged by that which he has not been prepared to think. In the interview with *Art Présent* the implications of experimental cinematic practice are discussed, in relation to undermining both conventions of time and the "conviction" that dogs conformist thinking. More than a decade later, "The Other's Rights" and "The Affect-phrase" introduce the important conception of infancy into these discussions, infancy as that which is not given the capacity to speak but makes itself felt in an untimely manner. The intensity of these writings belies their svelteness. They are prime examples of Lyotard's thinking as a practice which does not accept the dominance of "the system" as inevitable, which seeks to listen for the inarticulate thing.

Critical practices irritate the established program from the perspective of what Lyotard recognized as "the same force of lightness obtaining in works of painting, music, 'experimental' cinema, as well, obviously, as in those of the sciences."[10] Such lightness resists the dominance of the system, the "publish or perish" mentality which presides over oceans of sameness. It is the apathy to which Lyotard pays—and directs—attention, in the speculative theories of Freud, in the works of Marcel Duchamp and in unexpected narrative forms, when they refuse to bow to the conviction of the already made and the politics of unquestioned conviction. At their core, if critical practices may be said to have anything in common, it is the desire to seek out this lightness and listen for that which is forgotten in the clamor for certainty. And uncertainty is not the end of the story of thinking, but its beginning. What does this mean in a world in which action and other kinds of responses are so urgent (critical)?

What resists thinking

This collection came into being under the shadow of the global pandemic which began in 2019 and shaped our lives from that point forward. The consequences of this event for education excite Derek Ford's opening remark in the first chapter: in spite of so many superficial, procedural changes, what is alarming is the absence of actual change in pedagogy. This failure to reimagine the university is evidence of a constipated or bankrupt system. Nothing is taught except for that which is already known, even in a time of multiple crises, even in one that purported to "change everything." Ford's response urges an ungrasping exploration of the zone, following the metaphor taken by Lyotard from urban studies. The zone is where the dominance of the megalopolis is resisted, a wayward place where communicability is challenged by the untameable secrets of infancy. In highlighting the themes of listening and voice for contemporary pedagogy, Ford sets the tone of this section about thinking: where there is resistance, there is attraction.

In their commentary on the North Atlantic right whale, Grebowicz and Zurkow take up incertitude and attraction as well. Their collaboration proposes rapport and "the interesting" as central ethical categories, mapping Lyotard's potential to respond to the catastrophe that is current interspecies relations. But the catastrophe itself emerges as an interlocutor, challenging the limitations of Lyotard's revolutionary acknowledgment of the rights of all speaking creatures. This chapter invites a revisiting of listening and voice in the current interspecies critical landscape, focusing on "the animality of the speaking creature, the one to whom rights are owed." This is followed by Nouvet's careful tracings of the Thing, its unwelcome presence in a world tuned to the maximization of performativity for profit without care for that which drains away as a consequence. *Can art exist in such a culture?* she asks, establishing a theme to which many of the contributors respond. She also opens a consideration of incertitude as a mode of the sexual, as a major animating feature of Lyotard's relationship to psychoanalysis. In asking who has the "right to speak," Nouvet draws on a central concern of the two Lyotard texts which follow this section: "The Other's Rights" and "The Affect-phrase."

"The Other's Rights" was first presented as an Amnesty International lecture in 1993; as Nouvet reminds us, amnesty derives from forgetfulness, an etymology with which Lyotard is particularly concerned. The importance of "working through" such forgetting in a process of anamnesis involves an approach to temporality that disrupts the chronological and refuses the archival as the simple scraping away of layers. We might recall the famous image of Rome's historical fragments coexisting within one space as a figure of the unconscious's disregard for chronologically separated instances of time, as illustrated by Freud in *Civilization and its Discontents*. It evokes a psychological resistance to linear temporality, which is the focus of Georges Van Den Abbeele's chapter, completing Part 1 "What resists thinking." Layers are laid down but never fully hidden; the uppermost surface awaits its disturbance.

Van Den Abbeele is one of Lyotard's most important translators into English. It was his translation of *The Differend* that fueled a certain revival for Lyotard among anglophone philosophers towards the end of the last century. Van Den Abbeele's chapter lays out Lyotard's response to the painting practice of Albert Ayme written in 1980, during the years of *The Differend*'s long gestation. It is an essay about time, and the underexplored role of time in Lyotard's thought. The layers of semi-transparent paint laid down by Ayme do not exist except in a parachronic temporality, resisting separation; even on the reverse of the canvas, all that bleeds through is that "which Ayme felicitously calls its 'memories.'" Ayme's discontinuity of time contrasts with the need to gain time as observed in *The Postmodern Condition* and later made manifest in *The Inhuman* as the inhuman aspect of the system. Van Den Abbeele's chapter begins to plot the implications of such a deconstitution of time in the "*passage* from the aesthetic to the political."

Lyotard supplement I

There are four short pieces by Lyotard included in this collection, presented as two "supplements" between the different parts. As supplements, they are aside from yet central to the whole, but they also play on the subtitle of "The Affect-phrase (from a Supplement to *The Differend*)," which refers to Lyotard's intention to write a supplement to *The Differend*, the extant elements of which are collected in the posthumous collection *Misère de la philosophie*.[11]

Supplement I reprints both "The Affect-phrase" and "The Other's Rights," from 1990 and 1993 respectively. The former began its life as a spoken presentation under the title "*L'Inarticulé, ou le différend même*,"[12] judiciously echoing the odd, one might say "errantly written" title of Duchamp's *Large Glass* (*La mariée mise à nu par ses célibataires, même*) and allowing both "the differend even" and "the differend itself" as implied meanings, or as Geoffrey Bennington has commented "the being-differend of the differend."[13] The essay is a provocative reconsideration of a key element from *The Differend*, taking the question "Is feeling a phrase?" as a point of departure. In alerting us to the presence of that which cannot articulate itself but only signal its presence, the affect-phrase is prone to be wronged by attempts to articulate it, yet demands not to be forgotten.[14]

"The Other's Rights" is about the political implications of the seemingly paradoxical concern for that which cannot be articulated. It makes them clear within the framework of the organization that hosted its presentation in Oxford, UK. The two essays share several themes, including references to the Aristotelian distinction between articulated speech and inarticulated voice, the silencing of the latter by the former but also the other rendered silent by virtue of its strangeness. The right to speak is presented here also as the "right to speak only if the speech can say something other than the *déjà dit* (what has already been said)." Our hope is that the pairing of these two texts, together with their surrounding responses and commentary, is able to enact such a right.

Long views and distances

Part 2 suggests possibilities for considering aspects of Lyotard's thought in relation to other thinkers, traditions, and from different viewpoints, and in overt, deliberate retrospects—from various "here"s, as it were. As mentioned above Drabinski approaches from African American studies through a comparativist approach that highlights the possibilities offered by what he names the *afropostmodern*. He highlights themes common to Lyotard and the tradition provoked by Frantz Fanon to expose the profound decentering of imagination by the violence of the Middle Passage. The afropostmodern forces a reconsideration of the European postmodern and the "quiet, yet persistent racial metanarrative [that] sits in the definite article of the phrase 'the postmodern.'"

To describe Lyotard's own encounter with the colonial situation in Constantine in 1950s Algeria as a decentering might be accurate, especially if we emphasize the multiple temporalities with which the experience affected his thinking. As Lyotard reflected in 1989 in "The Name of Algeria": "I owed and I owe my awakening, *tout court*, to Constantine. The differend showed itself with such a sharpness that the consolations then common among my peers (vague reformism, pious Stalinism, futile leftism) were denied to me."[15] The dominant association of Lyotard with so-called post-structuralist thinkers leads to an ignorance of both his militant Marxist past as a member of the group Socialisme ou Barbarie and his writings on Algeria for the journal of the same name during the period of the struggle for independence. This is one of the reasons behind our desire to emphasize Lyotard's writings and critical engagement prior to *The Differend*, where the name of Algeria is figured.

Pagès has made extensive study of this period of Lyotard's practice as an activist. During Lyotard's life (1924–98) the war in Algeria was never officially recognized as such, euphemistically termed "internal operations to maintain order." Only in 1999 did the French state officially recognize the conflict as a war and whilst some officials have recognized the state's extensive use of torture, the issues of commemoration, reparations, and recognition still remain contentious today.[16] Pagès's archival research also foregrounds little-known work, such as the study of Islam and colonialism in North Africa which Lyotard embarked on in the mid-1950s but never completed, and the later reflections on Algeria which accompanied both the collection of his writings on the subject in 1989 and contributions in the context of contemporary events in 1995.

In a chapter that offers a "look back" at Lyotard's changing position on capitalism, from the "revolutionary" 1950s and 1960s, to the "ecstatic" 1970s, to the "inhuman" turn of the late 1980s, Bartosz Kuźniarz asks: Why was capitalism itself not explicitly considered a metanarrative at the time of *The Postmodern Condition*? He draws conclusions that Lyotard was reluctant to draw, arguing that the libidinal attachment to capitalism, diagnosed by Lyotard in his early works, is not incidental, but rather indicative of the fact that capitalism develops one of the authentic possibilities inherent in our existence. This leads Kuźniarz to articulate what he calls the dilemma of growth—a tragic conflict of two authentic human potentialities, whose resolution can never be innocent or definite in some absolute ethical sense; it can only be partial and therefore political.

The last chapter in this part continues to draw on some of Lyotard's thought-experiments from *The Inhuman* and the adulation of the techno-scientific which was then embryonic but is now commonplace. In a paper first written for the symposium "40 Years after *The Postmodern Condition*," which Yuk Hui organized at the China Academy of Art in Hangzhou, Hui revisits aspects of the postmodern as misunderstood or confused by the Chinese context whilst explaining its critical role in understanding the contemporary situation. He describes the importance of paralogy as key to resisting the system of totalization (including open systems) and promoting that which the system is unable to "grasp."

Lyotard supplement II

"Outrageously out of date"—this is Lyotard's delirious verdict of Louis Marin's book on Pascal's contribution to *Port-Royal Logic*, and it is cited by Van Den Abbeele. It may seem that this second supplement is similarly out of date: "Apathy in Theory" is from the 1977 collection *Rudiments païens* and the interview from *Art Présent* which follows is dated Autumn 1978. Yet it is not simply the excitement of presenting these pieces for the first time in English which directed their inclusion. Rather there is something almost uncanny in their being out-of-time.

As previously mentioned, "Apathy in Theory" describes the hesitancy of Freud's writing as that which struggles against the pervasive accepted conventions, knowledge, and approaches of the contemporary. It is a celebration of the willingness to listen to that which does not fit, or to listen for the paralogy, as Hui has described it. In *The Argonauts*, Maggie Nelson's reaction to Freud's wanderings (this time on the case known as the "Wolf Man") is set with the same astonishment as Lyotard's: "Such freely confessed swerves into the provisional are the pleasure of reading Freud; the problem comes when he succumbs—or we succumb—to the temptation to mastery rather than remind ourselves that we are at deep play in the makeshift."[17]

Further background notes to these two pieces are included in the makeshift that is the final chapter of Part 3, by Kiff Bamford. The *Art Présent* interview is one of many occasions where Lyotard performs a response to the question that motivates our final section: *why art practice?*

Why art practice?

In many ways, this whole collection may be conceived as a series of responses to this question, not only in this section and not only through art practice as narrowly defined, but through all critical practice, understood as responses to the inarticulate voices that discourse fails to hear.

Part 3 begins with the line of Gibbon's drawings as it seeks to reconnect the military hardware she encounters with the soft tissue of its ultimate victims. Ashley Woodward and Stephen Zepke continue to take the inarticulate as jumping-off points for their readings of Lyotard's affirmative aesthetics, and whilst they navigate similar currents at times—his work on Duchamp, Jacques Monory, and *Les Immatériaux*—we might say that they arrive at different shores.

On the one hand, Woodward acknowledges the divergence between contemporary artistic theory and practice and Lyotard's views. He acknowledges the different critical responses to Lyotard by Jacques Rancière and Bernard Stiegler, but puts these aside to construct an alternative image of Lyotard's focus on art. It is Lyotard's consideration of the effects of science and technology around which Woodward builds his argument for an affirmative transformation, one which opens up "not a simple negation or loss, but a new type of sensibility." This involves reconsidering Lyotard in contemporary contexts, beyond the world and politics he could have known.

On the other hand, Zepke borrows the title of his chapter from Lyotard's extreme ventures in *Libidinal Economy*—"hang on tight and spit on me"—in order to try to understand what the price of Lyotard's affirmative aesthetics might be in terms of contemporary art's ideas about itself. Zepke reflects that although he and Woodward share similar concerns, Woodward focuses on philosophical implications while Zepke chases after the more "passionate" moments "where aesthetics and politics collide." "It is the yin and yang of Lyotard perhaps ..."¹⁸ Zepke concludes, though perhaps without the implied harmony and balance.

In the final chapter, Kiff Bamford takes up the limping figure presented in both "Apathy in Theory" and the related interview with Alain Pomarède from *Art Présent*. Glossing the genealogy, context, and neglect of both texts, a hesitant figure acts as guide—the one who fails to fly through lack of conviction. Interspersed are several encounters with an uncertain "feeling" in contemporary art contexts, meshed with Freud's use of Arabic poetry, the sound play of artist Rana Hamadeh and, finally, a performance of Lyotard's last words on Augustine of Hippo.

The ground is uneven. Critical practices are those which immerse themselves in this unevenness in order to undermine the conviction and certainty masking the simple repetition of the same.

Notes

1. The album cover incorporates the 1958 photograph by Robert Frank, *Tattoo Parlor, 8th Avenue, New York City*, which shows a collection of photographs taped to a wall, likely in Hubert's Museum and Flea Circus, 42nd Street, New York.
2. An 80 per cent stake in the English Premier League football club Newcastle United was sold to a consortium led by Saudi Arabia's sovereign wealth fund in October 2021; most fans welcomed the injection of capital and ignored issues of human rights abuses, including the murder of United States-based Saudi journalist Jamal Khashoggi, in which the Saudi ruler and senior officials were incriminated.
3. Jean-François Lyotard, "Les Immatériaux: A Conversation" [1985], tr. unknown, in Kiff Bamford (ed.), *The Interviews and Debates* (London and New York: Bloomsbury, 2020), 77.
4. Ibid., 83.
5. John E. Drabinski in this volume, 85.
6. Jean-François Lyotard visited Colombia in March 1994 and 1995; the letter quoted is from December 1, 1997, held in the Doucet archive [JFL 529/15]. See also Amparo Vega, *Le premier Lyotard: philosophie critique et politique* (Paris: L'Harmattan, 2010).
7. Jean-François Lyotard, *Libidinal Economy*, tr. Iain Hamilton Grant (London and New York: Continuum, [1974] 1993), 94; Jean-François Lyotard, "Adrift" [1973], tr. Roger McKeon, in Roger McKeon (ed.), *Driftworks* (New York: Semiotext(e), 1984), 13. See also Jean-François Lyotard, "Notes on the Critical Function of the Work of Art" [1970], tr. Susan Hanson, in Roger McKeon (ed.), *Driftworks* (New York: Semiotext(e), 1984).
8. Jean-François Lyotard, "Anima Minima," *Postmodern Fables*, tr. Georges Van Den Abbeele (Minneapolis MN: University of Minnesota Press, [1993] 1997), 235–6.
9. Lyotard in Pagès in this volume, 108.
10. Lyotard, "Apathy in Theory," in this volume, 141.
11. See Dolorès Lyotard, "Avant-propos," in Jean-François Lyotard, *Misère de la philosophie* (Paris: Galilée, 2000), 9–11.
12. See Geoffrey Bennington, *Late Lyotard* (CreateSpace, 2005), 48. n. 47.
13. Ibid., 49.
14. See Julie Gaillard, Claire Nouvet and Mark Stoholski (eds), *Traversals of Affect: On Jean-François Lyotard* (London and New York: Bloomsbury, 2016).

15 Jean-François Lyotard "The Name of Algeria" [1989], in *Political Writings*, tr. Bill Readings with Kevin Paul Geiman (Minneapolis MN: University of Minnesota Press, 1993), 170.
16 See Raphaëlle Branche, *Papa, qu'as-tu fait en Algérie? – Enquête sur un silence familial* (Paris: La Découverte, 2020). In 2020 the French President commissioned a report by historian Benjamin Stora to address the memory of French colonialization, the Algerian war, and recommendations for reconciliation; the President of Algeria's appointee to the dialogue, Abdelmadjid Chikhi, regretted the lack of consultation on the resulting report.
17 Maggie Nelson, *The Argonauts* (London: Melville House, 2015), 85.
18 Stephen Zepke, personal communication with the editors, January 2021.

Part One

What Resists Thinking

1

Listening to the Mute Voices of Words: Errant Pedagogy in the Zone

Derek R. Ford

The COVID-19 pandemic hit some countries, including the United States, in the middle of the spring 2020 academic semester, forcing a phenomenal interruption in university life. Much has been written on the "shift" or "pivot" online that followed, and what it meant for students, professors, staff, administrators, parents and guardians, and the "future of the university." The empirical effects of the reorganization—the issues of labor and precarity, autonomy and economics that surfaced, the changes in the educational experience—felt sudden and radical. There were just days or, in the best cases, weeks to depopulate the university and figure out how to reorganize the semester, to retool and reskill faculty, change curricula and syllabi, acquire, implement, teach, and learn new software, develop different teaching strategies and methods, find new work and study spaces, make new arrangements between school, life, and work, study, care, and health. Yet what struck me most of all was the *absence of change*. The pandemic, I was told, was upending life as I knew it, and probably forever. But the biggest shock wasn't from an *interruption* but from a radical *continuity*. While the particulars were altered, the educational apparatus proceeded: classes, lectures, discussions, meetings, defenses, and reviews persevered, assignments submitted and graded, diplomas conferred. If the university was once seen as an ivory tower detached from society, the pandemic offered irrefutable proof that today it is not only part and parcel of society, but one of the social's most flexible, dynamic, and even paradigmatic institutions.

What accounts for the university's immediate subsumption of the interruption, and what the subsumption worked to rescue, was a distinct pedagogy, which doesn't refer to any individual way of practicing education, but the general modes of relating to the practice, the underlying logics and organizing ontologies of it. Any attempt to reimagine the university or education will necessarily fail without a pedagogical investigation, and any efforts at such a rethinking must entail pedagogical experimentation. In this chapter, I approach this problematic by writing about Lyotard's writings relating to space, literacy, and sound. The intention here (which isn't mine) is to encounter a suspension that can't be overcome, a pedagogical force that disseizes the mind and renders education subject to the (in)audible matter of words.

Grasping the zone

In his later works, Lyotard identified a new prevailing mode of urbanism that he termed the megalopolis, which has its origins in the city and the town–country relationship and resulted in part from the expansion of the city. This augmentation wasn't the domination of the city over the rest of the territory such that the outskirts and countryside became the city, but rather the incorporation of the territory into the megalopolis's expansive logic such that the city is no longer a unique coherent region. The megalopolis, that is, isn't a spatial form but a spatial process, an indeterminate zone that "does not have an exterior and an interior, being both one and the other together."[1] The expansive logic at work here is that of development and efficiency, a logic organized by the principle of exchange. This principle, which the megalopolis owes to the economic and political city, is what allows the megalopolis to consume the city, the suburbs, and the country, as all differences between and within each are rendered fungible. Just as important in this lineage is the zone, which denotes "a belt, neither country nor city, but another site, one not mentioned in the registry of places."[2] The zone, lodged between the city and its outside, was the sphere through which the principle spread, until there was only exchange. The megalopolis is an urban *process*, and the zone is the urban *form* and *style* the process generates. While the zone was once an unnamed yet distinct wayward and errant place as opposed to the named and ordered regime of the city, the operations of the megalopolis overcome the distinction through a kind of blurring that mobilizes the wayward and errant properties under the regime of development. If the zone was an indistinct place formerly, it was only because of its relationship to the city and the country.

One paper probes the contours of the megalopolis in relation to what it conquered: the *domus*, a form of domestic community or common, the household, under a monad of "space, time and body under the regime (of) nature."[3] There's a sense of belonging in which exclusions aren't necessary. Here, language, life, and association are rhythmical and progressive, meaning they are both developmental and repetitive. It's a rhythm of constant and spontaneous work at the service of nature. The child is one such form of rhythm, work, and the natural: "Within the domestic rhythm, it is the moment, the suspension of beginning again, the seed. It is what will have been. It is the surprise, the story starting over again. Speechless, *infans*, it will babble, speak, tell stories, will have told stories, will have stories told about it, will have had stories told about it."[4] Under the *domus*, the child is a fresh beginning that ensures continuity and repetition, that which maintains coherence through the possibility of beginning again. At the same time, and because of this, the child enacts the interruptions and excesses of the *domus*. There can be no domestic community without something to domesticate. The domestic rhythm, to put it differently, doesn't suture or heal interruptions, but "*scars* over" them.[5] Neither suppressed nor absorbed, unpredictable and unintelligible disruptions are simply a structural part of the natural realm under—and for—which humans produce their domiciles. Nature, impossible to subject to cognition, is fate.

Lyotard says he can only write about the *domus* from within the megalopolis, an urban form of community that's not based on a relation to nature but to exchange. There's no more memory, narrative, or rhythm, just databanks and algorithms. The megalopolis, in other words, is the geographic manifestation of what he terms "the system," which operates according to the logic of performativity where, driven by the demand to maximize the efficiency of inputs and outputs, "everyone seeks and will find as best s/he can the information needed to make a living, which makes no sense."[6] The megalopolis has replaced the order of the *domus*, has broken apart its rhythmic and spatial belonging to introduce a process of communication and commerce between individuals. In the place of an order dictated by the mystery of nature it installs a democratic and capitalist system based on reason, rationality, and exchange. The system prohibits mystery and interruption not through repression or exclusion, but through incorporation and development. Everything can and must be brought within its structure.

The spokespeople of the megalopolis tell us that this is progress and justice. By making everything transparent and communicable, by bringing the *domus* inside, after all, we can resolve all problems, address all wrongs, repair all divisions. Such inclusion, however, ultimately works to transform the untameable interruptions that pervaded the *domus*: "What domesticity regulated—savagery—it demanded. It had to have its off-stage within itself."[7] Whereas the *domus*, haunted by interruptions, accepts opacity *qua* opacity, the megalopolis consumes interruptions, rendering opacity as nothing more than an unrealized transparency. This consumption is fundamental to its development: "Secrets must be put into circuits, writings programmed, tragedies transcribed into bits of information ... The secret is capitalized swiftly and efficiently."[8] There is no service to mystery, no submission to interruptions that would compel us to construct a domicile. There is no need for shelter without the threat of the untameable, and the zone's internal spatial divisions are inessential, being merely rooms in a massive museum that can shift, collapse, or emerge as more objects accumulate. What is essential is "the multiplicity of competing figures," which provides the megalopolis with "an air of critique thanks to the comparison possible between 'good objects.'"[9]

Here we can approach the pedagogical apparatus that accompanies and facilitates the spread of the megalopolis. To compare is to subject different objects to a common measure, and is predicated upon according or giving a form to something. In according a form, something is placed under an existing category or concept, while in giving a form, a new category or concept is created. Both "forms and concepts are constitutive of objects, they produce data that can be grasped by sensibility and that are intelligible to the understanding."[10] This pedagogy of *grasping* is the motor of the megalopolis, which positions everything as a potential object to be known and exchanged. Under the *domus*, the child is both a child and a future adult, a something and a someone. Simultaneously an interruption into and a legitimation of continuity, the *domus* serves the child. In the megalopolis, the child is merely a deficient adult, one that doesn't need to be tamed but needs to be developed by grasping, through which the child learns how to grasp as it itself is grasped. The child or the student is not some*thing* that *will* speak (as in the *domus*), but some*one* that *can* and *must* speak.

The educational methods and contents—the information, knowledge, politics, habits, or beliefs they represent—are (largely) irrelevant. While specific instances of grasping are guided by specific ends, grasping itself is a never-ending process, a constant development that never stops for the individuals of the megalopolis as we expand the museum. In the university of the megalopolis, then, it is less significant *what* one grasps and more important that one learn *how* to grasp. This accounts for the refrain of administrators, admissions counselors, and public relations officers: we are preparing students not just for jobs that don't yet exist, but for an entire world that doesn't yet exist. By "world," they mean the specific internal configuration of the museum, which doesn't yet exist because it is the object of endless development, an end in itself, an end without any end.

The flexibility and openness of the megalopolis corresponds with that of its pedagogy. Anything and everything is only a new possibility to be realized, a new unknown to be grasped. How exciting! Even the worst of problems can be accommodated, for each new dispute or tragedy "requires new regulations, other forms of community that must be invented."[11] Every x is exchangeable and capable of entering into the circuits of the megalopolis, and if an x isn't so at the present moment, then through grasping it will be so in the future, at which point it will be placed, compared, and evaluated alongside the other objects in the museum. This will happen efficiently through the individualization and diversification of learning styles, objectives, outcomes, assessments, and evaluations. Any gap between possibility and actuality must be bridged by the imaginary as quickly as possible. All learning is therefore active learning, whereby x is transformed into a known variable, rendered transparent, known by the mind, and placed alongside other in-different objects for comparison in the endlessly expanding museum of the zone. Nothing is outside the power of imagination or the mind's ability to grasp. Everything is directed toward the individual of the megalopolis, in need of decipherment and comparison.

If Lyotard can only write what he does about the *domus* from within the megalopolis, it's not because it was a previous, empirically definable stage of history that demands a distance for comprehension. He doubts it ever actually existed as a form of community. Instead, it has to do with the very struggle over pedagogical relations, and the resistance to grasping in and for the zone. There is always something that resists development: the *domus*, which exists within the megalopolis as the force of impossibility, which "is not only the opposite of *possible*, it is a case of it, the *zero* case of possibility."[12] The way to inhabit the megalopolis is "by citing the lost *domus*,"[13] by inhabiting the zero case of the possibility of childhood. The *domus* exists as "the child whose awakening displaces it to the future horizon of his thoughts and writing, to a coming which will always have to be deferred."[14] Childhood—which is linked with thought and writing—includes but is more than a beginning and passing stage of life, and also refers to a recurrent state that runs counter to and interrupts development. Biological childhood is when the human is inhuman, when we're radically dependent on others yet without the capacity or means to recognize, account for, or respond to this dependency. The child isn't a human yet because there is no "I" that can speak. As a recurrent state, childhood or infancy is an interruption in the subject's humanity, in which we can't participate in the debate, dialogue, reason, or exchange that are so essential to the megalopolis. The child is, in short, stupid, and the stupidity of the child is the pedagogical stake of education in the zone.

Illiteracy in the zone

The trajectory of development in grasping proceeds from ignorance to knowledge. Ignorance is the possibility of communicable and exchangeable knowledge. The ignorant student is one who doesn't know but can learn how to answer. The object of ignorance, even if that object is a subject, is an opacity that can be rendered transparent. Through grasping, ignorance develops into competent and articulate knowledge. Ignorance, like grasping, is always active, constantly on the move toward mastery, destined for its proper place amongst "the billions of padded messages" in "the immense zone."[15] Stupidity, which can never be developed, threatens this trajectory. Stupidity never has an answer, and isn't even sure what the question is, let alone the proper referents. This isn't the absence of thought, but another mode of thinking altogether, thought's internal other, chronically disobedient incapacity to actualize and articulate. As Lyotard defines it at one point, it is "a no-saying amid the always already said."[16] Such a no-saying isn't the refusal to speak—which would necessitate the ability to speak—but the very impotence and failure of speech, its permanent opacity. It is only, Lyotard writes, in a state of stupor that we can access this impotent energy, "because it consists only in the timbre of a sensitive, sentimental matter."[17]

Organized around the pedagogy of grasping, the zone's museum has "no need for writing, childhood, pain" because it is "an economy in which everything is taken, nothing received. And so necessarily, an illiteracy."[18] There is no service or surrender to the untameable, no obligation to live with interruptions. Childhood as a recurrent inhumanity and writing are inessential to the megalopolis because they can't factor into exchange. They are relegated to the zone's ghettos, which aren't planned by the metropolis as spatially distinct areas, but instead are the result of "prodigal thought" that "*secretes* the wall of its ghetto."[19] The ghetto walls, that is, are the discharge of the secret, marks of stupor that can't be grasped. Illiteracy, on this reading, isn't the negation or suppression of literacy, but instead a development of literacy as grasping, through which forms and concepts constitute objects under the mind's direction and the subject's will. These traces are what the megalopolis could do without and are the reason it tries to develop the child as quickly as possible. They are also what can open an alternative pedagogy beyond grasping, which I want to sketch by turning to some of Lyotard's writing on writing and sound, to gesture toward an errant literacy.

In his letter ostensibly addressed to David Rogozinski, Lyotard comments on Claude Lefort's analysis of George Orwell's *Nineteen-Eighty-Four*. What is of significance to Lyotard, first, is that Orwell's book isn't a work of criticism but of literature. Criticism, as we have seen, is perfectly acceptable to, and even desirable for, the megalopolis. The kind of writing Lyotard is after is one that "demands privation" and thus "cannot cooperate with a project of domination or total transparency, even involuntarily."[20] Orwell's hero, Winston, writes the novel not as a manifesto or theoretical excursus, but as a private diary, an act that begins as a resistance through which Winston encounters his "secret universe."[21] Yet as he writes his innermost thoughts—driven by an attempt to escape the system—he *articulates the secret*, therefore obliterating it and facilitating its swift and efficient capture in the megalopolis. The capture and defense of the secret hinges on the relation between language and writing, which are both allied and opposed to each other. "One writes against language, but necessarily with it. To say what it already knows how to say is not writing. One wants to say what it does not know how to say, but what one imagines it should be able to say."[22] We can only write *with* language, but we write *with* language to move beyond or outside of it.

When the secret is absorbed into the megalopolis through articulation, writing is subsumed by language. But this domination is never really total as long as writing takes place, because writing is "one region where restlessness, lack, and 'idiocy' come out into the open."[23] This is the childish stupidity that emerges through writing, which always indicates there is something that language can't capture, that can't be reduced to information. There seems to be a kind of writing that's most open to stupidity, which Lyotard finds in Walter Benjamin's writings on childhood, which don't *describe* childhood but indicate "the childhood of the event and inscribe what is uncapturable about it."[24] In describing childhood, I might seek to articulate something new about childhood, to show how it's unique. But this would remain tied to the megalopolis's logic of development, in which an event is transformed into an innovation, something new that can be sold or circulated throughout the infinite exchange routes of the megalopolis. Each innovation is a child that has grown up. Instead, childish reading-writing is about an *initiation* into childhood—an unknown that remains unknown and only appears through traces. Instead of the diary, then, the more appropriate act of resistance in the novel is the production of idiom, singular words that can't be translated or transferred, which articulates that which can't be captured and, in so doing, never quite succeeds at signaling what it names. Because the idiom always fails, it's the experience of initiation without development. The idiom is singular but also shared, a common point of contact in which we share in the secret. In love, there is "the never-ending search for a different idiom of sensibility, this vertigo where my idiom and yours falter, where they look for exchange, where they resist and discover each other."[25] The idiom is never complete, can never capture what it wants, and hence cannot grow up into an innovation, destined always and only to the experience of initiation.

The megalopolis is not reducible to the totalitarian system in *Nineteen-Eighty-Four* but what the two share in common is the reduction of writing to language. The megalopolis doesn't seek to eliminate writing, but to translate its singularity as an initiation that *must* grow up into an innovation. Lyotard will later affirm this after the triumph of the liberal-capitalist-imperialist system, which did so precisely because it was *open* to writing, it *needed* writing and the secret, without which there would be nothing new to inscribe in its circuits. But it needs a particular kind of writing: innovative writing, adult writing, transparent writing.

Writing and listening to the voices of words

In several texts, particularly after he began writing about sound and music, Lyotard introduces a sonic dimension to literacy. In "Address on the Subject of the Course of Philosophy," for example, he linked philosophical literacy to listening.[26] Because philosophy isn't an object or a corpus of knowledge, but rather the activity of thinking and questioning, philosophical literacy is "an exercise in discomposure in relation to the text, an exercise in patience," the patience of never being done reading, discovering "that you have not read what you have read," such that "reading is an exercise in listening."[27] In a short foreword to a collection of his works, which later appeared in

Postmodern Fables, Lyotard introduces three sonic dynamics of literacy, which each corresponds to a particular kind of writing.

First, there is *hearing* writing. When you hear yourself write, "you hear only something that has to be written," are confident in the writing, "ahead" of it.[28] Hearing writing is a transparent communication between sound and text, the words in the head and the words on the page—where language and writing are allies. You're confident that you're writing what you're hearing. Second, there is *listening* writing, which is uncertain writing, when you hesitate to write because of the suspension or gap between what you hear and what you write. This hesitation, Lyotard says, can lead in two directions. On one hand, you might "strap it down, make it severe, classical, academic," arguing your points against another; on the other hand, it can also lead to a neglect of the writing.[29] If you're uncertain, that is, you might disrespect the adherence of writing to language insofar as the links between the two are lost. This ambiguity ensures that you'll have continue to listen to the writing, continue to write again. Third, there is *not listening* writing. You're not listening to the writing, but *for* something else entirely, beyond reading and thinking through words and language: "You lend an ear only to what comes along."[30]

We can take these distinctions as different relations to thought, with different temporalities. Hearing writing is a correspondence to formulations, or an immediate harmonization between language and writing. Listening writing is an interruption in the harmony, one that desynchronizes language and writing, thought and articulation. The relationship between thought and articulation is suspended, ambiguous, and unsettled, but still present nonetheless. Not listening writing is a sonic openness to the present, or an obedience to noise. Meaning is absent and without any relation to the writing. The reason why Lyotard ascribes illiteracy to the megalopolis, then, is that it is organized solely around hearing and listening. There is only information to be exchanged and knowledge to be produced. You can hesitate, yes, as long as you produce something intelligible. There isn't a hierarchy of values within the three modes of sonic writing, however; it's not as if hearing and listening must be resisted. In fact, the three modes might be either heterogeneously blocked together or viewed along a continuum. Like childhood, thought is something that's recurrent, that's within and beyond formulation. But it is through not listening that childhood is birthed. The child, after all, doesn't hear words, but noise. The words are still there, of course, but they are unrecognizable, indeterminable, without any links or chains between them. They are words as not-words, words as charges, affects, or mute matter.

Just as there are different sonic forms of writing, there are different sonic forms of words. And if it is possible to not listen to writing, it is because the voice (of the word or of the thought) is mute, or muted. In an article on Freud's writing, Lyotard notes that *mu* or *mut*, the root of "mute," appears in a variety of words that designate sounds emitted by a closed mouth, such as "*to moan, to mutter, murmeln, murmurer, mugir*," and in a parenthetical note writes that, "in French, even the word for word, *mot*, comes from this root, *muttum*."[31] Lyotard names this voice mute not because it is silent, but "because, whatever its timbre, it always muffles the *lexis*."[32] *Lexis* is articulated speech that appears when words are heard as arbitrary signs whose only meaning rests entirely on the real object they correspond with and represent. It's *lexis* that we hear when we're hearing writing. *Lexis* is an entire schema of writing, reading, speaking, and listening organized around meaning that comes from and is expressed by one subject to another. The meaning might not be transparent, in which case it would be subject to development by, for example, the teacher of the megalopolis. The task here is to discern inflexions of the voice, measuring them against their natural, simple, or "zero" state in order to find information and make the subject cohere: "I say *this*, but I think that you really mean *that*," or "You're starting to find your natural writing voice!" Feedback like this assists in training the student to hear writing, helps develops the subject, its voice, its words, and its words' voice into exchangeable information to be transmitted, circulated, and further developed, so that the student can participate in the endless construction of the megalopolis through communication.

There's another voice that doesn't change by degree but jumps in tone. *Phōnē* is a voice that escapes from the legible, the *timbre* or *nuance* of the voice that doesn't transmit any messages, doesn't refer to something outside of itself, and is concerned with neither senders nor receivers. It makes sense without recourse to representation, without articulation, and signals only itself, and does so immediately. It's the voice that comes from *pathema*, the passion and pain of animality and affectivity, the capacity to receive and manifest affect through sounds. It's therefore not subject to debate or the rules of discourse. The human has both *phōnē* and *lexis*, the former being the inhuman of the human, the infancy of the adult. The child, Lyotard writes here, "has a voice, but doesn't articulate. Non-referential and unaddressed, the infantile sentence is an affectual signal, pleasure, pain ... *In-fans* does not have the means to *reply* to an articulated sentence that addresses it or refers to it" by the order of the *lexis* in which it has been placed before its birth."[33] The *phōnē* renders childhood atemporal and incapable of development, for there is no "you" to address, to respond, or to request an address. When infancy recurs, it appears through *phōnē*.

Phōnē isn't metaphysical or "absolutely outside" of discourse, but rather accompanies *lexis* by lending it its nuance. *Phōnē*, that is, "can infiltrate a given place in the articulated structure, a given linkage, *without being heard*, precisely without inflecting the good order, and thus without having to reflect it."[34] It isn't heard because it happens in an instant, and there is no "one" there to synthesize it. Lyotard says that interior monologue is close to the atemporality of mute discourse, because the constituent elements of discourse occur simultaneously and thus without temporalization, synchronization, and conceptualization. Yet if we *don't listen* to the word, we might hear the inaudible *phōnē*.

What forms of sonic writing, then, can attend to the demand of childhood? One place Lyotard goes is Freud's encounter with Ernst, or the Rat Man, a case that initiated Freud's practice of free association and a new mode of sonic writing. When Rat Man reports that his parents knew a thought he had, but which he didn't articulate, Freud at first tries to reduce the *phōnē* to *lexis* because he's trying to *hear* the thought, and he does so by taking up the position of the addressee in a position of knowing in order to put the rules of exchangeable discourse in force, so that a developmental process can take place where Rat Man and Freud learn the truth. With the shift to free association, however, there is a shift from hearing to listening. Freud loosens his role as a knower and abandons his role in the exchange of discourse, which gives the *phōnē* of the words a greater presence, not only through the individual words but, more importantly, through the relations of words amongst themselves. The inaudible and audible words appear in his notes during the session and after the session, to find a new kind of writing. "All writing," Lyotard says here, "is this attempt to bear witness, by way of the articulated *lexis*, to the inflexible *phōnē*. Writing has a debt of affect which it despairs of ever being able to pay off."[35]

Elsewhere, Lyotard proposes two forms that writing takes, which we can see as running along this general framework. The first is rewriting as remembering, in which one tries to write again in order to get closer to the truth, to discover even more precisely the degree of inflexions in the words, and thus to get as close as possible to hearing writing so there are no errors, no excesses. The second kind is rewriting as working through, which he associates with free association. In this kind of writing, one suspends knowledge and decision to allow things to appear without links or meaning, and therefore as ungraspable. For this rewriting, "the only guiding thread at one's disposal consists in sentiment or, better, in listening to a sentiment. A fragment of a sentence, a scrap of information, a word, come along."[36] In the first mode, *phōnē* is *developed* and made to speak to the hearing writer, who ever-more precisely learns the real *lexis*. Meaning can be secured, the real beginning and end can be identified. In the second, *phōnē*'s force is merely allowed to show itself, and the writer both listens to the tone of articulation and becomes deaf to its tone so that it can hear the inaudible. By not listening to the *lexis* or the appearance of *phōnē* within it, the writer can let the inaudible *pathema* of the word through. Yet owing to the impossibility of the first kind of writing, we might, like Freud, discover the need for the second kind.

Words as silent teachers

Because the mute word can't be developed, one can't learn to listen or not listen to writing. We can only learn hearing writing. This is, in part, because we can *know* what hearing writing is: there are words, they mean things, and these meanings can be ordered, interpreted, and deciphered. This is the writing of the megalopolis, in which all differences and initiations are only new variables to be named, rendered transparent, and circulated. What is an appropriate pedagogical mode, then, for the other sonic forms? If they're not learned, then how can they be taught?

Teaching errant literacy is a paradoxical pursuit in which teachers and students "suspend the activity of comparing and grasping" in order "to become open to the invasion of nuances, passible to timbre."[37] This requires "a mindless state of mind, which is required of mind not for matter to be perceived or conceived, given or grasped, but *so that there be* some something."[38] Literacy here entails an inversion of the current relationship between the subject and words. In the zone, the subject is the one who grasps words and, through composition, appropriates and exploits words. In errant literacy, we are the subjects of words. But words are not there *for* us to use, to inspire us or allow us to accord or give form. After all, "words want nothing. They are the 'un-will,' the 'non-sense' of thought, its mass."[39] The excess of the word relative to meaning and signification is not a challenge to be overcome (anyway, it can't). The lesson their disobedience teaches us is our obedience. Hearing writing casts the excess aside, while listening writing flirts with excess, and not listening writing allows the secrets of the words to do their work. To be passible to the matter of words, however, isn't to be passive. It's not a matter of teachers and students throwing up their hands and surrendering the university to words. The writer still picks up the pen or places their hands on the keyboard.

Rather than grasp what this kind of literacy is, I'll instead offer some examples. The first is from Lyotard's second book on André Malraux. Lyotard writes that Malraux's writing is "a writing at the limit of writing."[40] Limit writing, which he also terms *absolute* writing, is done under the sovereignty of the word, is an act that "is authorized by no voice, aims at no end."[41] Writing, in other words, is done to write, to express the *fact* of writing and to change this *fact* into an *artifact*. The fact is an action, a charge of matter that guides writing, which seizes on and disarticulates the written words to produce the artifact, its objectification that still contains a signal or energy within it. Malraux teaches us this through his conception and deployment of ellipses, on which, he says, "all art is grounded."[42] The ellipsis is an anacoluthon that enacts or signals the incompletion and failure of a sentence. In doing so, it "imposes silence on the verbiage of intrigues and allows to murmur the mutism that it covers."[43] We might think, first of all, of the ellipsis as an "etcetera," or that which indicates an addition of words to a phrase, which are thereby included through their exclusion. While we might assume their exclusion stems from their assumption, there is no way of confirming even the most standard and routine linkages. The etcetera not only signals an indeterminate and infinite number of words, but also remains mute as to their linkages. It follows that the meaning of the articulated *lexis* is likewise suspended or rendered ungraspable through errantry.

The ellipsis is mute in that it's neither silent nor articulated. In this way, the ellipsis might be an instance of what Lyotard calls the "affect-phrase," which "is distinct in that it is *unarticulated*."[44] Being unarticulated, the affect-phrase can't be linked with other phrases, and instead can only "suspend or interrupt linkages."[45] Its sense, that is, doesn't arise from a referent and doesn't emerge from the will of the sender, although, as in the elliptical case, it can emanate from the failure of the will and of the grasping drive. The ellipsis, that is, demonstrates grasping as an illusion. In an essay on Michel Butor, Lyotard gets at this pedagogical tension between grasping and errantry in the zone through the figure of the list. Butor's writing Lyotard considers is linked with travel and discovery, in which the list serves as a kind of zone between *lexis* and *phōnē*. "The list," Lyotard writes, "is the luminous imperial system's edging: an impossible place (an edge is unthinkable: it is that by means of which one thinks) where what the empire will compose and what the confessor will cause to speak are held in reserve."[46] Listing is an articulation of words in the absence of articulated linkages, and it can move us between hearing, listening, and not listening writing. The ellipsis is a testament to the latter, a documentation of the failure to document *phōnē* through *lexis* that, as an affect-phrase, renders words mute as it "eclipses the apparent movement of meaning," which also eclipses "the ego—its support."[47] Ellipses mute words and subject, rendering the latter passible to the charge of the former. Within, against, and beyond the chatter of the megalopolis where, through exchange, words blur into each other, the ellipsis cuts or gashes the space around a word to set it apart, orphan it, establishing a zone between words that is neither inside nor outside of the word. As readers and writers subjected to the ellipses, we're stupefied and interrupted, drawn to the timbre and nuance of the word, which we can only try to think. The errant matter of words comes from that according to which I don't matter, and passes through me, leading me elsewhere but not developing me. A secret pedagogy secreted onto the ghetto walls in the zone: "..."

Notes

1 Jean-François Lyotard, *Postmodern Fables*, tr. Georges Van Den Abbeele (Minneapolis MN: University of Minnesota Press, [1993] 1997), 24.
2 Ibid., 18.
3 Jean-François Lyotard, *The Inhuman: Reflections on Time*, tr. Geoffrey Bennington and Rachel Bowlby (Stanford CA: Stanford University Press, [1988] 1991), 191–2.
4 Ibid., 193.
5 Ibid., 192.
6 Ibid., 194.
7 Ibid., 201.
8 Ibid.
9 Lyotard, *Postmodern Fables*, 27.
10 Lyotard, *The Inhuman*, 140.
11 Ibid., 31.
12 Lyotard, *The Inhuman*, 197.
13 Ibid., 200.
14 Ibid., 201.
15 Lyotard, *Postmodern Fables*, 31.
16 Lyotard, *The Inhuman*, 202.
17 Ibid., 201.
18 Ibid., 199.
19 Ibid., 200.
20 Jean-François Lyotard, *The Postmodern Explained: Correspondence 1982–1985*, tr. Julian Pefanis and Morgan Thomas et al (Minneapolis MN: University of Minnesota Press, [1988] 1993), 88.
21 Ibid.
22 Ibid., 89.
23 Ibid., 90.
24 Ibid.
25 Ibid., 92.
26 "Address on the Subject of the Course of Philosophy," in Lyotard, *Postmodern Explained*, 99–107.
27 Ibid., 101.
28 Lyotard, *Postmodern Fables*, 150.
29 Ibid., 150
30 Ibid.
31 Jean-François Lyotard, "Voices of a Voice," tr. Georges Van Den Abbeele, *Discourse* 14, no. 1 (1992), 130.
32 Ibid.

33 Ibid., 132–3.
34 Ibid., 133.
35 Ibid., 138.
36 Lyotard, *The Inhuman*, 31.
37 Ibid., 139.
38 Ibid., 140.
39 Ibid., 142.
40 Jean-François Lyotard, *Soundproof Room: Malraux's Anti-Aesthetics*, tr. Robert Harvey (Stanford CA: Stanford University Press, [1993] 2001), 10.
41 Ibid., 32.
42 André Malraux, cited in Jean-François Lyotard, *Signed, Malraux*, tr. Robert Harvey (Minneapolis MN: University of Minnesota Press, [1996] 1999), 87.
43 Ibid., 62.
44 Jean-François Lyotard, "The Affect-phrase" (from a Supplement to *The Differend*), in this volume, 67.
45 Ibid., 68.
46 Jean-François Lyotard, "False Flights in Literature," tr. Robert Harvey, in Lyotard, *Toward the Post-Modern,* ed. Robert Harvey and Mark S. Roberts (New York: Humanity Books, 1993), 129.
47 Lyotard, *Soundproof Room*, 62.

2

Animal Testimony: Cetaceans Between the Interspecies and the Inhuman

Margret Grebowicz and Marina Zurkow

What enters through the blazon of the body, sensations, aesthesis, is not just the form of an object, it's the anguish of being full of holes.

—Lyotard, "Music, Mutic"[1]

Blazon

This pair of banners (Figure 2.1), each 7 feet tall, represents the endangered North Atlantic right whale and cyamids, the tiny crustaceans who live on them. Each banner contains about half a whale at a little more than one-quarter scale. The distinct markings are composed of crustaceans, who remain in these configurations for the life of the whale.

Figure 2.1 Marina Zurkow, *A Swarm is My Bonnet* (2018). Nylon banners, 84" x 42" each. Installation view, Cape Cod Modern House Trust. Image: Dylan Gauthier.

Identification of the right whale relies on this distinct pattern, known as a callosity, that each whale displays like a blazon on the back of its head. These are rough skin patches—callouses. Whale hunters called them "bonnets." Each whale is born with its distinct callous formation, which grows pitted and grooved like volcanic terrain over time. Callosities would not be visible were it not for the species of cyamids who colonize them, eating algae and the whale's sloughing outer skin. Whalers used to think these cyamids were lice, and the name stuck ("whale louse"), but they are actually amphipod crustaceans. The right whales' cyamids are white or yellowish, or orange, whereas the callosities are gray like the rest of the right whale.

In effect, the cyamids allow humans to uniquely identify each whale. Scientists do this from surveying airplanes, which flattens the whale and its blazon into a shape seen from the air. This identification is important to humans, in order to track, quantify, characterize—and, some might suggest, *care more about*—the whales and their success or demise as a species. One could say the cyamids are producing signs that humans want to read. In fact, it's a nuanced set of signs:

White bonnets: the whale is healthy.
Orange bonnets: the whale is ill, injured, or dying.

Figure 2.2 Right whale callosity. Image: Iain Kerr Ocean Alliance.

The poetry of this isn't lost on anyone working in the field: cyamid species move around and relocate when the right whale is sick: *Cyamus erraticus* move out of their genital folds and creases and migrate into the wounds, signing Sickness.

> On each right whale around 5000 *Cyamus ovalis* coat the callosities and give them their white color. In the spaces between the raised callosities live around 500 *C. gracilis*. On adult whales approximately 2000 *C. erraticus* live in the genital and mammary slits. *C. erraticus* is highly mobile though, often occupying wounds, and living in large concentrations on the heads of young calves. Of these *C. gracilis* is the smallest with ~6mm long adults and with the other two species measuring #at12–15mm long as adults.[2]

Cyamids spend all phases of their life cycle on their cetacean hosts. The cyamids that live on North Atlantic right whales know no other species or environment. They can't swim. They are passed from whale to whale—from a mother to her calf, or while mating.

These banners honor a colony of commensal animals who, by living on the whale, inadvertently sign the whale's individuality to humans. Humans, who love both science and story, tend to tune in more when they can identify individuals. The bonnets become the grounds for calling these whales Cassiopeia or Starboard, and tracking them over their lifetimes. They become the "face" of the whale for humans working in whale and ocean conservation.

Animal

And yet, whales have much more in common with humans than with cyamids. They have been shown to be uniquely highly social and vocal, endowed with massive brains and highly complex and extensive communication systems. In the case of baleen whales, that communication happens thanks to vocal cords.

In many ancient Arctic whale-hunting societies, it was understood that whales not only spoke their own language with each other, but that they also communicated with humans. This was among the primary reasons that it made perfect sense to refer to them as a kind of people.[3] Today, some cetacean rights advocates are still quite focused on the idea that whales have language and thus deserve rights.[4] But their argument for whale personhood seems to have lost the dimension of communication *between* whales and humans. It seems like something out of a fable, at once too fantastic and too literal.

Much of today's critical animal studies literature, which rejects the category of the human and is often grouped together to indicate a general "nonhuman turn," suffers from the same blind spot. Posthumanist or interspecies work in the arts and humanities reorients the stakes away from what once governed the realm of rights—language, individuality, subjectivity, and personhood—to semiosis (Eduardo Kohn), materiality (Manuel DeLanda, Elizabeth Povinelli), and various ecospheric imaginaries of comingling (Una Chaudhuri); from companionate dyads (Donna Haraway) to packs and swarms (Gilles Deleuze) to biomes, metabolic flows, and other kinds of assemblages (Anna Tsing, Karen Barad, Elaine Gan, Hannah Landecker). And yet, whales don't make any special sort of appearance in this literature, as if their communication with each other amounted to no more or nothing different than the communication between insects or mice.

But whales are the paradigmatic *animal*, i.e., a subjectivity teetering at the imagined human/animal boundary. Such a subject tests the foundations of the nonhuman turn. It also offers a unique opportunity to revisit and perhaps revise the notion of the inhuman that fueled so much of Lyotard's later work.

Lyotard wrote almost nothing about animals. One of the few times animals make an appearance in his work is in a brief, powerfully stated paragraph in *The Differend*, a book dedicated entirely to the question of how to bear witness to injustice in the absence of a universal language or a meta-language. The paragraph concludes as follows: "The animal is deprived of the possibility of bearing witness according to the human rules for establishing damages, and as a consequence, every damage is like a wrong and turns it into a victim *ipso facto* ... That is why the animal is a paradigm of the victim."[5]

Like all Western philosophers, Lyotard assumes that nonhuman animals cannot testify for themselves, because, in some real sense, they lack language. But what if there are nonhuman animals with language, like whales? Are whales deprived of the ability to bear witness according to the human rules for establishing damages?

Testimony

There are approximately 400 right whales remaining in the North Atlantic. In the nineteenth century, their numbers were estimated at 21,000. It's almost funny that we are discussing personhood and the rights that come with that status, considering the whale's name: the right whale. Named by New England whalers, they are docile, slow, and feed near shore; blubber-rich, they are the "right" whale to kill.

Tragedies appear on both individual and species levels for North Atlantic right whales, often caused by interaction with human forces. Cyamids offer a form of legible testimony to these tragedies, for humans "listening." And while the humans may think they are "seeing through" the whale's bonnet (composed of living animals) in order to perform a very human kind of individuation, the communication that makes the individuation possible actually requires the presence and agency of all three parties.

The North Atlantic Right Whale Catalog was the source for the drawings in this chapter.[6] The catalog itself is an extensive document of individually identified whales and their cyamid symbionts. The accompanying whale data states "last seen" or "death year." These sketches, made by researchers surveying whales from small airplanes, whose purpose is *to keep track of* individual whales, evince the tensions between humans' capacity to care and to not-care, and their predilection to prefer nameable species to the nameless or "uncharismatic" swarm, which they invariably shun.

The banner drawings focus on and amplify the swarm, elevating the cyamid to its rightful place as key interlocutor. These cyamid portraits were uncomfortable to assemble. What makes the swarm truly "other" is that it cannot be reduced to a whale's

Figure 2.3 Image of Stumpy (#1004) from the North Atlantic Right Whale Catalog. Image: Anderson Cabot Center, New England Aquarium / rwcatalog.neaq.org

"bonnet." These are animals living together, eating dead skin, clinging on to callouses for their lives, and crawling over each other; they are not simply signs.

Cassiopeia's and Starboard's histories are recorded in the catalog. They are compressed into neat facts, identifying blazon, other "coding" in the form of scars, birth year, parentage, years and locations sighted, and death, if known. Cassiopeia (#4041) was born in 2010 in Georgia. She was last seen in 2019 in the Bay of Fundy. She has a slim, symmetrical bonnet (blazon). Her mother is #1241 (also known as Bugs,

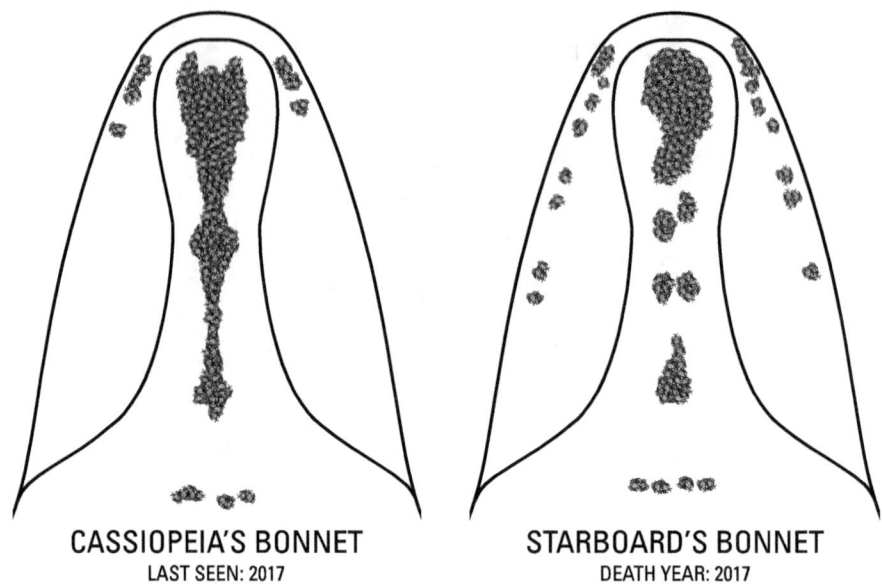

Figure 2.4 Marina Zurkow, *A Swarm is My Bonnet* (2018). Digital drawing.

presumably for the cartoon-face that her blazon resembles). Cassiopeia's grandmother, #1240 (Baldy), was born before the North Atlantic Right Whale Consortium's survey began in 1978. Over 700 whales have been cataloged, aerially tracked, and many have gone missing.

In this three-way of cyamids, whales, and humans, the cyamids are the equivalent of a scar or a tattoo; they are present and accounted for only to offer a sign among others. As sign-makers, the cyamids are not individuals; they are not even a swarm. The unique signature to which they contribute, which also includes deformities and amputations, coalesces into a whale's individual identity, legible only to humans interested in the dynamic and increasingly risk-filled lives of whales. In such a three-way relation, who testifies? To whom? About whom?

Starboard (#3603), b. 2006, has a known mother and father: Trilogy (#1503), b. 1985 and #1712, b. 1987. Starboard died in 2017. She had significant scars, a quarter fluke lobe missing, and a "Memorable mark on upper jaw only (including propeller wound)." Her blazon was described as a set of "broken islands."

Interesting?

In his essay "Interesting?" Lyotard announces that "nothing is less interesting" than what passes for conversation these days: "Bergson said, conversation is conservation. The same goes for the majority of interviews, discussions, dialogues, roundtables, debates, colloquia for which our world has such an appetite. They serve to assure that we are indeed 'on the same wavelength' and that it's going OK. Nothing is less interesting." This has profound aesthetic consequences for Lyotard: "The only interesting thing is to try to speak the language of another that you don't understand."[7]

But it also has profound political consequences. In "The General Line," he asks: "Why would we have the right to freedom of expression if we had nothing to say but the already said?"[8] Personhood, rights, humanity—all of these depend logically on having something to say beyond the conservative bla bla of conversation. What human rights protect—indeed, what the very idea of the human protects—is the same thing that makes a being worthy of interest. It is what makes us "listen up." And language, rather than being the condition of the human, comes second, as its logical consequence. In other words, the human is the creature that may (in the future) have something to say.

Today's animal rights literature has turned away from claims that animals have language, lest that become a requirement of having rights. In contrast, Lyotard believes language is in fact at the heart of the notion of personhood. Protection of the person is indeed the protection of language. However, this is not language understood as "the already said" (or what we can understand); in protecting the person, rights *in fact* protect what we don't understand, or what has yet to be said.

In "The Other's Rights," Lyotard goes to some lengths to describe the difference between animal and human languages. The distinction, for him, has to do with the utmost importance and centrality of the capacity to speak, rather than what is being said. He goes so far as to call the right to speak the most fundamental human right.[9] But that conclusion takes on a very particular tone in light of the fact that the Lyotardian argument for rights—which are always human rights—is actually an argument for the protection of the nonhuman or inhuman.

Starboard's bonnet is useful for conservation science. But does it—can it—testify to a wrong?

Following Lyotard, it would not be the absence of language, but the condition of being constitutionally unable to "give an account of themselves" (to quote Judith Butler) despite the *presence* of language that opens this space of the wrong and the victim.[10] Given that scientists can say with ever more scientific certainty that cetaceans "have" language, they provide a paradigmatic case of the following: a victim is a victim only if there's a *there* there, something to be wronged in the first place. Thus, the animal is a victim precisely because that animal is also, in some real sense, a person, the kind of being whose claim to being wronged is intelligible in principle. In other words, it's not the animal language itself that literally testifies to the wrong; the capacity for language is a testimony to an inner life that is the condition for being wrong-able.

What makes cetaceans persons—higher-order intelligence, language, long life spans, and what always follows those, namely complex and profound social ties—is also what makes their victimhood a living possibility. But the argument requires that its reverse also be true: the person is a victim precisely because that person is also an animal, in Lyotard's sense of animal, as the being bereft of the means to testify to the wrong that has been done to it.

Even if we take for granted what he spells out with such care in "The Other's Rights," that language is not natural but requires civilization, and that this requires man to forget his "animal nature," Lyotard argues that what such a shift requires first of all is "a moment of silence." This is a process of estrangement, of "saying something other than what I know how to say."[11] In "The General Line" he writes that "rights and respect for rights are owed to us only because something in us exceeds every recognized right."[12] This excess is an inner life that cannot speak for itself.

What is the relationship between the moment of silence and man's animal nature, always forgotten? Is this silence really an absence of sound, or is it rather what Lyotard invokes in "The Affect-phrase" as "mixed (or confused) voice," which is proper to all animals?[13]

The "charisma" we see in megafauna is real, not just an anthropomorphic projection, and what follows from it is that we can say intelligibly that (at least some) animals are persons. This renders much anthropomorphism just as appropriate as it is problematic. If "mixed (or confused) voice" is truly a voice and not just a sound, then this animal voice is also proper to all *persons*.

In humans' ongoing overtures to whales and other charismatic animals, personhood is not only a legal construct, or an idea. At its heart lives a complicated tangle of affects that points to everything about language that is not reducible to logos, and to the secret life of which no one can in fact give an account. In the end, that tangle itself is a sign that persons are in the proverbial house, creatures so like humans—while at the same time not-human—that it's uncanny. An uncanny reminder that human animals are also, at the same time, not-human. Why else would we find each other interesting?[14]

Swarm

Humans have all sorts of big feelings for whales. The swarm of crustaceans, on the other hand, is grotesque because their form and mass behavior are so alien to humans. And yet, with their accidental labor of signing to humans, the swarm creates conditions for humans to recognize marine animals. Right whales are too large and submerged for a non-aquatic species like humans to identify with in any other way than with both the aid of tiny crustaceans and the distancing means of aerial photography. It's the grotesque swarm that allows humans to not only care for but actually care more about right whales.

The swarm is both alien and the ground of intimacy between subjects, a pathway back to human predilection to correlate individuality with the capacity to care. This situation is ironic, complex, and beyond the simple logics of *the individual* that modern, Western, neoliberal humans tend to embrace. It's an opening to that entanglement that includes our love of/need for naming, identifying, and identifying-with and allows the beauty of non-linguistic signing to emerge.

The present triangulation facilitates arguments for whales' existence in the courts, in front of ocean regulatory bodies. It exists only in order to identify whales, their life spans, and lives of hardship amid noise pollution, propeller indifference, fishing, and transport boats' insistence on their high place in the hierarchy of matter and matters. But this identification is hardly innocent; it allows the primacy of the individual to

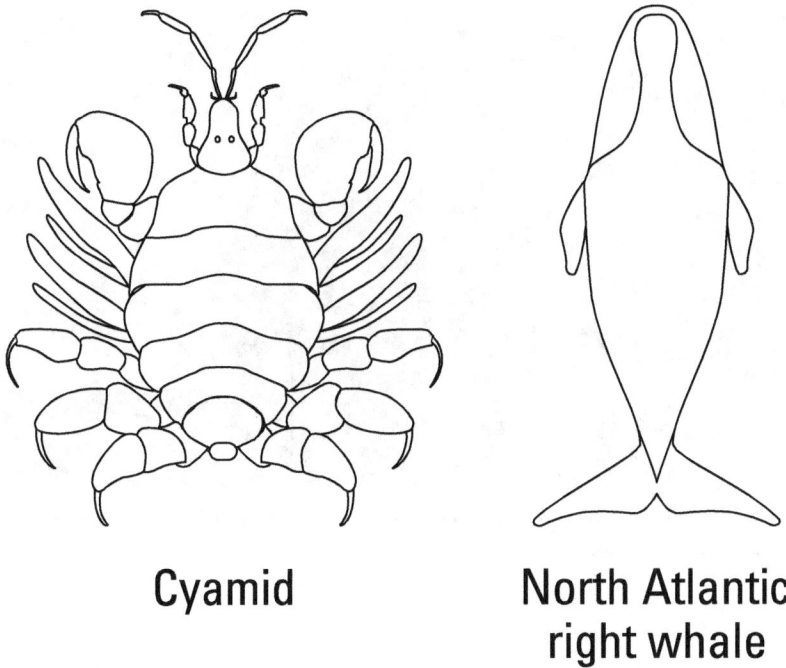

Figure 2.5 Marina Zurkow, *A Swarm is My Bonnet* (2018). Digital drawing.

persist. In a battle against anthropocentric entitlements, the triangulation nevertheless turns away from its own transcendence of anthropos.

If this entanglement came to be taken seriously as a three-way relation—as the true swarm—by the institutions that currently engage with (study, protect, exploit) cetaceans and thus shape cetacean–human interactions, there would be no more need for discussions of personhood, or for testimony to inner life. Claims to justice would have to find their basis in something other than the wronged person, or the person understood as that which can be wronged.

If the swarm includes humans, whales, and cyamids, does it produce something even less known and less identifiable than what we now call semiosis? What would law look like if it took that less known thing seriously?

Secret

In the end, it seems that only individuals can have the inner life to which Lyotard is so committed. Perhaps the secret life is not so secret after all. It signals the presence of the individual, the integrity of the subject that can be wronged and that is thus worthy of protection by rights. Or: perhaps there is a secrecy beyond the secrecy of interiority, to which the animal has yet to lead philosophy.

Figure 2.6 North Atlantic right whale breaching. Image: Anderson Cabot Center, New England Aquarium.

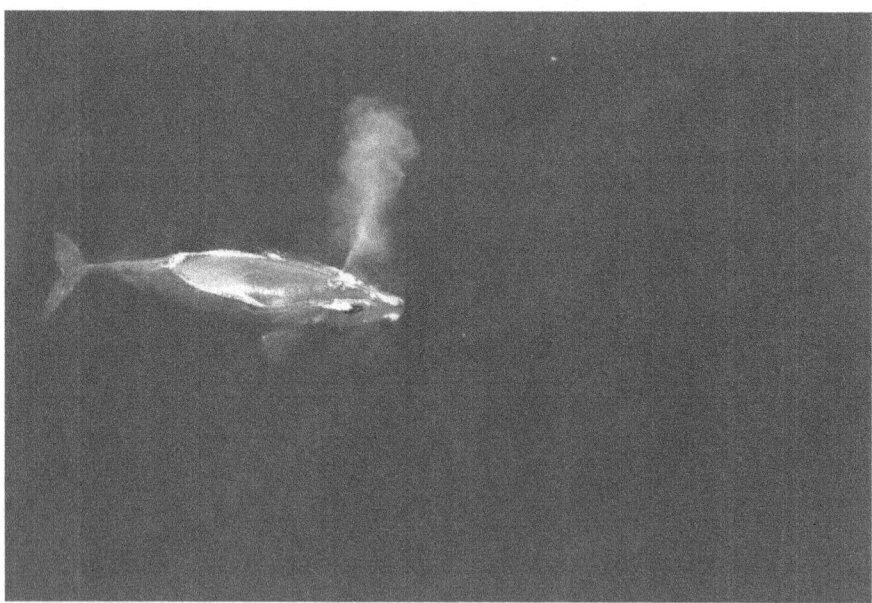

Figure 2.7 Aerial photograph of a North Atlantic right whale. Image: Northeast Fisheries Science Center, taken under MMPA Permit #17355.

Perhaps the present framing of some animals—ones as sagacious and charismatic as whales—as the most human of animals is not the best way forward for them. But the error is not that of anthropomorphism, or of a fundamental misunderstanding of animal nature. No: the error lies simply in the fact that even as robust a notion of the inhuman as Lyotard offers does not go far enough. It does not give voice to the animality of the speaking creature, the one to whom rights are owed. When the inhuman is limited to the secrecy that conditions the subject, this obscures the possibilities of another inhuman, the animal. Rather than human rights being the paradigm of rights, to which every "animal rights" discourse can do no more than attach itself, perhaps the future of rights in fact belongs to the animal in us all.

Notes

1 Jean-François Lyotard, "Music Mutic," in *Postmodern Fables*, tr. Georges Van Den Abbeele (Minneapolis MN: University of Minnesota Press, [1993] 1997), 231. Copyright 1997 by the Regents of the University of Minnesota. Originally published in *Moralités postmodernes*. Copyright 1993 by Éditions Galilée.
2 Kaliszewska ZA, Seger J, Rowntree VJ, et al. "Population histories of right whales (Cetacea: Eubalaena) inferred from mitochondrial sequence diversities and divergences of their whale lice (Amphipoda: Cyamus)," *Mol Ecol*, vol. 14, no. 11 (2005): 3439–56. doi:10.1111/j.1365-294X.2005.02664.x
3 Krista Langlois, "When Whales and Humans Talk," *Hakai Magazine*, April 3, 2018. Available online: https://www.hakaimagazine.com/features/when-whales-and-humans-talk/ (accessed January 31, 2021).
4 Cetacean Rights: Fostering Moral and Legal Change. Available online: https://www.cetaceanrights.org/ (accessed January 31, 2021).
5 Lyotard, *The Differend*, tr. Georges Van Den Abbeele (Minneapolis MN: University of Minnesota Press, [1983] 1988), 28.
6 The North Atlantic Right Whale Catalog. Available online: http://rwcatalog.neaq.org.
7 Lyotard, "Interesting?" in *Postmodern Fables*, 61.
8 Lyotard, "The General Line," in *Postmodern Fables*, 121.
9 "The Other's Rights," in this volume, 77.
10 See Judith Butler, *Giving an Account of Oneself* (New York: Fordham University Press, 2005).
11 Ibid., 77-8.
12 Lyotard, "The General Line," in *Postmodern Fables*, 121.
13 Lyotard, "The Affect-phrase," in this volume, 70.
14 For a related, extended discussion of personhood, intimacy, animality, language, and human rights, see Margret Grebowicz and Zach Reyna, "The Animality of Simone Weil: I Love Dick and a Nonhuman Politics of the Impersonal," *the minnesota review* 97 (2021): 77–94.

3

Under Threat: Rights and the "Thing"

Claire Nouvet

Art claims an "absolute right": the right to subject itself to the grip of what Lyotard calls "*la Chose*," the Thing, a right that it exercises apart from the human community and the ethical obligations owed to its members. But if this is the case, what of the Thing in the age of development? Is there any room left to relate to it? As for the right that art claims for itself, is it simply heterogeneous to the rights, the human rights, that one must defend within the community? Lyotard, I will argue, complicates this apparent heterogeneity, most notably in "The Other's Rights." To insist on maintaining a relation to the Thing (as art does even in the age of development that threatens any relation to the Thing) is to remember that which provides the very ground on which human rights rest.

But first, what is the Thing to which art claims the right to relate? And why does Lyotard phrase this relation as a "seduction," a notion borrowed from the psychoanalytic register? "Seduction" is the term that Sigmund Freud applied to sexual traumas inflicted by pathologically perverse adults onto children and that Jean Laplanche depathologized in his own theory of "generalized" seduction in which seduction becomes a "normal" because unavoidable, although still traumatic, process. Seduction occurs within a fundamental situation marked by a radical asymmetry. Dependent for its survival on an adult's caregiving, the infant is subjected to the sexual unconscious of this adult, which infiltrates the relation and implants in the infant signifiers that are "enigmatic" in the sense that neither sender nor receiver knows what is signified. This sexual enigma "compromises" the message, since it is that which, within the message, cannot be signified, and which, as such, generates excitement. Although the infant tries to make sense of this enigma by translating it, this translation is doomed to leave untranslatable residues that constitute what Laplanche calls the "source-objects" of the drives, objects that are the sources of an internal excitation that demands an endless work of translation. As Dominique Scarfone points out, Laplanche proposes with these source-objects his own elaboration of the Thing, *das Ding*, which Lacan highlights in a passage of *Project for a Scientific Psychology* in which Freud signals the presence, at the core of the fellow human being, of an uncognizable and unassimilable component. For Laplanche, the traumatic encounter with the other's enigmatic sexual unconscious provokes a process of translation that leaves its own untranslatable residues, the Thing, which is not the copy of the other's enigmatic unconscious core, but the remnant of its failed translation.

Lyotard concurs that it is necessary to posit an originary seduction, as he refers in a footnote to Laplanche's *New Foundations for Psychoanalysis*: "Seduction, in the current sense, the one Freud initially gives, is not necessary. What is necessary is a passibility, that is called excitability, which, in chronological or phenomenological terms, is 'constant.' Seduction is necessary only in the sense that it is necessary that this excitability be excited."[1] But seduction is not just any occasion to get a passibility excited, nor is it limited to chronological infancy. One is "seduced" whenever one is affected by some "thing" for which the psyche is radically unprepared and against which it cannot therefore defend itself. This condition of unpreparedness defines seduction as an incommensurable relation: one is asked to relate to that to which one cannot relate since it exceeds one's abilities. Such relation relegates one to an infancy no longer to be understood merely as a chronological stage. As Lyotard points out, infant comes from the Latin "*infans*," indicating the child who cannot yet speak, as distinct from the "*puer*," the child endowed with this ability. One is struck by an infantile muteness whenever one relates to the Thing that exceeds what one can name or represent.

If the Thing is without representation, how does one sense its presence? For Lyotard, it presents itself through the unconscious affect it inflicts. To give an analogical sense of this affect, he uses the Freudian language of dynamics. A mind seduced into a relation with the Thing is shocked, i.e., affected to such an extent that "the quantity of energy transmitted by this shock is not transformed into 'objects,' not even inferior ones [...] but it remains potential, unexploitable, and thus ignored by the apparatus."[2] Like a "cloud of energy particles," the unconscious affect resists formation. Since it cannot be formed into "sets that can be thought in terms of words or images," it does not belong to the unconscious formations produced by secondary repression[3] and indicates the presence of the originary unconscious that Freud hypothesized, an unconscious "without representational formations."[4]

In the Latin "*ducere*" (to lead) of seduction, a strange movement must therefore be heard: the "'duction' toward the inside of something (of energy) that remains outside of it."[5] The Thing seduces insofar as it forcefully introduces itself in the psychic apparatus as an affective excitation that cannot be inserted within its unconscious representative formations. Within the psychic apparatus while remaining outside of its formations, the unconscious affect lingers as an indeterminate, unqualifiable, and dispersed energy which cannot be put to work: "The deposit left behind by 'excessive' excitation [...] is not a localizable object in the typology of the soul. This deposit is dissipated, widely dispersed like a thermal state of the system, which, remaining undetermined, is not workable."[6] It is "'before' all work," "*chômé, chômant*," "unemployed, unemployable,"[7] since it has not been formed into a representation that could be included in the networks of unconscious representative formations that provide the material for the psychic work of transformation, such as the dream work. It could be compared to "a thermal state, to a cloud of unqualified heat,"[8] which diffuses itself through the unconscious networks of repressed formations without being localizable within them or exploitable by them.

If the Thing cannot be put to work within the psychic system, what becomes of it in the age of "the system," i.e., of a liberal, technocratic capitalism that no longer even pretends to serve the progress of humanity, but instead "guarantees development"?⁹ The system has only one directing principle: the optimization of its efficiency that it ensures by opening a vacuous "blank"¹⁰ within itself, "a margin of uncertainty" or "chance." In this opening, constant testing is taking place to select the "winning strategies" that the system can integrate in a virtually infinite process of self-revision and self-construction,¹¹ venture programs are launched to see what they might yield, disinterested research is funded because it might after all prove to have been useful, criticism—including criticism of the system—is encouraged since the system needs it in order to adjust its performance. It is in this opening that intellectuals perform their reflection and exercise the responsibilities "normally" expected of them: "'Normally,' insofar as these practices are authorized and even encouraged by legislation or, at least, by the formal and informal rules that regulate that status. Society permits us, requires us to act accordingly: because it needs us to contribute, in that order that is our own, to the development of the global system."¹² As for the hardships inflicted on the most underprivileged, they will be alleviated if it can be shown that failing to do so exacts a destabilizing cost on the system greater than the expenditures involved in alleviating them.¹³ Even the aesthetic "sigh," the brief exhalation through which the pressure of efficiency is momentarily suspended, can improve overall efficiency.¹⁴

As it self-improves and self-constructs, the system becomes increasingly complex, i.e., better able "to control and exploit 'natural' or 'human' energies that were previously dispersed."¹⁵ This exploitation extends to the mobilization of psychic energies for which liberal democracies are preferable to autocratic regimes since their openness increases their exploitative efficiency. As Ashley Woodward puts it when he summarizes Lyotard's argument:

> Liberal democracies, in allowing a great deal of openness and flexibility in the social organization itself, allow the most efficient way of exploiting energies and ensuring the preservation and increasing complexity of the collective human system. This system proved to be much more efficient at exploiting energy than closed systems with fixed social hierarchies.¹⁶

No wonder, then, if the "open" system accommodates itself quite well with democratic regimes even as its development ignores the national borders within which these democracies confine themselves. Liberal democracies provide a greater reservoir of exploitable psychic energies. Everything, including character traits, can be put to use. And the liberal Ego participates quite willingly in its own exploitation:

> even in intimacy the Ego reconstructs itself on the productivist model of the organic composition of capital. Character traits are to be exploited in the social, economic, and cultural circuits of exchange, like apparatuses of production, like productive goods. And, Adorno writes in *Minima Moralia*, the Ego becomes their director, landlord, and manager, an abstract instance.¹⁷

Hence, the famous unstructured question of job interviews, "So tell me about yourself," for which, as a Google search reveals, multiple trainings are available. From what I can gather, it is not recommended to answer with one's life story or a repetition of one's CV. Rather, one should identify, evaluate, and foreground the subjective characteristics that in one's "self" might be useful to the hiring enterprise. As for the weaknesses that one may also be asked to identify, they should be exploitable subjective defects such as one's "creativity" or exacting "honesty." The subject's Ego is asked to function as the manager who assesses its own psychic exploitability. In these simple questions can be heard the ever-pressing request of the system to mobilize and administer one's psychic energies for optimal efficiency of one's "self," a "self" conceived as a complex apparatus of production at the service of the system's efficiency. And since the system is endlessly self-improving, it follows that nothing one does will ever simply be good enough. One is constantly asked to criticize one's performance and the performance of others; there is always, always, room for "improvement," since endless self-improvement participates in the endless self-improvement of the system, its ever-expanding development. As Lyotard points out, "having problems" is viewed as "suspect," a failing to be eliminated in the shortest possible amount of time. Hence, the proliferation of self-help books and the devalorization of psychoanalytic therapy, which takes too long and does not promise to achieve the desired result: the elimination of all problems that could compromise the optimal efficiency of a fully mobilized and administered psychic apparatus.

For a system driven by the requirement of efficiency, to maintain an affective relation to the Thing can therefore only be "bad," and for several reasons. First, the economic law that rules development requires that all objects be turned into quantifiable units. Such law is bound to ignore the Thing insofar as it is not an object. The economic law "ignores what is not an object or what has no object—and thus the soul, if 'soul' means a spirit disturbed by a host that it ignores, nonobjectal, nonobjective."[18] The nonobjectal and nonobjective host which affects the mind that it inhabits and, in so doing, turns it into a "soul" is the affective presence of the Thing which the system can only ignore, since it is precisely not an object that could ever be quantified. Second, the Thing is that which, far from improving work productivity, radically disrupts the working capacities of the mind. Its affective presence is a *"mal,"* i.e., an "evil" and a "sickness," insofar as it disables the mind: "This affect is evil, it is undetermined, it does not enrich the system in any sense; it leaves it without the capacity to work, that is, to transform supplied information into any effectuation destined to ameliorate the performance of the system or to saturate its competence."[19] Better then to forget the Thing, to get rid of it.

It is such a radical oblivion that the system would be performing through the mobilization of psychic energies. Such a mobilization not only distracts from the Thing; it performs a psychic *"vidange,"* a term that connotes draining, emptying, cleansing. The draining of one's energies seems indeed to be a very efficient way of cleansing the psychic apparatus of the unworkable Thing that inhabits it:

> The request to mobilize the forces of the psychic "apparatus" in the present-day world engenders a kind of *emptying* or *draining* [vidange] of that apparatus. And first of all an anesthesia, an invalidity in perception. The mind is only "sensible" to the impact of shocks, to the sensational sensation, to the quantum of information.

Except for the most shocking, nothing is any longer perceived; the nuances and the timbres lose their quality of "material" singularities.[20]

Fully mobilized, the psychic apparatus is thoroughly depleted, too exhausted to provide any internal idiosyncratic representation to which its unconscious energies could fix themselves: where there should be an internal representation, nothing. Hence the feeling of internal void, of desolate emptiness, that opens up in a psyche working overtime in the service of the system. The depletion of psychic energies results in a depleted spectrum of sensations, an insensibility to nuances, a sensorial anesthesia, which in turn calls for "sensationalism": one can only sense ever more shocking sensations.

This "industrial devastation of the intimate" provokes a "transfer," the "placing outside, in media (aptly named) of the concerns of representation, of the (industrial) work of providing unconscious energies with representatives on which they will come to fix themselves."[21] Unable to do the work of representation, a depleted psyche delegates to sociocultural apparatuses the task of providing representatives onto which its unconscious energies can be "fixed" and therefore repressed, since secondary repression presupposes representation.

As for the representatives provided by these sociocultural apparatuses, they are boring. As Lyotard puts it, the main function of the communicational networks of modern social media is to preserve existing meanings: "They are boring to the extent that they teach us nothing."[22] They teach us nothing since they do not teach anything that we do not yet know how to understand. Even the disagreements that they stage are phrased in terms whose meaning is preserved. In so doing, they suffocate the relationship of the mind to the Thing and the anxiety that it fuels.

The ever-spreading extension of communal interlocution also contributes to the forgetting of the Thing, to its "*vidange*." As Lyotard points out, the right to express oneself has become an ever-pressing invitation, an oppressive obligation to "publish" oneself. Self-publication is not limited to the obligation to write, to the "publish or perish" of a modern university increasingly ruled by performativity: more published products in less time, products whose "excellence" is evaluated by their ability to meet the marketability criteria set by "recognized" presses and by the number of citations they accrue—a number that specialized entities aggregate in order to identify for university managers those research trends that deserve funding. To publish oneself is also to make one's "self" ever more public, to engage this "self" wholeheartedly in the active public life where one must incessantly communicate and exchange with others. Such proliferation of interlocutory exchanges leaves no time to engage in what Lyotard calls the "second existence" where one tries to listen to the affective echo of the Thing.

But it is precisely this relation to the Thing that art insists on maintaining. It does so by withdrawing from communal exchange into the reserved space of the "second existence." To enter this space, closing the door is not enough. One must clear a psychic space—an increasingly challenging task, as one's economic survival increasingly depends on one's engagement in the proliferation of activities that benefits the system. Nor is this psychic space a simple break from one's busy life, a peaceful retreat in the ivory tower of art, an aesthetic "sigh," the momentary alleviation of the pressure of the system for the sake of renewed performativity. It only opens when one endures the intimate terror of relating to a Thing which exceeds one's representative, cognitive, and even sensorial capacities, since it is "within sensation the 'presence' of what escapes sensation."[23] This presence induces an anesthesia, a radical incapacity: one simply does not have the words or colors to give a sense of that which strikes. And with this anesthesia comes the threat of nullity: one will never again be able to phrase anything. To sense the "presence" of the Thing is to confront a "blank horizon" that annihilates what one knows how to see and speak. This blank horizon is not the vacuous opening that a system, which claims that "everything is possible," must reserve within itself to test the possibilities that might improve its performance. It signals instead the threat of an impossibility: that nothing might happen, no more phrasing, verbal or non-verbal. Artists must confront this anesthetic annihilation: aesthetics "*arises* from anesthesia, belonging to it, recovering from it."[24] Triggered by the terror of annihilation, art tries to recover from it by working its way through the screens of available representations to find some way to give a sense of the Thing in its resistance to representation. Since the Thing retracts itself from all representation, this artistic labor is an interminable "working through" which differs from the type of inventiveness that the system requires to improve its performance. The working through that the relation to the Thing triggers is not the kind of working out that benefits the system, since the mind is forced to work in relation to something that will remain unemployable; no amount of work will ever manage to work the Thing out, to get rid of its unworkability. As for the artistic products of this working through, they are precisely not "products" since they do not provide the kind of "information" that the system can use for the improvement of its performance.

Can art still maintain its anesthetic relation to the Thing in the age of the system? At first, it may seem that it is reduced to echoing the anesthesia that the system induced.

> Now, this industrial devastation of the intimate, this placing outside, in media (aptly named) of the concerns of representation, of the (industrial) work of providing unconscious energies with representatives on which they will come to fix themselves, this transfer of the dreamwork, of the symptom, to "cultural" work—this very thing, this cleansing that has made "having problems" outdated and suspect—*this*, abstraction and minimalism can echo.[25]

While the refusal of representation in abstraction echoes the inability to provide an internal representation for the Thing, the sensorial reduction of minimalism echoes the sensorial impoverishment of a psychic apparatus thoroughly depleted by its mobilization. But if lack of representation and sensorial impoverishment are the signs of the intimate devastation perpetrated by the system, this sickness can be made to point to a much more "archaic" malaise:

> For the displacement of the tasks of secondary repression onto the sociocultural apparatuses, this reification, this abjection, reveal in the emptiness of the soul the sickness that Freud prophesied would increase with "civilization." A more "archaic" anxiety, and one that is precisely resistant to the formation of representations. It is

this, and only this, extreme resistance that can nourish the resistance of contemporary art and writing to the "everything is possible." Anesthesia to fight against amnesia.[26]

The postmodern inability to provide any internal representation of the Thing reveals a more archaic sickness: the anxiety triggered by the "extreme" resistance that the Thing opposes to representation. It is this resistance that "nourishes" the resistance of contemporary art, which uses "anesthesia" to fight "amnesia." Contemporary art echoes the signs of the postmodern sickness but, in so doing, diverts them, turning them into the very index of the presence of the Thing they were meant to evacuate. In abstract art, the lack of internal psychic representation produced by the system is made to signal the resistance of the Thing to representation. In minimalism, the sensorial anesthesia of a depleted psychic apparatus is made to signal the sensorial anesthesia inflicted by a Thing which "escapes sensation." Anesthesia, the sign of the oblivion to which the system's efficiency condemns the Thing, becomes the index pointing to its very presence as that which resists representative as well as sensorial capacities. The void of postmodern anesthesia, its desolate emptiness, opens onto the presence of the nonobjectal and nonobjective Thing and the unbound anxiety it generates.

To this anxious confrontation with the intractable Thing, art claims an "absolute right": "The absolute right of the 'second existence' must be well recognized."[27] Its exercise does not, however, dispense artists of the obligation they owe to the human community. As Lyotard insists, it is one's responsibility to defend human rights. Submission to the muting of the Thing cannot be used to ignore the muting imposed by political terror. If art should not be used to forget the ethical obligation to others, ethics should not be used to forget the aesthetic obligation to the Thing, a forgetting that Lyotard nevertheless detects. In the age of the system, even the defense of human rights can be used as a defense mechanism against the Thing, as a means "to forget that, in every mind and in the ensemble of minds that is the republican community, there is something that has no rights that needs to be affirmed, but that, beyond the just and the unjust, exceeds the mind of each and all."[28]

With the denunciation of these two forgettings, Lyotard sharply differentiates two distinct rights: the artistic right to relate to the Thing, to this inhuman Other which is "utterly other than the 'others,'"[29] and the rights owed to the human others. These rights are exercised in two apparently separate spaces: the reserved space that art carves for itself aside and apart from the human community, and the interlocutory space of what Lyotard calls the "Republican community." This Republican community is a contractual community that constitutes the other as the interlocutor who has the right to speak and the community as the result of this civil debate: "The one and the other can come to an agreement, after reasoning and debate, and then establish their community by contract. This is the principle of the Greek *politeia* or the modern *republic*. The citizen is the human individual whose right to address others is recognized by those others."[30] The republic posits the other as an interlocutor to whom is given the right to speak—to participate in the reasonable debate through which citizens constitute their community by defining that which they have in common. Republican debate establishes indeed the commonality which is the basis of its community.

Neither the republic nor its civil interlocution derive their legitimacy from any relation to the Thing. Based on the principle of civil interlocution and deliberative argumentation, the republic does not need to refer to an Other to guarantee either its authority or the respect for the human rights that it grants to its citizens. It is such a cut from the Thing that Lyotard sees literalized in the beheading of the king that inaugurated the French Republic. With this royal cut, the republic founded itself upon the severing of all relation to the heterogeneous Other from which the old regime derived its legitimation. The king received indeed his authority from God—or, as Lyotard puts it, from an Other, the Other that Augustine lodged at the very core of the ego. Within the ego but split from it, this Other is "deeper than the ego" "insofar as the ego cannot comprehend the Other."[31] While Augustine wanted to believe that this heterogeneous and unassimilable Other was a God of love who "wished only the good," Lyotard insists that "God" might be one of the names for a Thing which is "Evil" not because it is the opposite of the Good, but because it is indeterminate, below the determination of Good and Evil: "Evil is not the opposite of Good, it is the indecidability between Good and Evil."[32]

The republic founds itself on the negation of this Other: "The republic, and hence interlocution, can only be founded upon a deicide; it begins with the nihilist assertion that there is no Other."[33] As it inaugurates itself by severing all relation to a Thing which it negates, it also severs civil interlocution from it. Lyotard seems to endorse this republican elimination of the Thing from the sociopolitical field. In order to constitute and preserve the body of the *polis* as "'a commonality' of humans,'" politics must "forget" the Thing, which, as he puts it, is "not communicable or communal or common at all" and "not shareable."[34] The relation to the Thing is indeed absolutely singular, idiomatic even. As such, it is that which the members of a community based on commonality can neither share nor exchange.

But it is also that which makes every member singular and therefore irreplaceable. To cut one's singular relation to the Thing is therefore "to become perfectly interchangeable, without remainder, within the conditions of public and private law."[35] Insofar as it prohibits exchangeability, singularity becomes, for Lyotard, the basis of the respect for human rights that the community owes to its members: "Rights and respect for rights are owed to us only because something in us exceeds every recognized right."[36] What makes each member of the republican community worthy of civil respect is ultimately her intimate relation to that singular and uncivil part, the Thing, which constitutes her singularity and, in so doing, prohibits her exchangeability. To sever the relation to the Thing, as the republic claims to have done, is therefore to sever a relation that is both separate from civil interlocution and essential to the respect due to the singularity of its members. It is in this sense that Lyotard can assert, somewhat enigmatically, that "the absolute right of the 'second existence' must be well recognized, since it is that which gives the right to rights. But as it escapes rights, it must always be content with an amnesty."[37] The relation to the Thing "gives the right to rights" although it "escapes rights." The relation to the Thing, which grounds the civil respect owed to its members, is indeed not a right that the civil community can either promulgate or preserve. Since it is beyond the just and the unjust, this uncivil Thing has no right to claim within civil interlocution.

If the relation to the Thing "gives the right to rights," it is nevertheless difficult to see how it could ground the legitimacy of the right to speak on which the civic interlocution of the republic relies. As Lyotard insists, "This is the principle of the Greek *politeia* or the modern republic. The citizen is the human individual whose right to address others is recognized by those others."³⁸ This right to speak and to address is conceived as a "natural" right not derived from any relation to the Thing, but instead grounded upon a capacity. I am authorized to speak, not because I have earned this right by learning, for instance, how to speak, how to share in a dialogue with the other members of the republic, but because I am naturally endowed with the faculty of speaking. But, as Lyotard notes, by declaring that I am authorized to speak simply because I can, public law "confuses" a capacity with an authorization: "this legality conceals a confusion between a capacity, the aptitude for speech, and a legitimacy, the authority to speak."³⁹ Lyotard nevertheless judges the illegitimate confusion that grounds the right to speak to be "good:" "By authorizing every possible speaker to address others, the republic ... forbids that anyone be arbitrarily deprived of speech. It discourages terror."⁴⁰ Terror names the crime of arbitrarily silencing another, a crime that Lyotard repeatedly and insistently denounces throughout his writings. Against the threat of this arbitrary silencing, the members of the republican community invoke their right to speak which they derive from their natural capacity to speak. It is in the name of this right based on a capacity that they forbid the terror of arbitrary silencing and that the republic, in principle, extends the right to speak to any other while the "*demos*" restricts this right:

> The *demos* is not a contractual but a natural and cultural community. The individual of the *demos* is recognized as such not for his right to speak, but for his birth, language, and historical heritage. These individuals form a *nation* ... whose principal characteristic is the homogeneity of its constituents. Interlocution does not engender this community.⁴¹

Although Lyotard admits that he "oversimplifies" the difference, he does so "to bring out the essential opposition between the *demotic* and the *civic*" in terms of the position assigned to the other. As he bluntly puts it: "The people keeps the other out; the city interiorizes the other."⁴² The city interiorizes the other by extending in principle to any "other," any "outsider," a right to speak based on a capacity. This extension makes possible the work of organizations such as Amnesty International, which started as a "plea for amnesty" that asked public law to pardon, that is, to forget the wrong that it had condemned. As Lyotard reminds us, "*Amnestos* meant he who is forgotten."⁴³ "Amnesty" derives "from Greek *amnēstía* 'forgetfulness, oblivion, deliberate overlooking of past offenses,' from *amnēstós* 'forgotten, forgetful.'"⁴⁴ While the extension of the right to speak to any "other" might be good since it allows to plead for a deliberate forgetting, Lyotard nevertheless points out that the derivation of this right might itself proceed from an unacknowledged forgetting.

Is the right to speak indeed based on a capacity? Lyotard overturns its seemingly natural derivation. The right to speak does not derive from the possibility of speech, but from the intimate experience of its impossibility. If I claim for myself, and for any other, the right to speak, if I defend this right against the threat of despotic terror, it is not because I am assured of my capacity to speak but, on the contrary, because I know the terror of being incapable of speaking. After all, I did not start in life as a member of the speech community. As an *infans* who had not yet learned how to speak, I was relegated to its margins. While I was affected by the speech community that surrounded me, I was unable to speak within it or to it. In the midst of the speech community, I was abandoned, alone, to the distress of an affectability that I could not speak.

It is to the terror of this mute infantile distress that we owe, according to Lyotard, "our need to be welcomed, the request that we be authorized to enter the speech of the community."[45] Lyotard reminds the members of the community that they all were once an infant excluded from the speech community, an infant abandoned to the muteness of affectivity, and who begged to be delivered from it by being welcomed as a speaker. Only because this infantile plea was heard, did they become a speaker in the community.

Infancy pleads to be accepted within the speech community, to be given the right to speak within it. This plea is not a chronological past that can be forgotten. The inarticulate plea of *infantia* inhabits all the articulated questions and assertions that civil interlocutors address to each other: "In interlocution a drama is played out between *me* and *you*; it is the drama of authorization. The question or assertion that we address to others is invariably coupled with an entreaty: Deliver me from my abandonment, allow me to belong among you."[46] Any speech that I address to the other is still begging this other to "deliver" me from my abandonment, from the mute affective distress that my ongoing and absolutely singular relation to the Thing inflicts upon me.

It is in this infantile plea to be delivered from a terrifying muteness that, according to Lyotard, "resides the foundation of the right to speak. For it is this right that assures me that my request will be heard, and that I will not be rejected into the abjection of *infantia*."[47] This foundation of the right to speak is not a legal authorization; it is its condition of possibility. I now have the "right" to speak because my inarticulate infantile plea to enter the community of speakers was heard. In so doing, the speech community declared a Law of sorts: that one should not be abandoned to the mute distress of *infantia* by being denied access to interlocution. It is from obedience to this Law (which precedes all legislative authorization) that the members of the *polis* derive their "right" to speak. But admittance to the speech community does not mean that the threat of terror is left behind. Every civic interlocution is performed under the threat of a muteness which lingers through its civility and threatens to interrupt it at any moment. As they defend their right to speak, the members of the republic are therefore also reasserting their right to be delivered from the ongoing terror of this internal threat. It is the affective charge of this infantile terror that also grounds the plea for the right to speak to be granted to the designated outsiders of the *demos* and that fuels the resistance to the silencing of political terror.

At the border of the speech community, Lyotard asks us to hear the inarticulate scream of infancy. The speaking members of a community are always, and at the same time, terrorized infants who beg at its margins for admittance, for a reprieve from their mute affective distress. If this is the case, then the silence imposed by despotic terror is always coupled, in a way, with the refusal to respond to the inarticulate scream of infancy. This coupling can be exposed, literalized. One can, for instance, make sure that two overlapping sounds come from the borders that delimit the community of the citizens: the articulated requests of adults who ask for admittance within it, and the inarticulate screams of infants who beg to be delivered from the terror that is inflicted on them. As both requests are simultaneously rejected, a terrifying point is made, exposed as it were: that to deny admittance into the community of civic speakers is also to refuse any relief to infantile terror. As for the citizens who might believe that they witness, in the relative safety of their citizenship, the terror that is inflicted out there, on the outsider, the foreigner, it is up to them to hear—or not—in the infantile screams that come from the border the echo of their own inarticulate infancy, of their own infantile plea to be admitted within the community, a plea on which is grounded their very right to speak—here and now.

Notes

1. Jean-François Lyotard, "Emma: Between Philosophy and Psychoanalysis" [1990], in *Lyotard. Philosophy, Politics, and the Sublime*, ed. Hugh J. Silverman (New York and London: Routledge, 2002), 40, trans. modified. [The term *passibilité* in French is rendered as "susceptibility" in the English translation by Michael Sanders; the cognate "passibility" is now more often used to maintain the specificity of Lyotard's usage in relation to being open to affect, capable of feeling or suffering, in an active way, open to the possibility of event.—Eds.]
2. Jean-François Lyotard, *Heidegger and "the jews,"* tr. Andreas Michel and Mark Roberts (Minneapolis MN: University of Minnesota Press, [1988] 1990), 15.
3. Ibid., 15.
4. Ibid., 11.
5. Ibid., 17.
6. Ibid., 15–16.
7. Ibid., 20, trans. modified.
8. Ibid., 40.
9. Jean-François Lyotard, *Postmodern Fables*, tr. Georges Van Den Abbeele (Minneapolis MN: University of Minnesota Press, [1993] 1997), 199.
10. Lyotard, *Postmodern Fables*, 77.
11. Ibid., 200.
12. Ibid., 68–9.
13. See Jean-François Lyotard, *The Postmodern Condition*, tr. Geoff Bennington and Brian Massumi (Minneapolis MN: University of Minnesota Press, [1979] 1984), 62–3.
14. Lyotard, *Postmodern Fables*, 58.
15. Ibid., 200.
16. Ashley Woodward, "The End of Time," *Parrhesia*, no. 15 (2012): 89.
17. Lyotard, *Heidegger and "the jews,"* 48. The internal reference is to Theodor W. Adorno *Minima Moralia: Reflections from Damaged Life*, tr. E. F. N. Jephcott (New Left Books: London, [1951] 1974), §147–8.
18. Ibid., 41.
19. Ibid., 40.
20. Ibid., 48. The internal quotations are from Adorno, *Minima Moralia,* §150.
21. Ibid., 48.
22. Jean-François Lyotard, "The Other's Rights," in this volume, 79.
23. Lyotard, *Postmodern Fables*, 244.

24 Ibid., 232.
25 Lyotard, *Heidegger and "the jews,"* 48.
26 Ibid.
27 Lyotard, *Postmodern Fables*, 122.
28 Ibid., 193.
29 Ibid., 121.
30 Lyotard, "The Other's Rights," in this volume, 76.
31 Lyotard, *Postmodern Fables*, 213.
32 Ibid., 213.
33 Ibid., 211.
34 Ibid., 186.
35 Ibid., 121.
36 Ibid., 121.
37 Ibid., 122.
38 Lyotard, "The Other's Rights," in this volume, 76.
39 Ibid., 78.
40 Ibid., 80.
41 Ibid., 76.
42 Ibid., 77.
43 Ibid., 78.
44 Merriam-Webster's Collegiate English Dictionary, 11th ed. (2014)
45 Lyotard, "The Other's Rights," in this volume, 81.
46 Ibid.
47 Ibid.

4

A Matter of Time: Color, Affect, and the Suffering of Thought

Georges Van Den Abbeele

While the aesthetic and political dimensions of Jean-François Lyotard's thought have been subject to significant discussion, his major contributions as a philosopher of time have received less attention.[1] The thought of time is fundamental throughout his long and varied career. This preoccupation extends from his first publication (significantly in *Les temps modernes*) whose title bears its own time stamp, "Born in 1925," and from the early book on *Phenomenology* all the way through to the later work on infancy and anamnesis.[2] While explicitly basing himself in phenomenologically derived concepts of time, he also challenges its classic iterations as either the eternal present caught between the intentionalities of retention and protention (Husserl's revision of Aristotle), the finitude that structures our being-unto-death (Heidegger), or time consciousness as a function of narrative (Ricoeur).

Despite a narrative of changing positions and distinct phases that would periodize and temporally manage the vicissitudes of Lyotard's work, there is, nonetheless, a remarkable consistency to his analysis of time. Major shifts in his thinking have involved less a change than a deepening of his thought, as it pits the Husserlian model against the atemporality of the Freudian unconscious, the Marxian critique of exchange as the temporal basis of capitalism, the peculiar historicity of the *post*modern, the actuality of the event, and so on.

As good a place as any to grasp Lyotard's philosophy of time is a work from the middle of his career, namely his 1980 art book, *Sur la constitution du temps par la couleur dans les oeuvres récentes d'Albert Ayme*.[3] Lavishly illustrated with examples of Ayme's paintings and conceptual drawings, the book is as much a showcase of Ayme's work as it is the occasion for Lyotard to meditate on the sense of time provoked by the artist's distinctive painterly practice. Specifically, Ayme applies only the three primary colors of blue, yellow, and red in large, typically rectangular, swaths of a single color. After the paint dries, he may apply a new coat of a different primary color, thus creating an effect where the first applied color alters that of the second. A third or a fourth layer may then also be subsequently applied, but only once the preceding layer is fully dry. The colors are thus combined but not mixed, used dry but not wet, as in traditional painting where subtle shades of difference are generally produced by blending wet paint together on the palette before applying it to canvas. Instead of a continuum of colors, we are treated to the superimposition of one dried primary color on top of the other. The result is an abstract, non-representational work of art that inevitably yields varying gradations of brown, or even black, if enough layers are added to what began as a white canvas. Ayme's work thus follows the minimalist strain of abstract expressionism stretching from Malevich and Mondrian up through Barnett Newman and Mark Rothko.

What draws Lyotard to Ayme's work in particular is an art that proposes a visual materialization of time in the "constitution" of its colors. While the thickness, no matter how exiguous, of the multiple layers gestures beyond the presumed bi-dimensionality of the medium, the fact that these multiple layers are temporally separated in their application implies a four-dimensional work of art. To be sure, it is not the documentation about how the work was produced that matters. Rather, it is the specific shade of the color itself that reveals the phenomenality of time. What we are looking at in a painting by Ayme is not only time, but nothing other than time. For Lyotard, Ayme is not merely a painter but a philosopher who proceeds by brushstrokes rather than by words, thus breaking with the philosophical tradition that casts truth in terms of *logos*. It remains to be seen what Ayme's arduous attempt to "think" time means.

For Ayme is not only a philosopher by a different means, but his paintings can also be brought into direct philosophical dialogue with what for Lyotard remains the quintessential philosophical reflection on time: Edmund Husserl's *Vorlesungen zur Phänomenologie des inneren Zeitbewusstseins*, originally given as a series of lectures in 1905, but only published in 1928, with a preface by his student, Martin Heidegger. Despite Husserl's attempt to build upon Aristotle's insights in *Physics IV, sections 10–14,* to describe the origins of our perception of time as a *continuous* effect of consciousness and intentionality, his concept of time in its actual "Konstitution" (to use Husserl's term picked up by Lyotard) cannot help but imply an insuperable *discontinuity* of time, its becoming space, experienced as a set of distinct moments, each of which is marked by the retention of past moments in the form of memory and the protention of future moments via anticipation and imagination. This view of time is schematized via a triangular set of connections, where at any given moment T along a horizontal timeline, previous moments of T are retained no longer as present but altered as past T.

What one could call Husserl's quantum framing of time is fundamental to Lyotard's own thinking of temporality, and it is a frequent reference, often explicitly in its diagrammatical form, from his earliest through his latest work. In fact, his two most sustained critiques of Husserl's theory of time are to be found at opposite ends of his career: in the long, final chapter on "Phenomenology and History" in *Phenomenology* (1954), and in his last major work, the posthumous *Misère de la philosophie* (2000), where he explicitly confronts Husserl with Freud's views on temporality, a theoretical clash between phenomenology and psychoanalysis, which underlies Lyotard's philosophy of time (*Misère*, 70ff.).[4]

Nowhere is the Husserlian connection more pronounced, however, than in his book on Ayme, and it is precisely the realization in painting of a discontinuous notion of

A Matter of Time: Color, Affect, and the Suffering of Thought   53

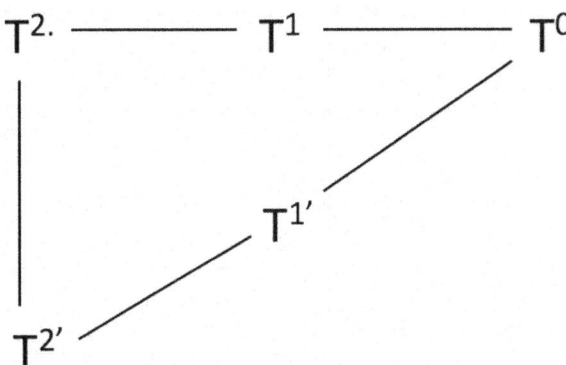

Figure 4.1 Diagram showing temporal positions, adapted by the author from a sketch by Jean-François Lyotard, after Edmund Husserl.

time, enabled precisely by the succession of discreet moments demarcated by each separate layer of paint, that brings that painter into philosophical dialogue with Husserl. Ultimately, Lyotard's Husserlian analysis reveals Ayme's work as in its own right a phenomenological investigation of time, if not as the phenomenality of time itself. Moreover, Ayme's work presents a world where the phenomenon of color describes not only the apperception of time but its "constitution" as such, as literally the standing together (*Zusammensetzung*) of time across its constituting moments.[5]

This *constitution* of time through color explains Lyotard's interpretation of Ayme's work not only as a philosophy of time, but *a fortiori* as a philosophy of time that rejects the continuous model of temporality as flow, be it the discontinuous flow of retention-protention, in favor of a combinatorics of time, with its own sets of permutations, reversals, and substitutions. There is no predictability to time for Ayme as he can begin with any one of the three primary colors, followed by further layers in any possible combination of the three, thus defining his opus as so many possible worlds of time, as parallel but equally potential temporalities. Lyotard quotes Ayme describing his work as "an attempt to abolish any discriminatory privilege among the three primary colors."[6] Time appears as so many ways of throwing the dice, without for that matter doing away with chance, to pastiche Mallarmé.

But this actuality of chance also points to Lyotard's contemporaneous rejection of classic phenomenology and his embrace of Wittgenstein's notion of language games, beginning with *Just Gaming* (1979). If phenomena appear as successive but unpredictable moves within a limited set of possibilities (be that the virtually illimitable set of options enabled by language, as opposed to the narrowed triad of blue-yellow-red), then the traditional study of the phenomenon of internal time consciousness (*inneren Zeitbewusstseins*) must yield to an analysis of the external relation between moves in a language game. In *The Differend* (1983), Lyotard thoroughly revises and transforms this concept into a "philosophy of phrases" based in pragmatics, specifically in terms of the kinds of rules that determine the linkage between phrases (understanding that phrases are not limited to discursive forms of language⁷).

It is no surprise, then, that Lyotard links onto Ayme's claim to a visual art that would "abolish any discriminatory privilege" among colors, with a question that also charts a *passage* from the aesthetic to the political, and beyond:

> Would a politics be possible following the same general paradigm? Isn't this what governed the institution of the rules for the political game of democracy in Athens at the time of the Cleisthenian reform? And an erotics? "The enigma that I am tracking through painting is that of woman," writes A.A. What then are the elementary units that it would be suitable to substitute for BYR [Blue Yellow Red] in terms of the womb? Sex organs, names of partners, positions, affects, partial drives…?⁸

While the leveling exchange between colors or between sexual behaviors can be readily understood, even if with reservations,⁹ how are we supposed to understand its application to politics? And specifically to democratic politics, if not as something like an equal exchange of governance among its citizens? Cleisthenes was a Greek legislator whose "reforms," according to Aristotle, made the constitution of Athens "much more democratic."¹⁰ Specifically, Cleisthenes redistributed the citizens of the four traditional tribes of Athens into groups organized by their *demes* or residences rather than by their family ties, even substituting a place-based nomenclature in lieu of the traditional patronymics that identified citizens by their genealogy:

> All who lived in any given deme he declared fellow-demesmen, to the end that the new citizens might not be exposed by the habitual use of family names, but that men might be officially described by the names of their demes…and so securing that more persons might have a share in the franchise [of the *polis*].¹¹

Athenian democracy thus instituted could indeed be said to be an attempt to "abolish any discriminatory privilege" among the four primary tribes, to channel Lyotard's rechanneling of Ayme.

But this general combinatorics of democracy, like the succession of colors in Ayme, is still fundamentally in a relation to time. In a 1982 exchange with Claude Lefort, Lyotard asserts that "democracy implies an 'invention in time,' and that the democratic experience should also be examined as an experience of time."¹² It is not just that there is an equal possibility for all deliberative outcomes, but that each one matters in its actualization, just as the specific sequence of colors in Ayme's work creates its own peculiar shade. Their democratic substitutability or exchangeability, like all exchange, invokes a distinctive relation to time, as Lyotard describes elsewhere:

> Someone (X) gives someone (Y) an object a at time t. This giving has as its condition that Y will give X an object b at time t'…the first exchange takes place if and only if the second is perfectly guaranteed, to the point that it can be considered to have already happened…the 'second' occurrence, the payment, is

not expected at the time of the first, it is *presupposed* as the condition of the 'first' ... Exchange [as presupposed time] requires that what is future be as if it were present.[13]

Exchange "value" is, of course, also the very principal of capital as the accumulation of (labor) time, or surplus value, within commodity production according to the famous Marxian schema of M-C-M frequently invoked throughout Lyotard's opus. And we can see the implementation of democratic combinatorics as similarly based in presupposed time, though not necessarily as a wager of increased value but rather as a guarantee of equal "franchise" to the *polis,* as the presupposition of an equality that is always still to come. On the one hand, it may just be a matter of time before a specific color is reached or a given citizen's voice is heard; but on the other hand, there may be other factors that thwart or challenge this democratic distribution. For instance, time in the form of speed itself may or may not make a difference. For Ayme, it only matters that the previous coat of paint has had time to dry, but other than that, the actual length of the delay between coats is irrelevant. There is no way to judge by looking at one of his paintings whether the lag between coats of paint is a factor of minutes, hours, even months or years. On the other hand, these time lapses may be highly determinative of distributive justice, especially if one must wait too long for one's turn, or is otherwise at some undisclosed statistical disadvantage. Consider, for example, the differing effects on democracy of systems where elections are rigidly set, as in the United States (one can vote for president only once every four years, no matter what the actions of that leader), in contrast to many parliamentary democracies, where elections can be called by the legislature at a moment's notice (typically when the timing suits partisan political advantage, to be sure).

There is another issue relative to speed and temporal rhythm, however, specifically the demand to make, save, or gain time (all three of which are succinctly captured by the French "*gagner du temps*"), or the desire to overcome time by doing more ever more quickly. Of course, the capitalist tropes of "time is money" and "speed is of the essence" loom large here. The rule of efficiency, of "performance," is how Lyotard actually defines the postmodern *condition,* as opposed to whatever "postmodernist" cultural/artistic/architectural/political practices are deployed in response to the givens of that condition. And that condition endlessly accelerates the speed of "development" while concomitantly casting an ever-deeper amnesia that effectively relegates not just the past but historical narrative in all its forms to irrelevance. It's precisely at this point, and perhaps at this point only, that Lyotard converges with Fredric Jameson in their otherwise divergent views regarding the meaning of postmodernism. The modalities of historical narrative have thus become either delegitimized for the one, or catastrophically forgotten for the other.[14] Regardless of how one adjudicates this dispute, a critical practice of anamnesis, or some kind of critical thinking that aims at an unforgetting, seems required.

For Lyotard, however, it is not simply a matter of peeling or scraping back the latest coat of paint to uncover the preceding primary color(s). As he writes in *Misère de la philosophie,* "A thinking that thinks is always in relation to what it does not know how to think."[15] Hence, for him, a thinking that really *thinks* cannot be content with a mere archaeology but rather must find a way to think in relation to what it cannot think, be it what under postmodern conditions can "no longer" be thought. This is the arduous task Lyotard undertakes in his later work, whether that intractability of thought is called infancy, or the Thing, or the inhuman. The intractable is what has somehow fallen out of time, or never entered time in the first place, what remains timeless like the Freudian unconscious, but which for that matter can also emerge unexpectedly, *in time*, as event, or as what is somewhat laboriously called in *The Differend* the "Is it happening? (*Arrive-t-il?*)."[16] It is, for example, the *temporal* experience of democracy as untimely insurrection that Lyotard chronicles in the popular Algerian uprising in 1960–1. This revolt, seemingly out of nowhere, so alarmed both the French government and the exiled FLN (Algerian National Liberation Front) as to trigger what he decries as their hastily and mutually self-interested brokering of the agreement granting Algerian independence. Other examples that loom large in Lyotard's thinking include the student–worker revolts of 1968 (which also took everyone by surprise, only to fade away just as quickly) and the "enthusiasm" Kant describes regarding the French Revolution precisely among those who had the least at stake, the most "disinterested."[17] But these are not in themselves cases of thinking the unthinkable, nor even of a collective anamnesis. On the contrary, they tend to be as quickly forgotten or suppressed as they emerge. Unexpected and unforeseen, they show how the unthought *happens* in all its untimeliness, as the very sign of history.

So what is the relation with a "thinking that thinks"? With the anamnesis that strives to reckon with what that thinking cannot think? A useful indication can be found in Lyotard's 1976 review of Louis Marin's *La critique du discours*,[18] a seemingly restrained account of early modern linguistic theory as it emerges in the *Port-Royal Logic* and in the philosophical work of Blaise Pascal. What could be less relevant or more dated (*inactuel*) for our contemporary concerns? In his review, Lyotard admits from the get-go that the work is "out of date" but in a true exercise of postmodernist paralogism, he argues that it is "outrageously out of date [*un inactuel fort*]." He claims that it is so out of touch, so "not with it," so out of synch with the times, as to question the very foundations of what we think is current, of what we think passes for relevant to our contemporary condition. It may be, *pace* Jameson, a characteristically postmodern attempt to think historically, but it also models a mode of historical thinking that conjures up a past so different from the past we think as past that it challenges the easy assumption we make in thinking the present to be disconnected from a past, which can nonetheless unexpectedly reemerge at any point *as* present.[19] Ironically, it is this twist of anamnesis that reveals the potential *return* of the past, its outrageous repetition, that the present is called into question through a resistance to the discursive temporality of retention-protention as a linear, unidirectional, and presumably progressive developmental flow. And that flow is what Lyotard describes as the inhuman "system" that precedes and supersedes human life itself and not at all to the latter's advantage. The danger is not merely the commonplace one of a late capitalist society overworked to utter exhaustion but rather the demise of thought itself, or at least, of a "thought that thinks."

The alternative is what Lyotard elsewhere calls "parachronicity," as in the concluding chapter of *Readings in Infancy*, where he articulates the difference between what now appear as two distinct kinds of temporality. On the one hand, there is the temporality that is "inscribed in the structure of the articulated phrase," the implicit temporality actualized by the pragmatics of phrases linked to others through various permutations and combinations:

> Now this faculty of permutation immediately entails a consecutiveness of the two sentences, a temporalization. In addressing itself to *you*, *I* expects a sentence to come, where the two names will be in reversed positions along the poles of address.—This disposition is the kernel of temporality in the phenomenological sense. (I note along the way that the failure of Cartesian or Husserlian thought in the elaboration of the problems of time and otherness results from the aberrant philosopheme that the Cogito is: an *I* without a *you*.) [20]

By way of contrast to this *discursive* "temporality of expectation and memory," incessantly caught between protention and retention, lies the apparent atemporality of unarticulated affect. Citing both Freud on the timelessness of the unconscious and Aristotle on the necessarily self-sufficient *eidos* of pleasure within itself, Lyotard posits the essential *now*ness of affect: "Pleasure would not be pleasure if it were missing something. It awaits nothing therefore for its completion. It requires no supplement of duration ... It is now."[21] Applying the same analysis to suffering as to pleasure, Lyotard concludes that affect is "singular, inflexible, incomparable" but also "for the same reason, it has amnesia."[22] Affect is only in the now, entire in its singularity as now and therefore immemorable except in its being now, "the affectual now is not framed by a *before* and an *after*." According to Lyotard, this is "the temporal paradox, the parachronicity" that Freud notes as *Nachträglichkeit* or belated after-effect, which we can also understand as the outrageously out of date (*inactuel fort*). Nothing precludes, of course, that the affect can be discursively rendered, but that it can be done so only in the third person, as the voice of some other: "An affect is like death and like birth: if it is thought, articulated, recounted, it is that of the other, of others."[23]

Death, birth, and affect point to what cannot be thought even by a thought "that thinks" and strives to reckon with that unthinkable. This is where one encounters affect *in* thought itself, as its "suffering."[24] Moreover, the split between discursive time and affectual untimeliness echoes what Lyotard provocatively calls the "conflict of inhumanities." On the one hand, there is the inhumanity of the system, of development as the institutionalized cruelty of endless acceleration, and on the other hand we have the inhuman within us, as what unthinkingly precedes or exceeds who we are, the infant we all were before we came into any sense of self and which continues to inhabit or haunt us even throughout our adult lives.[25] This infancy, as Lyotard notes in recalling the word's etymology, is literally unspeakable, yet its traces persist in what Lyotard reminds us only "passes as institutional: literature, the arts, philosophy." We recognize here what we continue to call "the humanities," precisely that suspect sector of the academic institution perennially accused of being childish or immature for its being the most resistant to the development incarnated by the technical, vocational university apparatus with its claim to "research in service to society." This is also where the self-anointed leadership of the humanities errs in desperately trying to make the case for their "value," practical or otherwise.

In a world where the system "has the consequence of causing the forgetting of what escapes it,"[26] and in particular, by the casting of infancy into and as oblivion (or what Freud called "repression"), we are caught between the discursive temporalities of "making" or "saving" time, in the name of "progress" and "development," and the figural parachronicities of what can only appear outrageously out of date, as lost time, as inefficiency, or as infantile resistance, to the extent that they recall what was forgotten by the inhumanity of ever more rapid development. Anamnesis would seem then to be the only thought that really "thinks," and, as Lyotard contends, the "other of acceleration and abbreviation."[27] Anamnesis is resistance, it is literally what re-states, re-situates, or re-constitutes what stood or what stands outside the system, what is or was forgotten, what re-stands or withstands it as the unsuspected strength of the "outrageously out of date" in its radical untimeliness. Or like the reverse side of an Ayme painting that reveals the once-white canvas stained by splotches of the colors that have bled through to the other side, and which Ayme felicitously calls its "memories."[28]

For Lyotard, the ruse or cunning of the system is in its innate neutralization of critique, which it absorbs or converts into greater efficiencies and speed. He thus anticipated what Silicon Valley likes to call "disruption" as the constructive spur to ever greater "innovation." But this ruse of development is what Lyotard pessimistically sees as "the very thing that takes away the hope of an alternative to the system from both analysis and practice,"[29] and thus deprives us of any utopian or revolutionary politics, of any alternative beyond mere resistance. That resistance, in turn, can only rely on the other temporality of parachronicity, the timelessness of what remains forgotten, unconscious, as the "debt to childhood":

> . . . what else remains as "politics" except resistance to this inhuman [of the system]? And what else is left to resist with but the debt, which each soul has contracted with the miserable and admirable indetermination from which it was born and does not cease to be born?—which is to say, with the other inhuman?
>
> This debt to childhood is one which we never pay off. But it is enough not to forget it in order to resist it and perhaps, not to be unjust. It is the task of writing, thinking, literature, arts, to venture to bear witness to it.[30]

Resistance is, in all senses, a *matter* of time, and relies for its efficacy on the profound untimeliness of philosophical reflection and artistic experimentation, and arguably those dimensions of the humanities that are the least relevant, the least disciplinary, the least professional or professionalizing.

To the objection that Lyotard leaves us with only a paltry and pessimistic politics of passivity that at best can merely "bear witness" to the intolerable inhumanity of our postmodern condition, one can answer in two ways. First, the general strategy of temporal disruption is a venerable successor to the earliest and yet still current forms of resistance to capitalism's endless need to overcome the physical limits of the working day by speeding up the process of production to extract ever more surplus value from labor. The first form of resistance, as Marx painstakingly describes in the first volume of *Capital,* was the work stoppage or slowdown, which existed well before the organized strike and has continued well after the destitution of officially sanctioned trade unions.

Likewise the "Luddite" destruction of machinery, even if Marx himself viewed that destructive action as a misrecognition of the machine for the capitalist standing behind it.[31] Some later Marxists, however, have viewed Luddite destructiveness in more positive and effective terms.[32] Other strands of leftist thought have stressed the right *not* to work, even the right to idleness and leisure, and more recently, discussions have arisen about the right to "basic income" regardless of work status.[33] I mention these modes of resistance because, even in his late texts, Lyotard is less distant from his Marxist roots in "Socialisme ou Barbarie" than is often assumed.[34]

The second answer follows from the first, just as the theoretical work of Marxism follows from the practical action of working-class resistance. In this case, the stereotypically frivolous or unproductive activities of "writing, thinking, literature, arts" mean that the lost time is doubly lost in the very process of anamnesis: "But writing and reading which advance backwards in the direction of the unknown thing 'within' are slow. One loses one's time seeking time lost."[35] Thinking that *really* thinks thus keeps standing, withstanding, or re-standing "in relation to what it does not know how to think." Of course, not *all* writing, or thinking, or making art is engaged in such parachronistic endeavor. Much of it resides directly in the service of the system, whether technical writing, administrative planning, or mercenary design, to achieve greater efficiencies and speed. For that reason, among others, critical anamnesis can only remain an ethical "task," an Idea in the Kantian sense, as Lyotard would say. It is not just a matter of time.

Rather, time itself is a matter of dispute, if not a matter for differends. The only possible relation between the two "modalities" of time, between discursive time and parachronicity, between (articulated) phrase and affect (phrase), between *logos* and *phōnē*, between meaning and pathos, between (adult) communication and (inchoate) infancy, is that of the differend: "*phōnē* and *logos* can only encounter each other, and not link onto each other. This encounter gives place to a differend. For the human animal, at least, this differend cannot be treated as a litigation."[36] Between a politics rooted in discourse and an aesthetics imbued in affect, the differend occasioned by the system is irresolvable. Moreover, as is the case for any differend, its attempted "resolution" or litigation only plays into the hands of the party that sets the rules: "A case of differend between two parties takes place when the 'regulation' of the conflict that opposes them is done in the idiom of one of the parties while the wrong suffered by the other is not signified in that idiom."[37] Criticism, whether constructive or disruptive—it matters little, as the discourse of Silicon Valley "innovators" would have it—always seems to serve the interests of development, of increasing efficiencies and accelerating performance.

On the other hand, though, the *suffering* or passion of thought before what cannot be thought, the pathos or affect of its knocking against its own limits, signals the attempt at a *passage*, if not a phrase, that can only avow what it cannot know, remember not what was never registered but more (or less!) simply that there is something that was never registered in the first place, not just forgotten historical memory but something that was always already forgotten. The pain of this suffering can never be alleviated no matter how unending the working through of anamnesis. This is the unforgivable but cherished scandal of the (in)humanities, the obligation of its Sisyphean task.

But the suffering of thought as anamnesis is in turn caught in the differend between the (ethical) demand of the voice and the (creative) command of the Thing. Both are forms of obligation, hence partaking in a modality of time,[38] but one radically different from the other. On the one hand, one hears but cannot understand the voice of the law that demands justice in the form of an indecipherable "you ought," framing our ethical responsibility by "saying to ourselves what the voice wants to say."[39] On the other hand, the "thing" that "preoccupies art and writing" could only be said to "command" but not to "demand" anything:

> This is how it differs so strongly from the voice. It does not address itself to you, it doesn't address itself at all. You are not its "you." It does not expect any realization from you because it is not even your interlocutor. It does not speak an unknown, untranslatable language. It does not speak at all. Let's say it lives within you but as if it were outside.[40]

The Thing, or the infant, or the inhuman, that commands the work (of art, of literature) is thus at one and the same time its undoing, or "unworking": "The work [*oeuvre*] is but a pause in the process of unworking [*désoeuvrement*]."[41] It is a deconstituting constitution, or the endlessly unworking work of working through that "allows for the opening of the path through which what has *not yet* come can come, the child, the past, here the line or the color-phrase, and what is nevertheless *already* potential human life, possible memory, or eventual chromatism and drawing."[42] It is what "strikes the eye, thus prepared for the unprepared, like an event."[43]

Thus, "the suffering of thought is a suffering in time, of what happens," and "if this suffering is the mark of true thought, it's because we think in the already-thought ... the unthought hurts because we're comfortable in what's already thought."[44] This is not the presupposition of exchange and the assumption of a future already made present, and certainly not the calculation of risks to assure maximum profits, but the possibility or *passibility* to what cannot be foreseen, the unexpected, the "is it happening?", the event. Which in turn gestures towards the very essence of time, its immaterial matter, not as hysteron-proteron, but as the instant of what has no retention-protection, neither no longer nor not yet. That gesture is the work of anamnesis, never-ending yet always beginning again, a suffering of the event not unlike the (in)visibility made visual in the occasional spillover of primary color at the edge of an Ayme painting, or as in the instantaneous irruption of Barnett Newman's vertical stripe descending across one of his monochrome backgrounds.[45] But if painting can thus occur *as* time for Ayme and Newman, then the color we see there affects us, in turn, as the chromatic matter that is the deconstituted constitution of a chronology never being itself, the very *matter* of time in its becoming space—*chronos* as *chromatics*—that commands the urgency of suffering the unanticipated event of a thinking that really thinks ...

Notes

1 Important exceptions include Peter W. Milne, "Temporality and the Lyotardian Sublime: Kant between Husserl and Freud," *Journal of the British Society for Phenomenology*, vol. 51, no. 3, 2020, 201–14; and Geoffrey Bennington, "Time after Time," in *Late Lyotard* (CreateSpace, 2008), 81–104.

2   Jean-François Lyotard, "Né en 1925," *Les temps modernes* 32 (1948), translated as "Born in 1925" in *Political Writings*, tr. Bill Readings and Kevin Paul Geiman (Minneapolis MN: University of Minnesota Press, 1993), 85–9; Lyotard, *Phenomenology*, tr. Brian Beakley (Minneapolis MN: University of Minnesota Press, [1954] 1991).
3   Jean-François Lyotard, *Sur la constitution du temps par la couleur dans les oeuvres récentes d'Albert Ayme* (Paris: Édition traversière, 1980). translated as "*On the Constitution of Time through Colour in the Recent Works of Albert Ayme*" (tr. Vlad Ionescu and Erica Harris), in *Textes dispersés II: artistes contemporains/Miscellaneous Texts II: Contemporary Artists*, ed. Herman Parret (Leuven: Leuven University Press, 2012), 312–49.
4   Milne likewise situates Lyotard's notion of temporality in the conflict between Husserl and Freud and, in a compelling argument, identifies the Kantian sublime as their inarticulable hinge for Lyotard. My own approach is to locate that hinge in Lyotard's recasting of Wittgenstein's concept of language games into his signature analysis of "phrases"—a move, it must be said, that also rejoins his analysis of the Kantian sublime in many of the ways astutely unpacked by Milne.
5   This actualization of painting *as* time is further elaborated in Lyotard's later study on Barnett Newman; see Jean-François Lyotard, *The Inhuman: Reflections on Time*, tr. Geoffrey Bennington and Rachel Bowlby (Stanford CA: Stanford University Press, [1988] 1991), 78.
6   Lyotard "*On the Constitution of Time*," 329, trans. modified.
7   See Jean-François Lyotard, *The Differend: Phrases in Dispute*, tr. G. Van Den Abbeele (Minneapolis MN: University of Minnesota Press, [1983] 1988), 70.
8   Lyotard, "*On the Constitution of Time*," 329, trans. modified.
9   Lyotard's rejoinder to Ayme's classically sexist eroticization of his art practice in terms of tracking the misogynist "enigma" of woman also gives pause in this all too typically male misunderstanding of female genitalia, confusing the womb or uterus (the French word, *matrice*) with the vagina and vulva, thus heteronormatively misconstruing procreation with eroticism. One could perhaps then justify the deliberately literalist mistranslation of "*matrice*" not as "womb" but as "matrix" by Ionescu and Harris (326).
10 Aristotle, *The Constitution of Athens* ¶ 21, in *The Complete Works of Aristotle*, ed. Jonathan Barnes (Princeton NJ: Princeton University Press, 1984), II, 2354.
11 Ibid.
12 A transcript of this intervention can be found in Jean-Luc Nancy and Philippe Lacoue-Labarthe, *Le retrait du politique* (Paris: Galilée, 1983), 87.
13 Lyotard, *The Inhuman*, 65–6; emphasis added, interjection in square brackets is mine. Exchange as such appears as the inverse of Freudian *Nachträglichkeit*, not an "*après-coup*" but a kind of *avant*-coup, playing havoc with protention just as the Freudian concept undermines the logic of retention. Instead of the delayed "return" of unconscious affect, capitalism posits the hastening of anticipated profits, the so-called market in futurities.
14 "It is safest to grasp the concept of postmodernism as an attempt to think the present historically in an age that has forgotten how to think historically in the first place." Fredric Jameson, *Postmodernism, or the Cultural Logic of Capitalism* (Durham NC: Duke University Press, 1991), ix.
15 Jean-François Lyotard, *Misère de la philosophie* (Paris: Galilée, 2000): 179, my translation.
16 Lyotard, *The Differend*, 79 and *passim*.

17 Jean-François Lyotard, *La Guerre des Algériens: Écrits 1956–1963* (Paris: Galilée, 1989), especially the chapter, "En Algérie, une vague nouvelle," 211–23. Curiously, this crucial chapter does not appear in Bill Readings's almost integral translation of that work in Jean-François Lyotard, *Political Writings*. See also my "Algérie l'intraitable: Lyotard's National Front," *L'Esprit Créateur* XXXI (Spring 1991), 144–57. On May '68, see especially "Unbeknownst," in Jean-François Lyotard, *Postmodern Fables,* tr. Georges Van Den Abbeele (Minneapolis MN: University of Minnesota Press, [1993] 1997), 185–97. And on Kant and the French Revolution, Jean-François Lyotard, *Enthusiasm: The Kantian Critique of History,* tr. Georges Van Den Abbeele (Stanford CA: Stanford University Press, [1986] 2009). In general, one sees in these political texts Lyotard's admiration for the kind of "spontaneism" associated with Rosa Luxemburg and embraced by "Socialisme ou Barbarie" that remains anathema to classic Leninist doctrine.
18 Jean-François Lyotard, "Humour en sémiothéologie: que le signe est hostie, et l'inverse; et comment s'en débarrasser," originally published in *Critique* 342 (1976), and republished in *Rudiments païens* (Paris: 10/18, 1977), 32–59. An English translation by Mira Kamdar can be found in Robert Harvey and Mark S. Roberts (eds), *Toward the Postmodern* (Atlantic Highlands, NJ: Humanities Press, 1993), 73–86.
19 As such, the *inactuel fort* wreaks appropriate havoc with what Hayden White calls "the practical past" in his book by that same title (Evanston: Northwestern University Press, 2014).
20 Jean-François Lyotard, *Readings in Infancy*, ed. Robert Harvey and Kiff Bamford (London and New York: Bloomsbury, [1991] forthcoming 2023). Lyotard, *Lectures d'enfance* (Paris: Galilée, 1991), 135.
21 Ibid., 136.
22 Ibid.
23 Ibid., 137.
24 Lyotard, *The Inhuman*, 19–20.
25 Ibid., 2–7.
26 Ibid., 2.
27 Ibid., 3.
28 Lyotard, "*On the Constitution of Time,*" 347.
29 Lyotard, *The Inhuman*, 7.
30 Ibid.
31 Karl Marx, *Capital,* tr. Ben Fowkes (New York: New Left Review, [1867] 1976), 553–64.
32 For example, Raya Dunayesvkaya, *Marxism and Freedom: From 1776 Until Today* (New York: Humanity Books, 2000), 266–87.
33 Eugène Marsan, *Éloge de la paresse* [1926] and Paul Lafargue, *Le droit à la paresse* [1880], reprinted as a single volume (San Bernardino: FV Éditions, 2012). On "basic income," see inter alia, Guy Standing, *Basic Income, and How We Can Make It Happen* (Harmondsworth: Penguin, 2017); Philippe Van Parijs and Yannick Vanderborght, *Basic Income: A Radical Proposal for a Free Society and a Sane Economy* (Cambridge MA: Harvard University Press, 2017).
34 Lyotard's most sustained self-reflection on his relation to Marxism can be found in *Peregrinations: Law, Form, Event* (New York: Columbia University Press, 1988).
35 Lyotard, *The Inhuman*, 3.
36 Lyotard, "The Affect-phrase" in this volume, 72.
37 Lyotard, *The Differend*, 9.
38 Lyotard, *The Inhuman*, 81.

39 Lyotard, *Misère* 104, my translation.
40 Ibid., 105–6.
41 Ibid., 103.
42 Ibid., 99.
43 Ibid.
44 Lyotard *The Inhuman*, 19–20, trans. modified.
45 See Lyotard's remarks on this facet of Newman's painting in "Newman: The Instant," in *The Inhuman,* 78–84.

Lyotard Supplement I

5

The Affect-phrase (from a Supplement to *The Differend*)[1]

Jean-François Lyotard, 1990
Translated by Keith Crome

1. Is feeling a phrase? And if it is, to what sort or family of phrases does it belong? In §22 of *The Differend* we read: "The differend is the unstable state and instance of language wherein something which must be able to be put into phrases cannot yet be. This state includes silence, which is a negative phrase, but it also calls upon phrases which are in principle possible. This state is signaled by what one ordinarily calls a feeling. 'One cannot find the words,' etc."[2] And in §105: "The absence of a phrase (a silence, etc.) or the absence of a linkage (the beginning, the end, disorder, nothingness, etc.) are also phrases. What distinguishes these particular phrases from others? Equivocality, feeling, 'wishes' (exclamation) etc." It is not clear whether the feeling is a non-phrase, a negative phrase or a particular sort of phrase. Nor is it clear whether the feeling results from an impossibility of phrasing an event or, on the contrary, it is the cause of this deficiency. Do we remain silent because we are greatly moved, or find ourselves moved because the words are lacking and we are obliged to remain silent?— The question is badly formulated. It presupposes a relation of causality. It might be thought that this category is, in this instance, inapplicable.

2. Feeling is a phrase. I call it the affect-phrase. It is distinct in that it is *unarticulated*.— We read in *The Differend* that a phrase presents a universe (§§18, 25, etc.). A phrase universe is in principle (i.e., transcendentally) polarized according to two axes: the poles of addressor and addressee on the axis of address, the poles of meaning and referent on the semantico-referential axis (which Aristotle designates apophantic). According to the latter axis, something (a meaning) is phrased about the subject of something (a referent). According to the former axis, that of the address, this something (the meaning) is phrased by or in the name of something (the addressor) towards something (the addressee). We can say, in order to be brief, that the former connotes the semantic axis, the latter the pragmatic. A phrase universe is in principle arranged according to this double polarization. A phrase is articulated to the extent that it presents a universe.

3. It is necessary to say that this double polarization is a transcendental condition of the articulation of a phrase, rather than an empirical fact. Many given phrases neglect to

mark this or that instance or such and such a relation between instances. They presuppose them or imply them. Such omissions are not, in general, obstacles to linking. On the contrary, it is the foreseeability of linking (the rule of the genre) which makes them acceptable. The demand for an articulation that is as complete as possible characterizes certain genres of discourse. The questions which actualize this demand are: What exactly are you talking about? How do you know what you have said; who told you? What exactly do you mean by...? etc. One argues in response. In the cognitive genre, one seeks to establish not only *what* the referent, the addressor, the addressee and the meaning are, but also the *reality* of the first three, as well as the legitimacy of the linkages. Establishing these realities demands procedures which are specific to the cognitive genre and which link together groups of phrases bearing upon the meaning, upon the designation and upon the nomination.

4. In the "Preface" to *The Differend* we read: "A damage [*un dommage*] results from an injury done to the rules of a genre of discourse, but which is reparable according to those rules. A wrong [*un tort*] results from the fact that the rules of the genre of discourse according to which one judges are not those of the judged genre or genres of discourse."[3] And further on, in §7: "This is what a wrong would be: a damage accompanied by loss of the means to prove the damage."

5. Many noteworthy characteristics follow from the fact that the affect-phrase is unarticulated. Here are three: (1) The affect-phrase appears not to let itself be linked on to according to the rules of any genre of discourse; on the contrary, it appears only to be able to suspend or interrupt linkages, whatever they are; (2) The affect-phrase injures the rules of the genres of discourse; it creates a damage; (3) This damage in its turn gives rise to a wrong, because the damage suffered by discourse can be settled within the rules, but argumentation is in all cases inappropriate to the affect-phrase, if it is true that it does not give rise to a genre and cannot be argued. Consequently the damage that the affect-phrase makes the genres of discourse suffer transforms itself into a wrong suffered by the affect-phrase.—The articulated phrase and the affect-phrase can "encounter" one another only in missing each other. From their differend, there results a wrong. If articulation and inarticulation are irreducible to one another, this wrong can be said to be radical.

6. A phrase can be more or less articulated, its polarizations more or less marked. But the affect-phrase does not admit of these gradations. *Unarticulated* would signify: this phrase does not present a phrase universe; it signals the meaning; this meaning is only of one kind, pleasure and/or pain ("it's alright, it's not alright" ["*ça va, ça ne va pas*"]); this meaning is not related to any referent: the "it's alright" and the "it's not alright" are no more attributes of an object than are the beautiful or the ugly; ultimately, this meaning does not proceed from any addressor (I) and does not address itself to any addressee (you). The signal that the affect-phrase is, is tautegorical: *aisthēsis*, *Empfindung*. The affect-phrase is at once an affective state (pleasure or pain) and the sign of this state, which is what Kant said about aesthetic feeling. Equally Freud separated affects from representations of a thing or a word: they are testimonies, but testimonies that represent nothing to anyone.

7. One or more articulated phrases can take the affect-phrase as their reference. They can endow pleasure or pain with a referent: "the spectacle of this ... misery was intolerable"; and place them upon the axis of destination: "your friend's little comment was enough to get me down." Thus the affect is attributed and addressed in the same way as a cognitive signification.—It appears that this transcription is inevitable, if only because within the order of discourse the affect-phrase is inopportune, unseemly, and even disquieting. Your joy, your suffering, will be shown, despite everything, to have been legitimate all along; they would only have been distressing because their "logic" was misunderstood. It could almost be said that the affect-phrase demands to be articulated in this way, and even argued—as if the scandal that it causes for discourse was intolerable. Discourse does not appear to be able to support for long an unarticulated and unargued remnant remaining outside of its grasp.

8. Would it not be simpler just not to deal with affect-phrases? This appears to be easy since they are silences, and silence implies consent. Let's simply leave feeling to its mutism; "You were too emotional, you didn't know what you were saying (or: you didn't know what to say); pull yourself together."—We can neglect a particular feeling to the point of forgetting it. To this strategy of forgetting it is often objected that the feeling will come back. But how can we know that it is the same affect-phrase which returns, given that it cannot, unarticulated as it is, furnish any signs allowing it to be recognized? Could it be claimed that we can recognize a certain quality of melancholy or jubilation that we have experienced previously and elsewhere? This can be said, certainly, but it is not attestable. A question of "private language," but also of time.

And why would a forgotten (repressed) feeling necessarily have to come back? Is it necessary to admit the hypothesis, hazy even in the eyes of Freud, of a repetition compulsion? Of an eternal return of the same?

9. The time of feeling is *now*. An actual feeling—joyful, nostalgic, a mixture of both—could come to be associated with the articulated phrase which refer to a joyful past. How are we to establish that the joyful present, for example, is the same as that which was experienced before? The feeling cannot be identified with itself by itself. It can only be experienced, as we say: it signals itself, it is tautegoric in the moment that it occurs. In order to be recognized as identical to itself through time, it must be chronologically localized. Chronology is one of the nominal systems necessary for the recognition that establishes the reality of a referent. Dated, the feeling is fixed as a reference of cognitive phrases: "Do you remember the emotion that we experienced, on that particular day, when we first found this shore?" We can recall this emotion. That is not to say that we experience it again. We can actually experience an emotion in evoking a past emotion. We could say that a feeling appears and disappears as a whole in an instant; that it is ageless.

10. We read in the *Nicomachean Ethics*: "Just as the act of sight appears to be perfect [perfect, finite, *teleia*] at any moment ... this also appears to be the case with pleasure. It is, so to speak, entire [complete, *holon ti*] and in no moment of its duration can one find a pleasure whose proper being [*eidos*] could be rendered more perfect [more final]

by a prolongation of time" (X, 4, 1).[4] And further on: "It is the *eidos* of pleasure to be finished, perfect at any moment ... It comes under that which is entire [complete] and final ... In contrast to movement, which cannot be conceived outside of time, pleasure owes nothing to duration. Because what is in the now is, so to speak, entire [complete]" (X, 4, 4). An analogous observation drawn from the clinic: the hysterical attack (phobic phrasing, for example) is each time brand new. "Brand new each time" means: at each time the *jouissance*, pleasure and pain, what it is and what it signals, is complete. It awaits nothing.

11. We have to be careful about the "each" of "each time." It is not within the remit of that which belongs only to the *now*. The "each" demands memory and counted time, thus articulation. Aristotle writes of the pleasure-phrase that it is "in the now." We ought to say that it is now. It is the same for the "in" as it is for the "each." If there is an inside of the now, there is also an outside, i.e., the before and the after, the *hysteron* and *prosteron* of the *Physics*. I am not saying that there is not. There are clocks. But even the now framed by the *no longer* and the *not yet* of the temporalizing consciousness must not be confounded with the now of pleasure: the former is relative, it is a differential measure; the latter is absolute, a "one" without two.—Such is the difficulty: to think the affect-phrase not outside of time, but outside of diachrony. *Pathēmata* do not know anything of the *dia-*.

12. How can you say that the affect-phrase is a phrase, considering that it is not articulated and does not present a phrase universe?—The ancient grammarians, who reserved the "articulated voice" (*phōnē enarthros*) for humans, conceded to animals a "mixed (or confused) voice" (*phōnē sunkekhumene*). This employment has its source in the *Politics* of Aristotle: "Alone amongst the animals, only man has discourse (*logos*). Without doubt, the voice (*phōnē*) is the sign of pain and of pleasure; thus it belongs to the other animals" (1253 a 10). All animals, man included, have the *aisthēsis* of pain and pleasure, and *phōnē* by which they signal this *aisthēsis* to one another (*sēmainein allēlois*). *Logos*, reserved to human animals, which Aristotle also names *dialektos*, appears heterogeneous to *phōnē*: to it belongs the capacity "to render manifest the useful and the harmful, and as a result of this the just and the unjust, and other similar things" (1253 a 15). It notably follows that a properly political community, where what is at stake is not only the signaling of pleasure and pain but also deliberating and deciding upon the useful and the just, requires this *phōnē enarthros*, this articulated phrase, that is *logos*.

13. There is, nevertheless, a communicability of pleasure and pain, of the *pathēmata*, without the mediation of *logos*, by the "confused voice" alone. Animals "signal their feelings to one another," says Aristotle. Certain ones, like birds, even divide the unarticulated voice into distinct sonorities, which make "a sort of *dialektos*" (*History of Animals*, 5335 a 27–8; I follow here the argument of Jean-Louis Labarrière in "*Imagination humaine et imagination animale chez Aristote,*" *Phronèsis* 29, 1, 1984).— We know what stakes will come to be attached, in Kant, to this sentimental communication. We can call it *mute* if we recall that the root *mu* connotes the closed

lips indicating that one remains silent or emitting a *mute* sound. From this root come *murmur, moo, mystery* and the low Latin *muttum* which has given us the French word, *mot*. This mute communication is made up of non-discrete inspirations and expirations of air: growlings, pantings, sighs. It spreads over the face and it spreads through the whole body which thus "signals" like a face. The essence of the face considered negatively (referred to by an actually articulated phrase) is that its lips are mute. Thus it will be necessary to extend *phōnē* as far as *gesture*.

14. Yet, even with birds and dolphins a continuous transition between *phōnē* and *logos* cannot be found. It is written at the beginning of *De Interpretatione*: "Even when inarticulate sounds (*agrammatoi psophoi*), such as the noises of the beasts, manifest something (*dèlousi ti*), none of them constitutes a name (*onoma*)" (2, 16 a 27–9). The name belongs to the voice that is divided into elements devoid of entirely conventional signification. It is this arbitrary sign that Aristotle calls the symbol. In contrast to *phōnē*, it has lost all immediate affective value.

15. Leaving the theory of language, which is not our concern, we follow rather the destiny of phrases. What happens to *phōnē*, the unarticulated phrase, when *logos*, the articulated phrase, is at work? It is banished from human language. Barbara Cassin shows that, from Aristotle to K. O. Apel, *logos* excludes *a priori* (transcendentally) all phrases and all genres of discourse which are not argumentative or, at least, arguable.[5] The exclusion of *phōnē*, of the affect-phrase, is the threshold of this exclusion: *phōnē* is not only unarguable, it is unarticulated.—Classically the process of exclusion is that of the dilemma: if *phōnē* belongs to language, it is articulable; if it claims not to be articulable ("my feeling is unsayable"), it at least argues this claim (just about what we are doing here), and thus places itself under the rule of the *dialektos*.

16. I will illustrate this procedure. Take the example of articulation that I have named the axis of destination. The affect-phrase is said to be non-destined. What would it be to respect its mutism with regard to its address? At the very least it would be to lend it one's ear. This is, notably, the Freudian rule of "free-floating attention," sometimes spoken of as that of the "the third ear." "Why aren't you saying anything to me?" In asking why this mutism is addressed to the person questioning it, the question articulates the silence by presupposing that it is at least addressed to the present interlocutor, the questioner. We call this presupposition of address a request. The questioner asks: "Why are you addressing your affect to me, without saying a word to me?" The questioner's request requires the mutism of the question to be addressed. Here the affect-phrase is transcribed into the pragmatic scheme. This, however, demands that phrases be articulated.

17. This transcription appears to be inevitable. It is called transference. The affect can *present* itself only by *situating* itself in the universe presented by an actual phrase. If it is not to remain the unattestable referent of a solely cognitive discourse, it must be actualized in the addressing [*la mise en adresse*] of what phrases itself now.—But, it will be asked, how is it possible to know that this present, transferential, address is indeed

that of the affect? Is it not imaginary? "You claim to love me or hate me, but your feelings are addressed to someone else." Following the direction thus indicated, one would attempt to go back as far as a reputedly *initial* phrase universe, where the affect is supposed to arise along with its genuine address. Hence Freud searched for the "primal scene." He will renounce this. It is not only that one never stops passing through screen-memories (of imaginary addresses and referents); it is rather that the presupposition itself is false: the affect-phrase is not originally sent to somebody. The capacity to feel pleasure and pain, affectivity, *aisthēsis,* is independent of its possible articulation. It does not await it (it is *logos* which declares that it awaits it), it has no need of it in order to perfect itself (this is what Aristotle says). It is perhaps indifferent to articulation. This is why the latter *wrongs* it.

18. *Phōnē* and *logos* can only encounter each other, and not link onto each other. This encounter gives rise to a differend. For the human animal, at least, this differend cannot be treated as a litigation. Certainly, the human being is born, like all animals, well endowed with *aisthēsis* and *phōnē.* But in contrast to other animals, excepting the domestic kind, it is born right in the middle of thousands of discourses, into the world of articulated phrases, and in contrast to domestic animals, it is granted to him to phrase in an articulate manner, after a certain time. This time before the *logos* is called *infantia.* It is the time of a *phōnē* that only signifies affections, *pathēmata,* the pleasures and the pains of the moment, without relating them to an object taken as referent, nor to the couple addressor–addressee. Pleasure and pain are signaled with vocalizations (and I would add: with gestures—*The Differend,* §110) provoked by objects that are not objects of thought, under the regime of a "narcissism" prior to all *ego.* This is what Freud has described under the two headings of polymorphous perversity and primary narcissism.—But this description (here mine, often that of Freud) remains anthropological. One would have to elaborate the transcendental status of *infantia.*

19. There is a *body* only as the referent of one or several cognitive phrases, attested to by the procedures for the establishment of reality. There are many sorts of body, according to the nature of the knowledge sought. Bodies, like existence, suppose *logos.* Only the logical animal *has* a body.—*Phōnē* does not have a body since it is not referential. The pleasures and the pains experienced in the adventure of the *infans* are only attributed to the excitation of this or that erogenous zone by the articulated discourse of adults, which takes the organism as its reference.—It is necessary to elaborate the status of the world or of the incorporeal chaos associated with the affect, the status of the Thing. And since it is not referential, *phōnē* is not addressed, from which point one might conclude that the concourse of voices, their sharing, does not make up a community properly speaking (which requires addressors and addressees) but a sort of communicability or transitivity of affects without expectation of a return. Freud might have persisted in wanting to name this infantile affectivity *sexuality,* yet it is certain that it is completely ignorant of the polarization linked to sexual difference.

20. The infantile *phōnē* is innocent not because it has not committed an error or been seduced, but because the question of what is just and unjust is unknown to it given that

this question demands *logos*. This question only poses itself with phrases that can present referents, addressors and addressees—that is, every instance necessary to the thought of distribution, equality, and the communicability of proper names on the instances of destination, which permit debate and argumentation. Infancy, like Adam, does not know that it is naked. And inasmuch as *logos* recovers *phōnē* (covers or dresses it up) rather than either suppressing or even domesticating it, this shameless innocence can always arise in the course of articulated phrases, in an impromptu manner.—But then one would make it ashamed of its nakedness. The impudence of the affect would be culpable. Innocence and culpability arrive together, under the name of anxiety.

Notes

1 This is a lecture delivered in January 1990 in Brussels under the title "The Inarticulate or the Differend Itself" during the colloquium "Rhetoric and Argumentation," organized by the European Centre for the Study of Argumentation. A first version of this text was published in the same year in the imprint of the University of Brussels, in a collection entitled *Rhetorical Figures and Conflicts*, edited by Michel Meyer and Alain Lempereur. The title chosen here corresponds to the name which Lyotard most recently gave this text. ["The Affect-phrase" translated by Keith Crome, in James Williams and Keith Crome (eds), *The Lyotard Reader and Guide* (Edinburgh University Press, 2006), 104–10, from the *Journal of the British Society from Phenomenology*, vol. 32, no. 3 (October 2001): 234–41. Originally published as 'La phrase-affect: d'un supplement au Differend' in *Misère de la philosophie*, © Editions Galilée, Paris, 2000, 43–54. Reproduced with permission of the Licensor through PLSclear.—Eds.]
2 Translator's note (TN): we have used Georges Van Den Abbeele's translation for all quotations from *The Differend*.
3 TN: Ibid., xi.
4 TN: for all quotations from Aristotle we have consulted the translations given in the bilingual Loeb Classical Library. We have, however, modified the translations in accordance with Lyotard's French where appropriate.
5 Compare B. Cassin "Parle si tu es homme," Introduction to *La Décision du sens: Livre Gamma de la Métaphysique d'Aristote* (Paris: Vrin, 1989).

6

The Other's Rights[1]

Jean-François Lyotard, 1993
Translated by Chris Miller and Robert Smith

"It seems that a man who is nothing but a man has lost the very qualities which make it possible for others to treat him as a fellow man."[2] With this sentence, taken from the study on *Imperialism* which forms the second part of *The Origins of Totalitarianism* (1951), Hannah Arendt defines the fundamental condition of human rights: a human being has rights only if he is other than a human being. And if he is to be other than a human being, he must in addition become an *other* human being. Then "the others" can treat him as their fellow human being. What makes human beings alike is the fact that every human being carries within him the figure of the other. The likeness that they have in common follows from the difference of each from each.

Thou shalt not kill thy fellow human being. To kill a human being is not to kill an animal of the species *Homo sapiens*, but to kill the human community present in him as both capacity and promise. And you also kill it in yourself. To banish the stranger is to banish the community, and you banish yourself from the community thereby.

What is this figure of the other in me, on which, it is said, my right to be treated as a human being rests? It is this question to which I devote the rest of my reflections.

"Nothing but a man," writes Hannah Arendt. That is, nothing other than an individual of the species *Homo sapiens*. A powerful species; in the struggle for life enacted in the theater of the world, *Homo sapiens* has emerged victorious over all other species. And it continues, successfully, to combat them, using hygiene, sanitary arrangements, the protection of the environment and so on. Each human being is a specimen of this species. He resembles any other member of the species, as a chimpanzee resembles a chimpanzee.

Is the figure of the other (ape) present in every ape? Apes are able to tell each other apart and to distinguish themselves from other species of animal. They can communicate amongst themselves by systems of sensory signals based on the five senses and motility. These systems constitute a sort of language which endows the animals with a sort of community in which affective states (Aristotle's *pathemata*) are exchanged, along with admonitions as to conduct.

This signal-based language is not wholly lacking in the human species, but its role is confined. Animals' capacity to communicate is determined by the genetic stock common to the species, and is of the order of instinct. Human beings have very few instincts. In comparison with their animal brothers, young human beings are slow to realize their capacity in the language of their fellow. And this human language is not common to the species. It functions not by bodily signals, but by signs. These arbitrary signs, combined according to rules which are also arbitrary, but which are fixed by syntactic structures, make it possible to designate any object, real or not, internal or external, as their referent, and to signify something about that object. Finally, and this is what interests us here, this signification is *addressed*.

It is what we today call the "pragmatic" function of human language which governs the formation of the figure of the other. Explicitly or implicitly, every human sentence is destined to someone or something. Some answer, some response, some link or follow-up is expected. The polarization is marked in our languages by the verbal "persons" and the personal pronouns. *I* is the one who is speaking now; *you* is the one to whom this communication is currently addressed. *You* are silent when *I* speak, but *you* can speak, has spoken, and will speak.

Animal communication is, we might say, homogeneous. By contrast, the distinguishing characteristic of interlocution is the relation of simultaneous similarity and disparity introduced between the speakers. The instances *I* and *you* cannot merge, since while the one speaks the other speaks no longer or not yet. *I* and *you* are deictics, and as such are correlated with *now*, and *now* designates the present of speech. From it, the temporality of past and future unfold. But relative to the capacity to speak, which by definition is not confined to the present but extends to every possible interlocution, *I* and *you* are alike. Persons capable of speech alternately occupy the instance *I* and the instance *you*. When they say *I*, they are a past or future *you*, and when they are in the position of *you*, they are so because they have spoken or will speak as *I*.

Interlocution thus implies that human beings cannot, as animals can, merge into a community based on signals. They do so only when the impossibility of interlocution reduces them to that meagre resource. In theory, the human *we* does not precede but results from interlocution. In this *we*, the figure of the other remains clearly present to each, to the extent that the other is his possible interlocutor. The one and the other can come to an agreement, after reasoning and debate, and then establish their community by contact. This is the principle of the Greek *politeia* or the modern *republic*. The citizen is the human individual whose right to address others is recognized by those others.

It is important to distinguish the republican principle from the democratic fact. The *demos* is not a contractual but a natural and cultural community. The individual of the *demos* is recognized as such not for his right to speak, but for his birth, language and historical heritage. These individuals form a *nation* (in the medieval sense in which one hears *nature*), whose principal characteristic is the homogeneity of its constituents. Interlocution does not engender this community; between the members of the nation, language and mores function as signals of recognition. Though possessed of interlocutory capacity, the demotic individual, whether a serf or a free man, uses the language to signal emotions and actions to other specimens of the variety of *Homines* to which they collectively belong. This relationship to language excludes the alterity implicit in civic interlocution. The other remains alien, and does not enjoy the rights reserved to nationals. The very Greeks who invented the *politeia* excluded *barbaroi*. The right of interlocution is not granted to every human being. The figure of the other is that of a threat weighing on the national community from without, which cannot help but undermine its integrity.

I oversimplify my description to bring out the essential opposition between the *demotic* and the *civic*. The difference between them is the consideration given to interlocution, which modifies the figure of the other. The people keeps the other out; the city interiorizes the other. In contemporary human communities, for various reasons, these two aspects are for the most part not distinguished: more or less nation, more or less republic. For example, the institution of a European community undoubtedly draws its justification exclusively from the civic principle.

In the republic, there is a principle of universalization which relates to the function, inherent in speech, of *addressing* the other. If a human being can speak, he is a possible interlocutor. The principle is not invalidated merely by the fact of his speaking a language foreign to the national language. *Homo sapiens* has always spoken a multitude of languages. But they are all human languages comprising the structural characteristics I have briefly outlined. These characteristics guarantee that an unknown human language can in principle be translated into a known one. I do not wish to take up here the difficulties and enigmas of translation. The theoretical possibility of translation is quite sufficient to extend interlocution to any human individual whatsoever, regardless of natural or national idiom. Civility may become universal in fact as it promises to do by right.

The form in which civility is in fact extended to national or demotic communities is a serious question. History offers a profusion of different modes, linguistic as well as political and economic. These include: an obligatory single language, an official language alongside which traditional languages are tolerated, compulsory multilingualism, effective multilingualism and so on. The pattern established depends on the balance of military, political, economic and cultural power. These relations determine how interlocution extends, but they cannot curb its extension. There is no limiting the function of destination inherent in the structure of sentences: one may beg a service of a tree or a river, and issue a command to a cat. If the addressee is human, he is immediately vested with the status of interlocutor, capable, in his turn, of addressing the first speaker.

There is no a priori limit to the interlocutory capacity. By its association with the recursiveness and translatability of human language, it cannot help but bind all human speakers in a speech community. From this effective (de facto) power there arises what I shall term an *effect of right* (*un effet de droit*). If any human being *can* be an interlocutor for other human beings, he *must be able* to, that is, must be enabled or allowed to. We move from the potential implied by competence to the permission implied by entitlement. We know, however, that capacity does not legitimacy make. But it is tempting to merge the two categories in the case of interlocution, both because the capacity to enter into dialogue with others is possessed equally by everyone, and because interlocution in itself implies reciprocity of speech. Reciprocity respects not only the alterity of interlocution but the parity of the interlocutors. It thus guarantees their respective liberty and their equality before the word. These are the characteristics of justice itself. The slippage here from the fact to the right resembles the contemporary confusion of democracy and republic. But how can we avoid it?

Let us take it that the capacity to speak to others is a human right, and perhaps the most fundamental human right. If the use of this capacity is forbidden, whether de facto, by some injustice of fate, or on principle, for example as a punishment, a harm is inflicted on the speaker thus constrained. He is set apart from the speech community of interlocutors. To no one is he any longer someone other, nor is anyone now his other. There are many ways of imposing silence. Amnesty International knows them better than anyone. Its vocation is modest but decisive. It is *minimal*. *Amnestos* meant he who is forgotten. Amnesty does not demand that the judgment be revised or that the convicted man be rehabilitated. It simply asks that the institution that has condemned him to silence forget this decree and restore the victim to the community of speakers.

Amnesty's task is in accordance with the provisions of the public law of the republican democracies. I nevertheless maintain that this legality conceals a confusion between a capacity, the aptitude for speech, and a legitimacy, the authority to speak. In other words, there is, strictly speaking, no natural right. It is of the essence of a right that it be merited; no right without duty. The same goes for the capacity to enter into dialogue. It is not true that it realizes itself spontaneously. It requires care and attention, an entire learning process. It requires precisely what is called civilization. The human being as such is no other than a member of the species *Homo*: an animal that can speak. It is true that its language is so constituted that it effectively contains the promise of interlocution. But if he is to bring out and respect the figure of the other that this promise bears in it, he must free himself from that in him which will not recognize the figure of the other, that is, his animal nature. Children do not spontaneously enter into dialogue. There is something in us which resists, something which does perhaps "speak," but in signals rather than according to the rules of interlocution.

Civilization, understood here as the process of learning how to share dialogue with *you*, requires a moment of silence. Aristotle said: the master speaks and the pupil listens. For that moment, the status of *I* is forbidden to me, I am assigned the position of *you* for the master, at the *tacit* pole of destination. *Tacit* does not imply *passive*. The exaltation of interactivity as a pedagogic principle is pure demagogy. The pupil has the capacity to speak; he has to win the right to speak. To do so, he must be silent. The suspension of interlocution imposes a silence and that silence is good. It does not undermine the right to speak. It teaches the value of that right. It is the exercise necessary for excellence in speech. Like the pupil, writers, artists, scholars and novices must enter into retreat in order to learn what they will have to say to others.

The master, whatever his title, exempts his pupils from the sharing of speech in order to tell them something that they do not know. He may even speak to them in a language that they do not understand. The master is not the figure of the general other, of *you*, but the figure of the *Other* in all its separateness. He is the stranger, the foreigner. How can one dialogue with the foreigner? One would have to learn his language. This question is in some measure analogous with that of literature and the arts, testifying to something that is "present" otherwise than as interlocutory expectation: something opaque, Beckett's the "Unnamable."

The silence that the learning process of civilization imposes is the moment of a labor of *estrangement*. It is a matter of speaking otherwise than is my wont and saying something other than what I know how to say. Through the alterity of the master, the strangeness of another logic is, in silence, imposed. He takes me hostage in order to make me hear and say what I do not know. Emmanuel Lévinas has elaborated this theme better than anyone.

From this brief analysis, it follows that the interlocutory capacity changes into a right to speak only if the speech can say something other than the *déjà dit* (what has already been said). The right to speak implies a duty to announce. If our speech announces nothing, it is doomed to repetition and to the conservation of existing meanings. The human community may spread, but it will remain the same, prostrated in the euphoria it feels at being on such very good terms with itself. It is the main function of the media today to reinforce the interlocutory consent of the community. They are boring to the extent that they teach us nothing. Interlocution is not an end in itself. It is legitimate only if, through others, the Other announces to me something which I hear but do not understand.

We should then distinguish three different levels of the "right to speak." First, the faculty of interlocution, a principle factually inherent in human languages; second, the legitimation of speech, due to the fact that it announces something other, which it strives to make us understand; and last, the legitimacy of speech, the positive right to speak, which recognizes in the citizen the right to address the citizen. The latter aspect merges the two former. But this confusion is good. By authorizing every possible speaker to address others, the republic makes it every speaker's duty to announce to those others what they do not know. It encourages announcements; it instructs. And, on the other hand, it forbids that anyone be arbitrarily deprived of speech. It discourages terror. In this way it governs silence in everyone's best interest, authorizing the silence of discipline and outlawing the silence of despotism.

This picture of the republic is idyllic, but the idyll conceals something far from idyllic. The threat of being deprived of speech is not contingent; it weighs constantly on the interlocutory right. This is precisely why the republic is indispensable. The human speaker is always afraid that a "keep quiet" will debar his words. He complains of the precariousness of his membership in the speech community. Even the good silence of the writer, the monk, or the pupil contains an element of suffering. Any banishment is a harm inflicted on those who undergo it, but this harm necessarily changes to a wrong when the victim is excluded from the speech community. For the wrong is the harm to which the victim cannot testify, since he cannot be heard. And this is precisely the case of those to whom the right to speak to others is refused.

The right to impose silence which the community grants itself as a sanction is always dangerous. The death sentence evidently does an irremediable wrong to the condemned man, even if he is guilty of a heinous crime. But in relation to our present topic, death is not necessarily the wrong done to him. There are, as the Greeks put it, "beautiful deaths," of which the citizens continue to speak long afterward. It happens that a speaker is more eloquent dead than alive, and does not therefore die for the community. So we must reverse the relation: it is the wrong which is the cause of death, since it implies the exclusion of the speaker from the speech community. The community will not even speak of this exclusion since the victim will be unable to report it and cannot therefore defend himself or appeal.

Those who escaped extermination in the camps are aware of this. Restored to the community, they can describe and narrate what the administration of death was. But how can they communicate the abjection to which they were reduced? It was first and foremost the severing of communication. How can one communicate by means of interlocution the terror of what it means no longer to be destined to anyone or anything? They were not spoken to, they were treated. They were not enemies. The SS or Kapos who called them dogs, pigs, or vermin did not treat them as animals but as refuse. It is the destiny of refuse to be incinerated. The ordeal of being forgotten is unforgettable. It reveals a truth about our relationship to language that is stifled and repressed by the serene belief in dialogue. Abjection is not merely when we are missing from speech, but when we lack language to excess. Our debt to announcement can never be acquitted. The Other in language, the Other that language is, does not say what must be said. It keeps silent. Does it even wait? Excluded from the speech community, the camp victims were rejected into the poverty, the misery of this secret. In that misery resides the true dignity of speech. Clearly, the ordeal of being forgotten cannot be expressed in the sharing of speech, which is, *ex hypothesi*, ignorant of it. Neither *I* nor *you*, the deportee is present in the language of his lords and in that of the deportees themselves only as the third person, who is to be eliminated. He is superfluous as any speaker is superfluous in relation to the Other. But precisely for that reason, absolutely responsible for himself.

The abjection suffered in the camps horribly illustrates the threat of exclusion which weighs on all interlocution. In the school playground, the child to whom the others say "We're not playing with you" experiences this unspeakable suffering. He suffers a wrong equivalent, on its own scale, to a crime against humanity. Even those who submit themselves to the ascesis of separation in order to exalt the annunciatory power of language run the risk of abjection. True, they forswear the company of others only in order to listen more intently to the foreign master. But this enslavement to the Other is perceived as a suspicious dependence on a power alien to the interlocutory community, as a sort of betrayal. The Latin *sacer* (sacred) expressed the ambivalence of the abject: human refuse excluded from the interests of the speech community, yet a sign, perhaps, in which the Other has left its mark and deserving of respectful fear.

In his analysis of the sublime effect, Edmund Burke termed *horror* the state of mind of a person whose participation in speech is threatened. The power which exceeds the capacity of interlocution resembles night. Though we seek to tame it by dialogue, it does not have the figure of the *you*. It may be well- or ill-disposed. We hear it. We cannot understand it. It may be God, it may be Animal, it may be Satan. In silence we strive to translate its voice in order to announce it to the community of speakers. In this way we seek to make our relation to the Other dialectical. But the strangeness of the other seems to escape any totalization. The effort of translation must be endlessly renewed. It is precisely when we think we have reduced the abject or the sacred to transparent meanings that it becomes most opaque and returns to us from without like an accident. The discontent from which contemporary societies are suffering, the postmodern affliction, is this foreclosure of the Other. It is the reverse of the triumphant identification with the Other which affects modern republics at their birth. Saint-Just enacted law in the name of the Other, and instituted the first totalitarian reign of terror.

Wiser than the dialecticians, the Jacobins and the deciders, Freud acknowledged that abjection was not an episode but a situation constitutive of the human relation to interlocution. As children, we are kept on the margins of interlocution, and condemned to exile. The situation of *infantia* is that of the incomplete human being who *does not yet* speak. The child is spoken to and spoken of, but is not an interlocutor even though he is plunged into the interlocutory community. The statements that concern him have no value for him except as signals or gestures; they are difficult for him to decipher because they are arbitrary, and he has little instinct. He is affected by them, but has no language in which to articulate his own affective states. These reside within him unconsciously, in a forgetfulness which is always present. They do not enter the temporality associated with the instances of destination *I* and *you*. They loom up in the course of the individual life history in apparently unmotivated ways. They block interlocution. With them, the inevitable wrong and abjection of *infantia* erupt into adult relations.

From our native prematurity a mute distress results. It is to this distress that we owe our capacity to question everything around us. But we also owe to it our need to be welcomed, the request that we be authorized to enter the speech community. In interlocution a drama is played out between *me* and *you*; it is the drama of authorization. The question or assertion that we address to others is invariably coupled with an entreaty: deliver me from my abandonment, allow me to belong among you. This entreaty allows of a wide variety of modalities: friendship, hatred, love, and even indifference. But in it resides the foundation of the right to speak. For it is this right that assures me that my request will be heard, and that I will not be rejected into the abjection of *infantia*. Yet at the same time, I have to announce to you the opaque Otherness that I have experienced, and still am experiencing, as a child.

The law says: thou shalt not kill. Which means: you shall not refuse to others the role of interlocutor. But the law that forbids the crime of abjection nonetheless evokes its abiding threat of temptation. Interlocution is authorized only by respect for the Other, in my words and in yours.

Notes

1 First published as Jean-François Lyotard, "The Other's Rights," tr. Chris Miller and Robert Smith, in Stephen Shute and Susan Hurley (eds), *On Human Rights: The Oxford Amnesty Lectures 1993* (New York: Basic Books, 1993), 135–47. Reproduced with permission from The Belgrade Circle (ed.), *The Politics of Human Rights* (London: Verso, 2002), 181–8.
2 Hannah Arendt, *The Origins of Totalitarianism* (London: Harcourt Brace, 1967), 300.

Part Two

Long Views and Distances

7

Citing and Siting the Postmodern: Lyotard and the Black Atlantic

John E. Drabinski

In a personal conversation recently, Carlos Amador remarked that Jean-François Lyotard is one of the most misread and under-valued philosophers. I found this an interesting and, at a certain level, perplexing remark. For those of us doing doctoral work in the early 1990s, Lyotard was at the center of post-structuralist theory, working in the same vein as thinkers like Jacques Derrida, Emmanuel Levinas, Michel Foucault, and others to dismantle pretensions of identity, identification, and the avalanche of hegemony that comes with such pretensions.

What is Lyotard's legacy today? Philosophy and critical theory, like all of intellectual life, moves in and out of trends. Generations shift and emerging interests supplant, often without critical engagement or reengagement, previous theoretical habits and languages. But I am not interested, here, in retheorizing the importance of Lyotard for contemporary European philosophy or contemporary trends in critical theory. That is a matter for different kinds of specialists. Instead, I am interest in how we might see in Lyotard's work having a complex relationship to what I want to term *the afropostmodern*, a post-Fanonian model of thinking in the Afro-Caribbean tradition that conceptually converges with so many of the motifs in Lyotard's work, in particular, his sustained critique of narrative and defense of the irreducibility of the differend—the signature pieces of Lyotard's work as postmodern.

In making this argument, however, I am not interested in using Lyotard's critical vocabulary for the sake of enhancing or elevating Afro-Caribbean discourse. It is an intellectual tradition comprised of its own vocabulary and conceptual innovations, so needs no such enhancement or elevation. Indeed, central to the tradition is an argument for the importance of its own vocabulary. Rather, as a comparativist in this essay, I am interested in two aspects of *engaging with* Lyotard from the perspective of the afropostmodern. First, I want to explore how Lyotard's critical vocabulary broadens the resonance of the postmodern *in* the afropostmodern, helping us distinguish what is *afro* about the afropostmodern as well as what is problematic about the notion of *the* postmodern. In other words, the engagement between Lyotard and the afropostmodern helps us see the distinctiveness of the afro- in afropostmodern *and* turns us back to *the* in "the postmodern" with a critical eye, now with a view toward the racialization of the

European experience, then conceptualization, of postmodernity. A quiet, yet persistent racial metanarrative sits in the definite article of the phrase "the postmodern." Second—and this is the endgame, so to speak, of my reflections here—understanding the afropostmodern in relation to the European postmodern helps us understand how to *date* or periodize the postmodern, to understand how the afropostmodern is born in the very same moment as European modernity. Understanding this dating of the postmodern underscores the global resonance of the term and its link to the Atlantic world's most enduring violence: the Middle Passage, and how it formed and deformed both the black Americas and white Europe.

So, to begin: how can we situate the afropostmodern?

The history of ideas in the Afro-Caribbean tradition moves quickly. This is no doubt in part due to the accelerated sense of cultural production begun in the middle of the twentieth century. The mid-century moment was a moment like no other: independence, anti-colonial struggle, and decolonization. Intellectual, cultural, and political life was explosive, responding to not only a long history and shadow of subjugation, but also revitalized by the ecstatic experience of liberation. What was liberated? How does liberation transform thinking? This is a matter of theorizing the energy of decolonial thought. And it could not be weightier or more urgent. The sheer enormity of the task of decolonization—the movement toward and articulation of a sense of cultural roots and political independence after centuries of enslavement and colonial domination—introduces a cluster of ideas, principles, and ethico-political debates that are increasingly attuned to the specificity of Afro-Caribbean experience, while also negotiating the complex nuances of European, African, Middle Eastern, and indigenous influences on language and thinking. This is profoundly decentering work, displacing the idea of a single-root and uniform cultural content—a colonial project of uniformity and assimilation—in the name of another logic of intellectual production. What that other logic looks like, what memories and histories it draws upon for orientation and content, is the substance of the tradition and its disputes. And it is important, especially for comparative work, that Afro-Caribbean thinkers emerged as decolonial theorists at the very same moment that so much European philosophy was moving toward deep critiques of the thought of the Same, of hegemony, of epistemological and political authoritarianism. Rooted in different experiences, yet similarly oriented as anti-authoritarian, counter-hegemonic, or hegemony-neutralizing modes of thought and praxis. In this intersection of *sensibilities* lies interesting points of contact and clarifying difference.

A curiosity: for those trained in the white European intellectual tradition, Frantz Fanon has emerged as a foundational figure of difference and diversification in thinking, theorizing, and understanding the margins of that tradition. It seems to me, in fact, that Caribbean thought, when routed through trends and tendencies in the European tradition, all but begins and ends with Fanon's thought in philosophical circles. Aimé Césaire, and perhaps also Léopold Senghor and Albert Memmi, regularly appear in such taxonomies of European thought and its critical horizons, but, more often than not, those thinkers (and perhaps a few others) function as foils for Fanon's revolutionary thinking and transformation of phenomenology, existentialism, and psychoanalysis. That says something important about the power of Fanon's thinking, that no matter how short his life, his intellectual production remains so utterly transformative that his short life and modest output (if we compare to thinkers with longer lives lived) is massively outsized by his impact and legacy.

But, of course, that is nothing like a proper picture of the Caribbean tradition. Fanon was a global event as a thinker—especially in his afterlife as an icon and foundation piece for postcolonial theory and practice. Even in his moment, however, Fanon was a controversial, disputed figure in an emerging Caribbean tradition; it is always worth noting that he left the Caribbean in the 1950s and, after *Black Skin, White Masks,* moved away from theorizing blackness and toward a more generalized notion of "the colonized." Fanon became a *global,* not *Caribbean,* event. This move is important, because it stands in contrast to, for example, Césaire's commitment to a Caribbean iteration of Négritude, a movement dedicated to the articulation of an African thread across the Black diaspora that dominated the immediate postwar period in Caribbean and black Atlantic theory. Césaire's approach was straightforward: Africa functions as a spirit animating the cultural life of the diaspora, threading cultural difference together with a single vital force and urge.[1] (Négritude's debt to French vitalism and life philosophy is significant.) Alongside that, René Ménil's transformation of French surrealism, attuning it to Caribbean senses of embodiment and landscape, argued for another paradigm, one rooted in the immediacy of experience and a vibrant sense of presence to the particularities of place and world. Against these trends, Fanon, showing the profound and enduring influence of Sartrean existentialism, embraces the capacity of subjectivity to disentangle from the past (via revolutionary violence at every level) in pursuit of the new: new identities, new senses of the human, and so a new humanism, as the closing pages of *The Wretched of the Earth* puts it. These disputes are in some ways a crystallization of the mid-century moment and its conflicts. In defense of, then repudiation of, and then proposals of radical alternatives to essentialist thinking, the mid-century debate between Césaire, Ménil, and Fanon takes on questions of the body and its relationship with history, time, and the thickness of embodied presence to the world.

Whatever these differences, such positions share a sense of temporality—namely, the compulsion and drive to repudiate the past and redeem the present with a conceptual-existential story about the past. The present is always abject; this is the consequence of centuries of slavery and colonialism, a total project that burrowed the violence of disidentification and dismantling of the self into the deepest recesses of singular and collective subjectivity. This total project was dedicated to the abjection of Black life in the Americas at every level of lived experience and communal, social, and political life. And so antiblackness comes to function as a base structure that informs the very foundations of social, political, and cultural being such that no sense of the future can be built on the terms generated in that space. However dissident, however interstitial the formations of community and life, what Négritude, surrealism, and existentialism in the Caribbean agree upon is that there is no foundation for meaning in what we know as the world and the person. Metanarratives, in the sense of ancestral origins (Négritude's atavistic race theory) or a metaphysics of embodied life (afro-Surrealism's sense of landscape) or apocalyptic violence and its temporality (revolutionary existentialism's vision of a pure break), adhere to the mid-century moment precisely because the time of the present has no stories to tell. No stories of redemption. No stories of world making and meaning. The story of stories, the insertion of a Caribbean sense of history into History, hopes to redeem the past and supplant the present. Revolutionary. Radical. Pulling time up by its roots. All in the work of one metanarrative or another.

This is the tradition's flirtation with the excesses of modernity, without a doubt, but with ecstasy instead of bureaucratic reason—with no small bit of unintended irony. The moment certainly shares a modernist impulse, telling a grand story, a metanarrative in the deepest sense, of how difference and pain is overcome by narratives of race, the senses, and/or revolutionary, anti-colonial messianism. Lyotard's note resonates here in important ways: "the metanarrative of a subject . . . guarantees their legitimacy."[2] What would make Caribbean life legitimate? Worth of living as a form of life? If the past and present are abject and that abjection is total, then only a "metanarrative of a subject" can overcome history and memory for the sake of a legitimated mode of being.

And this is met immediately with a counter-movement.

We can think here of three thinkers in particular—Édouard Glissant, Derek Walcott, and Kamau Brathwaite—who, by chance, belong to the same generation as Fanon, all having been born within a few years of one another. (Yet another example of how prolific the young Fanon was, and how short his life.) Generations, though, aren't really about numbers, are they? Fanon's indulgence of the metanarrative structure of revolutionary violence, seeing it as telling the biggest and grandest story of History's inversion and sudden, unprecedented form of liberation, turns on a flattening of the cultural and political space of the present. His *pessimism* (inflected though the lens of antiblack racism), as well as his optimism (expressed in messianic visions of the new, the future), work from one and the same premise: the Caribbean (and perhaps the black Atlantic world more broadly) is too saturated with antiblackness to find liberatory structures in the world formed over the previous five centuries. *What is the Caribbean?* and *Who is a Caribbean?*—these questions animate the tradition from the outset. And those issues are rooted in one of philosophy's most enigmatic questions: What does it mean to begin?

What it means to begin is in many ways the broad Atlantic world's mid-century crisis, whether in the north or south Atlantic world. The legacy of two world wars initiates the same sorts of queries in what becomes the European postmodern, especially the strains of that postmodernism that grow out of Heidegger's reckoning with technology, estrangement from place, and dissociation from language. But the legacy of those two wars tells a different story in the colonies. In the colonies, specifically in the Caribbean, Fanon notes[3] that the rapid defeat of the French by the German army in June 1940 revealed something crucial about Europe to colonized people: their vulnerability to defeat. Germany's subsequent isolation of French Caribbean islands during the war only furthered this revelation's capacity to debunk racial myths about colonizing power. Witnessing the defeat of France and its submission emboldened anti-colonial movements precisely because of perceived vulnerabilities, and this is felt immediately in the intellectual production coming out of Martinique—in particular with the publication of Césaire's poem *Notebook of a Return to the Native Land*. Césaire's conception of beginning is the poem itself, a response to the torpor and despair of colonial domination. *Notebook* opens with descriptions and evocations of colonial devastation lived on the body. Bodies asleep, bodies unable to move, bodies in despair. Beginning in that despair, out of devastation, drives the tradition's varied approaches to the problem of beginning. The repair model, which commences in the production of metanaratives of race, body, and violence, proceeds from just that: the presupposition that the past bequeaths to the world of the present only, or at least predominately, brokenness. *Notebook* sets the diagnostic stage for Fanon's conception of beginning and the new, Ménil's turn to the senses and body as sites of radical renewal and revitalization. Things are broken. Liberation is construction and configuration of the new.

But a sense of beginning out of brokenness on the model of repair, a sense of inherent and determinate deficiency, is what produces the modernist (however one processes that term) compulsion to create and embrace metanarratives of atavism, intensification of the senses, or messianic futures that put what is broken back together again. Or for the first time. Reconciliation or conciliation of self to self, self to others, and self to world. And yet, the post-Fanonian shift to the afropostmodern paradigm proposes a very different approach, one that eschews metanarrative and refuses adjudication of the irreconcilable affects, laws, epistemological elements that comprise what we might call the Caribbean *differend*. I have in mind here the opening pages of Glissant's *Poetics of Relation*, which stand as one of the most profound sustained meditations on the Middle Passage and memory. Glissant outlines three senses of the abyss manifest in forced migration. First, there is the abyss produced in/by the forced departure of/from western Africa: boarding the slave ship is the abyss of first loss, the loss of root and knowledge and communicability. Second, there is the abyss of the ocean in the belly of the slave ship, which Glissant evokes in such painful detail: the disorientation of darkness, the endless horizon of the sea, the foul pain of human waste and death in the belly, and of course the countless, nameless victims thrown overboard at the bottom of the Atlantic. Here, Glissant recalls Walcott's stunning poem "The Sea Is History," a sparse but devastating archaeology of the black Americas by way of a topology of the ocean's floor. Third, there is the arrival, the thought of the shoreline on which the abyss of the future opens up, bookended by the passage and its abyssal pain. The Middle Passage is the first breaking, the first sense of brokenness that is repeated and reproduced in plantation slavery and colonial domination.

This last sense of the abyss, the abyss of arrival, prompts Glissant to theorize the uncomfortable, yet also ecstatic sense of inheritance at the shoreline. The shoreline represents a certain kind of closure of time, clipping, however roughly, the present of island life from the immediate, then ancestral, continental past. It is in that sense a truly radical sense of loss.[4] And yet, life goes on. Life begins again after catastrophe. What does it mean to begin from and with loss? And what would it mean to begin from and with loss *without* configuring that loss as brokenness? To begin with *fecundity*, thinking with both productivity and melancholic loss, means embracing the paradox of history and memory, the contradiction of social death with vernacular culture and its expressive life, the differend of having been rendered subhuman and creating sublime human worlds. To see the unknowable pain of history as a condition of life itself, of the archipelago that is at once a geographical site and a figure for thinking. Glissant writes:

This is why we stay with poetry. And despite our consenting to all the indisputable technologies; despite seeing the political leap that must be managed, the horror of hunger and ignorance, torture and massacre to be conquered, the full load of knowledge to be tamed, the weight of every piece machinery that we shall finally control, and the exhausting flashes as we pass from one era to another ... there is still something we now share: this murmur, cloud or rain or peaceful smoke. We know ourselves as part and as crowd, in an unknown that does not terrify.[5]

Further, evoking the slave ship and the gorgeous spectacle of the shimmering sea under sailboats racing just off the shoreline, he adds, with a poet's touch:

For us, and without exception, and no matter how much distance we may keep, the abyss is also a projection of and a perspective into the unknown ... We take sides in this game of the world. We hail a renewed Indies; we are for it. And for this Relation made of storms and profound moments of peace in which we may honor our boats.[6]

We see the work of memory on identity in these passages, crucial work precisely because it puts *honor* at the center of reckoning with the pain of the past and present. It says *yes* to the West Indies *as* West Indies, which, when set in this broader Caribbean intellectual tradition of reckoning with pain, stands out as a transformation of the tradition because it refuses abjection. Glissant, and the afropostmodern movement of which he is a part, turns toward the story of *this place*, the West Indies, without recursion to metanarratives that might hope to redeem abject space. Such a turn does not deny what Césaire, Ménil, and Fanon documented as abject space, but instead interrogates the differential and deferring structure of life buried in, yet also at the forefront of, that exact same space. Life goes on *as life*, but without the purity one might want to imagine such a life composes and extends.

How, then, do we begin thinking in this space without recursion to metanarratives and their commitment to redemption stories? Stories of loss invite reconstructive narratives. The afropostmodern turn, however, articulates an orphan narrative that, in a peculiar twist, orphans narrative itself. Consider how Walcott closes his 1974 essay "The Muse of History" with a provocative refusal. He writes:

I accept this archipelago of the Americas. I say to the ancestor who sold me, and to the ancestor who bought me, I have no father, I want no such father, although I can understand you, black ghost, white ghost, when you both whisper "history," for if I attempt to forgive you both I am falling into your idea of history which justifies and explains and expiates, and it is not mine to forgive, my memory cannot summon. any filial love, since your features are anonymous and erased and I have no wish and no power to pardon.[7]

History, the discursive strategy that would want a narrative of contextualization-as-redemption, inserting a racial story about identity, is rejected by Walcott in the name of *his* story, the story of the archipelago as a form of thinking and geographic site, an orphaned identity and mode of knowing and being. An archipelago, here, that says yes to fragments *against* history and its commitment to stories of legitimation and adjudication. An archipelago in which life is forged in and by pain, but which is also a *gift*—a gesture both gratuitous and excessive generated from the most austere and melancholic history. Walcott continues:

> I give the strange and bitter and yet ennobling thanks for the monumental groaning and soldering of two great worlds, like halves of a fruit seamed by its own bitter juice, that exiled from your own Edens you have placed me in the wonder of another, and that was my inheritance and your gift.

The wonder of another. Therein lies a relation to alterity, in Walcott and the afropostmodern, that does not reconcile, equivocate, or adjudicate, but instead works from a relation of wonder, of astonishment at life itself, how it persists with obstinacy and fecundity. Wonder is not pleasure alone, however, or even foremost. Walcott's image of pieces of fruit seamed together is important here because the seam is bitterness—accounting for the pain of the embrace of violent origins—and also because it makes a sense of meaning out of contradiction. Violent contradiction made violent because it leaves the differend of what origin asks as differend.

This bitterness of the seam, then, gives affective texture to what we might call the historical-memorial differend—an absolutely critical notion for theorizing the Middle Passage and its transformation of time and space. The European and the African are, in historical memory, contradictions that suspend judgment, not out of mercy or forgiveness, but because the violence of the Middle Passage—initiated in the violence of sale, the violence of purchase—offers no legitimate rule of judgment. Reconciliation *might* be facilitated by either a supervening notion of the human or subordination of one "father" to another. But Walcott (and here is his afropostmodern ontology) rejects a universal, isolating instead the specificity and particularity of the Caribbean as an archipelagic geography of thinking. Fragments without reconciliation or reassembly of the original. "This gathering of broken pieces is the care and pain of the Antilles," Walcott writes,

> and if the pieces are disparate, ill-fitting, they contain more pain than their original sculpture, those icons and sacred vessels taken for granted in their ancestral places. Antillean art is this restoration of our shattered histories, our shards of vocabulary, our archipelago becoming a synonym for pieces broken off from the original continent.[8]

This figure of thinking intervenes, methodologically, in the question of paternity when Walcott refuses the verticality of relation; to choose the white father would be to choose colonial memory, to choose the African father would be to choose racial essentialism along the lines of Négritude. Walcott, in the afropostmodern gesture, restores with what he calls "love"[9] and always without reference to the original, only and always with reference to the bricolage and eclecticism of making life out of fragments.

What, then, can be told as a story—that is, how to tell it—without constant reference to History, without metanarrative? It means beginning work without structures of legitimation, without regimes of measure and correction that, in their coercive and curative work, (want to) redeem spaces of fragmentation.

The afropostmodern is oriented by and comprised of fragment work and fragment workers, an aesthetics and epistemology that reflects the work of the *djobber* in the Caribbean context. Glissant summarizes *djob* as "a method of cartage or transport and, in the wider sense, an 'odd job' that is free form and created afresh each day,"[10] a life and vernacular culture built up around the figure documented in Patrick Chamoiseau's compelling text *Chronicle of the Seven Sorrows*. If the *djobber* works odd jobs, is multiskilled and capable of shifting and moving from demand to demand, responsive with creative and technical knowledge to changing modes of labor, then the work of the afropostmodern enacts precisely that logic in the work of memory and history. Walcott theorizes this refusal of paternity in terms of fragmentation. Fragments, on the model of something like Négritude and its critics, including Fanon, are signs of loss and fracture, which in turns leads to the compulsion to repair. What is repair in this context? This question shifts and determines so much of Afro-Caribbean thought.

For Négritude, especially Césaire's iteration of it, the restorative power of Africa as a civilizational *spirit*—a conceptual move indebted to French vitalism and life philosophy—is critical for overcoming the estrangement from self and world rooted in pain, fragmentation, and the melancholy of centuries of subjugation. This imperative to think *against* fragments informs Fanon's derisive comments on vernacular speech (pidgin, creole) and culture (jazz, blues)—comments that draw on a conception of pessimism as fundamental ontology and reflect a hostility toward everyday life *as life*. Rather than seeing vernacular culture and expressive life as signs of an alternative mode of being, one in the interstices of colonial abjection, Césaire and Fanon see only brokenness and construct metanarratives of redemption from past or future. Whatever the differences, both thinkers imagine apocalypse and messianic forces as preconditions of any sense of repaired life.[11]

But there is another way of telling stories.

We locate story in the formation of identity, giving texture and contour and place. If we think with fragments, prioritizing the *djobber*'s sense of becoming rather than the calcification of being or reassembly of brokenness, then we have to conceive story on a different model. Indeed, one of the central arguments of Glissant's work in the 1990s is that the work of epic and myth has traditionally been anti-fragment labor, making difference subsume itself under identity. Reassembly or assembly that negates difference and differentiation. The way *Aeneid* tells a story that unites Rome under a myth of beginning, rendering Mediterranean difference secondary to Romanness as such or, better, an outright illusion. Africa played this role in Négritude, as we have seen, putting Caribbean difference under the rubric of a broader civilization and diasporic identity. In *Poetics of Relation*, Glissant casts epic and myth as arguments for *filiation*, a sense of link between singularities or diffuse and differentiated cultural groups and a broader identity, often a metaphorical or literal blood identity, erasing forms of alterity and post-dialectical remainder in the name of the Father, of irreducible relationship. This is how "the West"—a project, not a place—establishes its identity through an epic tale of ancient Greek origins, democracy, and then ultimately an ethno-religious region we've come to call "the continent." But that is a projection. Epics and myths *project*, and in that projection legitimate regimes of knowledge and identification. Glissant writes:

> In the Western world the hidden cause (the consequence) of both Myth and Epic is filiation, its work setting out upon the fixed linearity of time, always toward a projection, a project.[12]

Linearity is crucial here because the arrow of time, when it flies straight, sets boundaries and lines of descent that are filial in origin and intent. The stuff of fantasy. The stuff of the most catastrophic violence. Glissant writes, further:

> As Mediterranean myths tell us, thinking about One is not thinking about All. These myths express communities, each one innocently transparent for self and threateningly opaque for the other ... Either the other is assimilated, or else it is annihilated. That is the whole principle of generalization and its entire process.[13]

Glissant's evocation of annihilation is intentional and ought to evoke the genocidal impulse of political cultures rooted in epic stories. Indeed, in his *Introduction to a Poetics of Diversity*, published just a handful of years after *Poetics of Relation*, Glissant will link the metanarrative function of myth and epic and its capacity to adjudicate the differend of social and political life, linked to the fantasy of single-rootedness, to the genocidal impulse and reality, citing both the Shoah and the Rwandan genocide as examples. What replaces these stories is fragment work, partial stories, stories of becoming, stories that dis-assemble rather than reassemble. Glissant's poetry often does exactly this, returning again and again to the Caribbean shoreline to contemplate the convergence of the sublimity of its beauty with the negative sublime of its painful memory. This is a site of honor, but an honor that is solemn and ecstatic at the same time; neither affect overcomes the other, no third affect or triumphal narrative intervenes to re-tell and re-tool the contradictions of pain and beauty.

Afropostmodern because, attuned to the specificity of black experience in the Americas, it takes on the fragments without mythic and epic reassembly of fragments.

Afropostmodern because, attuned to the specificity of black experience in the Americas, it tells multiple stories without anxiety about difference and becoming.

Afropostmodern because, attuned to the specificity of black experience in the Americas, it refuses metanarrative in the name of a vertical proliferation of expressive life.

Orphan narratives have no recursion to parentage. Orphan narratives indulge the differend of affective life *after* loss and *after* the setting of roots, always plural, always proliferating, always becoming and never being.

The Middle Passage as beginning and the site of the afropostmodern.

Whence, then, the postmodern?

I think there is a persistent and not altogether inaccurate story of the postmodern that dates it simultaneously to Heidegger's attack on humanism and May 1968 in France.

This dating makes sense. Heidegger's critique of humanism came at a time of generalized crisis in Europe following two wars in which so many millions of people were killed and the category European Jew was reduced to a trace, at most, of its former meaning. Mass killing and genocide change the way a place thinks of itself. Always. Or it should. And the near dismantling of the bureaucratic, capitalist state in May 1968 signaled an emerging dismantling of identity and authority—at least in terms of values and aspirations—that fundamentally contested modernist notions of subject and state. That is, the postmodern emerges in Europe as a response to a mid-century crisis. A whole cluster of postwar thinkers reckon with Europe's internal violence, its terrifying reproduction of anonymity, sameness, and casual embrace of both spectacular and everyday violence, offering critiques that take alterity and its disruptive, sometimes ethical, force seriously.

The postmodern, in this account, emerges as a break with modernity and its pretenses, as well as the values and aspirations of modernity itself. If Adorno and Horkheimer were right in *Dialectic of Enlightenment*, then European modernity, for all its humanist promises, was elemental in the production of machineries of death. The war machine. The capitalist machine. The machine of genocide. So much death, and the ethical impulses of the postmodern are at least in part, if not near wholly, dedicated to contesting the machinery of death. This is no small bit of what animates Lyotard's *Heidegger and "the jews,"* a text dedicated to the critical function of the social-political-cultural other in establishing modernity's dream of fulfillment and development—always without boundaries, without being subjected to time. Mid-century Europe's reckoning with the violence of modernity, how the bureaucratic state is excessive and the mechanization of death and destruction are centerpieces rather than after-effects of modernity, generates the crisis to which the postmodern is a counter-position and from which it was generated as an ethical-political imperative.

But from where did modernity come? And what is that origin to the afropostmodern?

There is the European story of its own modern origins, tracing modernity back to certain innovations in philosophy—disputes between rationalists and empiricists that generate new models of reasoning and Enlightenment visions of the human person—and any cluster of scientific, political, and aesthetic revolutions that displace the enchanted world with a calculable universe. The mathematization of everyday life. The destiny promised by Euclid, fulfilled in Newtonian physics and all of its companion processes and modes of thought: bureaucracy, calculative reason, formalization of the material world. And yet there is another story to be told, one reconstructed from the colonies by Enrique Dussel, in which modernity is born not in a self-affecting intellectual movement in Europe, but in a bureaucratic crisis.[14] That crisis is begun when Bartolomé de Las Casas convinces the Spanish powers to free enslaved indigenous people in the Americas, a demand made because slaves had converted to Christianity in greater and greater numbers. Whatever its theological significance and political impact on indigenous life and its fate, it creates, for European powers, a managerial crisis: how can profit be maximized in the colonies if labor must be contracted for some sort of compensation? How can the labor force be organized and set to work with maximum profit as the outcome? A bureaucratic crisis.

The response is the origin of the Atlantic slave trade as we know it. If indigenous people could not be enslaved, then Africans would take their place. From this, genocide of indigenous Caribbean people and resettlement of the archipelago through forced migration follows in full force, a project fully realized. The Caribbean as the locus of the black Americas becomes a historical reality and, with that reality, comes the cluster of memories that make the hemisphere. Indeed, the very term "Americas" is a synonym for conquest and slavery. Modernity, Dussel argues, comes out of this transformation of the hemisphere because the combination of shocking greed with a diminished free labor source demands of reason just what reason becomes in modernity: calculating, bureaucratic, anonymous. Alongside that birth of modernity in a bureaucratic crisis is the origins of the black Americas: the Middle Passage. The two are inseparable in time, transformative of space, and specters of one another in each place: Europe, the Americas, Africa, and the Atlantic as sea, passage, death, memory. A graveyard of goodness. The birth of two paradigms of thought.

What I think this story from the colonies tells us is that the afropostmodern is simultaneous with the birth of European modernity. That is, when Europe responds to the emancipation of indigenous slaves with an intensification of transport of enslaved Africans to the Americas under a new rubric. At the opening of the sixteenth century, Iberian enslaving was bound by a simple condition: the enslaved, if they were to be taken to the Americas, must have been born under the domain of Christianity— converted, brought into the world, but under Christian dominion. But Charles V changes everything with a document in 1518 declaring that enslaved Africans may be taken from Sao Tomé and the Cape Verde Islands to the New World *without* the restraints of Christian dominion, birth, and rebirth. This changes everything because it initiates, in the fullest sense that we know it, the Middle Passage: the transport of millions of Africans from the coast of Africa to the archipelago, beginning with Hispanola and then of course to all of the islands and so many sites on the continent. If the afropostmodern is defined by fragment work, reckoning with the differend of beauty and pain, and an engagement with radical becoming without recursion to Being, then 1518 marks the inception of the conditions of that work—something intensified when the bureaucratic crisis initiated by Las Casas comes to its peak in 1542. Charles V prepared the terms for mass forced migration, the emancipation of indigenous slaves intensified and actualized that migration, and the afropostmodern emerges in the very same moment as European modernity.

And if we return to Lyotard, this site of modernity/postmodernity offers a twist on the story of the postmodern and the differend, shifting from the consequences of Lyotard's conceptions, in which anti-state and anti-imperial agitation works against the violence of modernity in our moment, and toward a notion of the afropostmodern as an originary interruption, disruption, and contestation of modernity's violence *in the very moment of its inception*. The question, then, is not simply how postmodern strategies mitigate and disrupt conventional forms of violence, but also how dating or periodizing the postmodern in the moment of modernity's emergence reveals an alternative mode of thought in the shadows of Europe's worst excess. Further, when we see this sort of emergence-at-origin, we catch sight of something utterly compelling and revolutionary: the creation of worlds-becoming that work *with* fragments, work *without* strategies of legitimation, and therefore work without what Lyotard calls the fantasied "universal genre of discourse" that regulates difference. I am thinking here of the opening pages of *The Differend* in which Lyotard sets out the problem:

> Given 1) the impossibility of avoiding conflicts (the impossibility of indifference) and 2) the absence of a universal genre of discourse to regulate them (or, if you prefer, the inevitable partiality of the judge): to find, if not what can legitimate judgement (the 'good' linkage), then at least how to save the honor of thinking.[15]

Thinking becomes, in the afropostmodern, a thinking of becoming—but always a becoming without reference to a possible being that stabilizes. Glissant, for that reason, characterizes Relation, his term for afropostmodern thinking, as rhizomatic and (on the model of theoretical physics) chaotic. Nomadic without the desire to set up a final or single root. A Deleuzean term, but one adopted in response to the demands of thinking in the wake of the failure of metanarratives of race, origin, or political principles to negotiate and neutralize contradiction, paradox—the threats to the modern order and its authoritarian impulses.

A final note

Where does this all leave us? No small question. Indeed, this is always the question asked back to the postmodern, whether the European postmodern or the afropostmodern, precisely because the delegitimation of knowledge through the dismantling of metanarrative leaves conventional, habitual forms of knowing, being, and doing without real weight. But those forms of knowing, being, and doing were always constructs in service of a particular vision of political order and cultural hegemony. The emergence of the European postmodern had exactly this in view when the deconstructive work of alterity did its work in readings of foundational texts from the tradition, as well as direct interventions against calcified traditions and exercises of power. The afropostmodern has a different temporality, however, dating itself back to the origins of European modernity and emerging as a consequence of forced migration and enslavement, rather than as a refusal of a given social order. Yet—and this is key—the afropostmodern was also a source of great anxiety for mid-century black Atlantic thinkers; vernacular culture and expressive life—creole, pidgin, other forms of everyday life—were not deemed abject because of an inherent character, but because what the mid-century moment inherited from European (and perhaps also African) traditions was a compulsion to tell a story of history in order to insert that story into History. The afropostmodern corrects course and sees, as Walcott put it, the *gift* that accompanied unspeakable pain and suffering. Whereas the European postmodern is generated as a critique and intervention of a given order, the afropostmodern turns to the everydayness of resistance and world making and away from aspirations to mimic the cultural excesses of modernity.

But what makes both moves so provocative, however different their orientation and intellectual origins, is a shared commitment to contest and refuse authoritarianism even at the level of everyday life. These forms of micro-resistance and dissent are no small matters. While they do not have the grandeur of revolutionary and messianic rhetoric, micro-resistance, especially when it permeates the entirety of world making and its pleasures, reminds us of the ecstasy of everyday life, of community and solitude, and so the work of unsettled life on thinking, embodiment, language, and cultural production. Heidegger was right: ours is an epoch of Enframing in which everything is flattened for the sake of forms of uniformity, sameness, and susceptibility to calculation. What it means to live under those conditions, to resist but also thrive—survival is never enough—is something opened by the European postmodern. And in that opening, when we see it in relation to the afropostmodern, we are reminded that fragments, chaos, and becoming might bequeath something more than remnants of life. In fact, they bequeath possibility itself. Open, unprecedented, unresolved. We should honor what that gives to thinking.

Notes

1 See Aimé Césaire, "Culture and Colonization," tr. Brent Edwards, *Social Text* 103, vol. 28, no. 2 (Summer 2010): 127–44.
2 Jean-François Lyotard, *The Postmodern Condition,* tr. Geoff Bennington and Brian Massumi (Minneapolis MN: University of Minnesota Press, [1979] 1984), 35.
3 See Fanon's recounting of this dynamic in "West Indians and Africans," in *Toward the African Revolution,* tr. Haakon Chevalier (New York: Grove Press, [1964] 1994), 17–28.
4 Documenting Glissant's sense of loss is the focus of the first two chapters of my *Glissant and the Middle Passage: Philosophy, Beginning, Abyss* (Minneapolis MN: University of Minnesota Press, 2019).
5 Édouard Glissant, *Poetics of Relation,* tr. Betsy Wing (Ann Arbor MI: University of Michigan Press, [1990] 1999), 9.
6 Glissant, *Poetics of Relation,* 8–9.
7 Derek Walcott, "The Muse of History," in *What the Twilight Says* (New York: FSG, 1999), 64.
8 Derek Walcott, "The Antilles: Fragments of Epic Memory," in *What the Twilight Says,* 69.
9 See Walcott, "The Antilles," where he famously writes: "Break a vase and the love that reassembles the fragments is stronger than the love that took its symmetry for granted when it was whole ... the cracked heirlooms whose restoration shows its white scars" (69).
10 Édouard Glissant, "Foreword" to Patrick Chamoiseau, *Chronicle of the Seven Sorrows,* tr. Linda Coverdale (Lincoln NE: University of Nebraska, 2003), vii.
11 I elaborate this sense of apocalypse in "Césaire's Apocalyptic Word," *South Atlantic Quarterly* 115, no. 3 (2016): 567–84.
12 Glissant, *Poetics of Relation,* 47.
13 Ibid., 49.
14 Enrique Dussel, "The 'World-System': Europe as 'Center' and its 'Periphery' Beyond Eurocentrism" in Eduardo Mendieta (ed.), *Beyond Philosophy: Ethics, History, Marxism and Liberation Theology*. (Lanham MD: Rowman & Littlefield, 2003), 53–83.
15 Jean-François Lyotard, *The Differend: Phrases in Dispute,* tr. Georges Van Den Abbeele (Manchester: Manchester University Press, [1983] 1988), xii.

8

Jean-François Lyotard's Marxism, in *Socialisme ou Barbarie* and the Algerian War[1]

Claire Pagès

In 1946, the "Chaulieu-Montal tendency" was formed by Cornelius Castoriadis, Claude Lefort and other members of the French section of the Trotskyist Fourth International. Based on the critique of orthodox Trotskyism, the tendency eventually broke away and developed a project for a journal. Titled *Socialisme ou Barbarie* (Socialism or Barbarism; SouB), the first issue was published in March 1949.[2] The group, which took the same name as the journal, included workers and intellectuals from Spain, the United States, Germany, the United Kingdom and Italy who had broken with the Fourth International at the end of the Second World War. First published bi-monthly, later quarterly, it ceased publication after its fortieth issue in June 1965. It was not until June 1967, however, that a letter was sent to subscribers announcing the end of the publication, by which time the group was dissolved.

Jean-François Lyotard joined the group in 1954 at the same time as Pierre Souyri, a former member of the Fourth International whom he had met in Algeria. In 1958 Lefort left, having questioned the reconstitution of a revolutionary party within SouB, and founded the group "Informations et liaisons ouvrières" with Henri Simon, later renamed "Informations et correspondances ouvrières" in 1960. In 1963–4, there was a second split between a "tendency" led by Castoriadis and Daniel Mothé, who retained the journal and the name Socialisme ou Barbarie, and a heterogeneous grouping including Lyotard and Souyri who adopted the name "Pouvoir Ouvrier" (Worker's Power). Pouvoir Ouvrier was short-lived: Lyotard resigned in 1966 and by 1969 the group ceased to exist.[3]

Who is this Lyotard when he joins SouB in 1954? Born in 1924, he is thirty years old. A young high school philosophy teacher, he has just returned from teaching at the Lycée d'Aumale in Constantine, Algeria, to take up a post in La Flèche where he teaches from 1952–6. On leaving university, he decides to complete his philosophical education by reading two authors who were excluded from the higher education program at the time, Thomas Aquinas and Karl Marx, but having started with the latter, he says, he never returned to the former![4] He is also trained in phenomenology and is the author of a short volume on the subject published in the popular "Que sais-je" series in 1954. In the Lyotard archives there is a series of works and conference papers, dating from the 1950s and 1960s, devoted to the relationship between phenomenology and history: "The problem of history from a phenomenological perspective" (1961), "The concept of rationality in history and phenomenological philosophy" (1959), "History and Phenomenology" (1959).[5] It is thus as a phenomenologist more than as a revolutionary activist that he is known in the 1950s and early 1960s, which reminds us of the limited reach of the SouB group and its journal at the time.[6]

Once admitted to SouB, he writes, "the struggle against exploitation and alienation became my whole life."[7] During these twelve years, 1954 to 1966, he devoted all his time "to the sole enterprise of 'revolutionary critique and orientation' which was that of the group and its journal."[8] This meant writing notes and studies of politics for the journal, and later for the mimeographed newspaper *Pouvoir Ouvrier* that was distributed at factory gates, but also clandestine support for Algerian militants.[9] In this commitment, Lyotard identifies an age-old desire "to be in touch with the stuff concrete history is made of ... to be open to events."[10] Virtually all research that is not related to the cause ceases, and it is only with the end of this militancy that he returns to academic publishing.

Because of their particular knowledge of the subject, Lyotard (under the pseudonym of François Laborde) and Souyri (under that of Pierre Brune) are respectively in charge of Algerian and Chinese issues in the journal. Thus "for seven years [between 1956 and 1963 he] wrote the Algerian chronicle of *Socialisme ou Barbarie*."[11]

Socialisme ou Barbarie

I shall confine myself here to recalling the main characteristics. The group took the name of the journal it published, a name whose meaning was clear at the time but which Lyotard felt he had to explain when he returned to the topic in 1986, speaking to an audience in California: "[this] name constituted a sentence ... 'Socialisme ou Barbarie,' which means, and it is not useless to be precise about this today, 'either socialism or barbarism.'"[12] The expression is Rosa Luxemburg's: this was how she and the Luxemburgists saw the alternative facing humanity. If the action of the masses did not succeed in bringing about socialism, society as a whole would regress to barbarity. How the group understood "socialism," however, needs further explanation.

SouB defined itself as a revolutionary group, an organization that was both political and theoretical, with a critical theory and practice. It was critical of all known varieties of socialism and class struggle: reformist, anarchist, Trotskyist or Stalinist. In particular it was critical of all forms which became bureaucratic; according to Castoriadis, SouB offered an analysis of "the historical destiny of Marxism."[13] As a result both Miguel Abensour and Lyotard were able to compare the objectives of Socialisme ou Barbarie to those of critical theory and the first Frankfurt School.[14] It was a question, by and large, of indicating how a project of emancipation can shift dialectically into its opposite, into one of domination, and of denouncing the most hidden and pernicious forms of this reversal. Theodor W. Adorno and Max Horkheimer analyzed such a reversal, most notably with the Enlightenment but also with the Marxism of their time. Similarly, SouB worked to illuminate the reversal of the Soviet project into its opposite.

Thus, Castoriadis analyzed the Soviet Union as a form of "State Capitalism" that appears to have broken with private property but that, paradoxically, also appears to demonstrate within itself the reinforcement of capitalist forms of power and domination.

SouB was still characterized as a form of spontaneism, hence the crucial reference to Rosa Luxemburg. This "organ of criticism and revolutionary orientation" presents itself as an instrument for the "avant-garde of manual and intellectual workers." But the internationalist reflection on "the guiding ideas of workers' emancipation" does not lead the group to want to direct their struggles. It is a question of being attentive to their inventiveness:

> the role of the revolutionary organization is not to direct workers' struggles, but to provide them with the means to deploy the creativity that is at work in them and the means to become aware of that creativity so as to direct themselves.[15]

In other words, it is a question of regenerating the framework of the workers' guiding ideas without intervening from outside, but by listening to the immanent logic of the struggles.

One of the tasks proposed by SouB's radical Marxist critique was "to analyze the dynamics of the struggles in underdeveloped countries."[16] Hence the need for an Algerian chronicle.

Lyotard and Algeria

Why is Lyotard in charge of covering Algerian issues for *Socialism ou Barbarie*? This is because he not only knows Algerian history but has lived in Algeria for two years. In 1950 he was appointed professor of philosophy at the lycée for boys in Constantine, then the capital of a French *département* in Algeria.[17] Almost thirty years later, he tells us that as a young teacher in Constantine,

> He was involved in both workers unions and the principal movements for the liberation of Algeria. Fascinated by the theological and practical power of dialectical materialism, this freshman in radical militancy was naturally convinced that a society as contradictory as Algerian society, one in which injustices were so flagrant, couldn't avoid resolving its aporia, no matter the means it would take or the amount of time this resolution might take.[18]

It was in Constantine that he met Pierre Souyri, who had taken up his first post as a history teacher in Philippeville, Algeria, in September 1949. He met him there after a trade union meeting. Speaking at a conference, at the beginning of the 1990s, he recalls another decisive meeting which took place at the time, with one of his pupils, named Bouziane:

> it was he who taught me Algeria in 1951, the improbable cultural and social fabric, the odious complacency of the administrators, the contemptuous paternalism of

the native French and the ignorance of metropolitans like me, the aberration of the Algerian Communist Party ("the independentists are in the pay of the big settlers"; I could explain the motive of this absurdity to the student) and the still secret resolution which was taking shape after the deportation of Messali Hadj to Bréhat, the decision that it would be necessary to take up arms. This delicate young Arab, full of cheerfulness, who read Merleau-Ponty, was killed seven years later at the head of his group of resistance fighters near Soukh Ahras, formerly Tagaste, the birthplace of St. Augustine.[19]

Lyotard's relationship with Algeria is multilayered. There is the Algerian experience itself, a crucial experience of which Lyotard wrote: "It had for me the importance of something that initiates one directly into the political."[20] However, this experience, to which we will return later, is first and foremost an experience of suffering:

What is this misery to an unexpectant gaze? where are its remedies? Anyone who has heard the chants of the naked beggar ... on the Sidi Rached bridge in Constantine, who has seen dead infants at the waxy breast of the Bedouin women squatting among the passers-by in the medina at Tunis; whoever has suffered the assault of the tuberculor boys at Touggourt, of the flies entering their mouths and their eyes, who has endured the spectacle of these markets of famine, everyone then, this question cannot fail to come to everyone. It is not a matter of conscience, it is not the peculiarity of the observer that makes it resonate or not; on the contrary it is because of what is universal in him.[21]

Then there are the analyses of the Algerian situation which will appear in *SouB*: thirteen texts, published between 1956 and 1963 (later collected as *La Guerre des Algériens* in 1989, and partially published in *Political Writings* in 1993). The documentation gathered to examine this dossier is astonishing. Thousands of pages of notes can be found in the archives: reading notes on the history of colonialization in the Maghreb and elsewhere, but also on the history of Islam since the eleventh century (for example, a huge file in "Working Papers and Courses" titled "Colonial questions Maghreb-Islam").[22]

However, Lyotard will also evoke the Algerian war in retrospect, after he has abandoned a Marxist perspective. He writes texts which evoke Algeria, texts of remembrance, written after the painful break with Marxism. Such texts include "Memorial for Marxism," devoted to Souyri in *Peregrinations* in 1988,[23] "The Name of Algeria," (1989) in *Political Writings*, and "La guerre des Algériens, suite," an unpublished text (1995). But the way in which he speaks of the struggles for independence in texts devoted to questions of the postmodern already indicates the change of perspective.

The Marxist grand narrative of emancipation from exploitation and alienation through the socialization of work—progressive or catastrophic emancipation of work (the source of value in capitalism)—would have placed legitimacy in a universal idea to be achieved, like in other grand narratives, in the contribution made to the emancipation of humanity. These—typically modern—narratives presuppose the existence of a suppressed voice in the discourse of "reality"; in this case, it is a question of replacing the emancipated proletariat in its position of subject unduly usurped by the impostor. There are many reasons why these grand narratives or meta-narratives have fallen into disrepute, many reasons for the failure of modernity, "the fall of metaphysics," Adorno would have said. But among them, Lyotard inscribes a form of resistance, that of "the multiplicity of worlds of names" or that of the "insurmountable diversity of cultures."[24] For Lyotard, the modern project of making men speak with one voice has failed and we see that the complete overcoming, resorption or *Aufhebung* of the particular in the universal cannot take place. He gives two examples of retreat into local legitimacy or resistance to it:

> The workers' movement is a particularly telling example of this failure. In theory, its internationalism meant that the legitimacy of the class struggle did not derive from local (popular or labor) traditions but from an Idea to be realized – the Idea of the worker emancipated from the proletarian condition. Now we know that, from the time of the Franco-German War of 1870–1871, the International was deadlocked over the issue of Alsace-Lorraine, and that in 1914 both German and French socialists voted for national war budgets etc. Stalinism as "socialism in one country," and the suppression of the Komintern, openly proclaimed the superiority of the nation's proper name over the universal name of the Soviets. The spread of struggles for independence since the Second World War and the recognition of the new national names seem to imply a consolidation of local legitimacies.[25]

If the Marxist grand narrative of emancipation comes up against local legitimacies, the latter had already made their resistances felt when Lyotard delivered a Marxist analysis of the Algerian war for *SouB*—as considered below.

He will also return to his reports on Algeria during a conference paper "La guerre des Algériens, suite" in 1995, delivered in Paris at the *Maison des écrivains* during the conference "Algérie-France, regards croisée." This event took place *after* the return of the Algerian question, prompted by the crisis of 1993, after the bloody civil war that marked the 1990s in Algeria:

> Thirty years after the end of the War of Independence, civil war has begun in Algeria. I accompanied the first by gesture and with political, social and revolutionary critique. As for the second, I feel helpless: for want of an alternative practical, international and local perspective, the means for a radically critical approach are lacking. An analysis of the Algerian situation remains possible, but it has ceased to be the moment allowing the orientation of a practice ... No situation today, no matter how critical it may be on the outskirts of rich countries, threatens the state of things or announces revolution. The word rings hollow. We cannot analyze the events in Algeria from this perspective. For some at least, myself included, that country remains an object of transference or, if you like, of love. The concern for the grace of beauty joined with the disgrace of fate can guide analysis, we know, as well as political engagement ... During the war of liberation, it was clearly right to support, as a Frenchman could and as a revolutionary Marxist activist should, the Algerians' struggle to impose their name on imperialism and, no less obviously, also to help them by critiquing the inconsistent bureaucracy that

led their struggle and claimed to govern their liberated country. Which we did. In the current civil war, the power of this bureaucracy has demonstrated its impotence for the past thirty years.[26]

The Algerian war

What characterizes the Lyotardian analyses of the Algerian war in *SouB*? In part, they are typical of the group. In part, they specify Lyotard's philosophical and political sensitivity at the time. The historical framework of Lyotard's analyses of the Algerian war is dictated by the major rhythms of the conflict: the texts thus run from 1956 to 1963 (in the aftermath of Independence, July 5, 1962).

1. It is firstly a question of putting French imperialism and colonialization in Algeria on trial, a violent and infamous imperialism, says Lyotard, a rotting imperialism which is a class imperialism, that of the French bourgeoisie:[27]

Few people have been ravaged like the Algerians by the French: rendered unfit for mere survival by expropriation and poverty, estranged from their name by ignorance and offence, made foreigners to their language and history by a fiction of French citizenship.[28]

2. First target of criticism, the position of the French Communists of the PCF (French Communist Party) on Algeria. As Lyotard presents it, the tactics of the PCF and Moscow—the French PCF was very weak in Algeria in the 1950s—are quite simple: it is a question of maintaining the links with the metropolis as a priority, which means keeping Algeria and giving the Algerian branch of the French PCF a chance. Hence the sabotage of the struggle against the Algerian war since 1954 by the PCF and the simply formal nature of the support it gave to the FLN (Algerian National Liberation Front). Thus, the PCF would rather help French imperialism to maintain itself in Algeria than see it dislodged by US imperialism.[29]

3. Secondly, it is a Marxist analysis of the Algerian war. It asserts that "there is no other alternative to exploitation than socialism,"[30] no other alternative to the exploitation of Algerian society by French imperialism and the bourgeoisie. Algerian society is contradictory and the rapid development of the situation depends on these "contradictions of the Algerian situation"[31] (more internal contradictions than geopolitical context). The Algerian situation, at the end of 1959 and the beginning of 1960, is "revolutionary" in the sense that "people no longer live according to the formally dominant institutions," because "the open and durable rupture of a class or of an ensemble of classes within the structure of society necessarily has revolutionary significance."[32] This does not mean that the revolution has been accomplished. It still remains to institute new social relations, to destroy the dominant class. What is more, it seems that Algerian society is organized in such a way that contradictions cannot succeed. If the armed struggle in particular has a new revolutionary content, the situation

in general does not reach maturity and the schema of permanent revolution remains inapplicable. Finally, we recognize here the Marxism of SouB: it is not a question of directing, orientating, or enlightening this revolutionary struggle, but of hoping that

> the colonial workers intervene *themselves, practically and directly*, in the transformation of their society, that they break off, effectively, without asking permission from anyone, the relations that crushed them, and that they provide an example of socialist activity personified to all the exploited and the exploiters: the recovery of social humanity by its own efforts.[33]

4. As is typical of *SouB*, Lyotard's analysis of the Algerian war highlights the criticisms of bureaucracy and the surreptitious reconstitution of a bureaucracy at the head of the national uprising. The FLN is in no way the incarnation of the Algerian proletariat for Lyotard. It constitutes a form of national front: uniting the peasants, workers, employees, and petty-bourgeois under a bourgeois leadership.[34] Between the peasants and the protagonists of this leadership, signs of class conflict would already be perceptible. It is apparent from the ideological poverty of the program that the leaders are in fact bourgeois.[35] Algeria can therefore join the list of societies which, in spite of the existence of an emancipatory struggle bearing a revolutionary spirit, sees a new bureaucracy forming within them.[36] And this bureaucracy, Lyotard says, whatever its origin—here it is national—always has the characteristics of class. The main risk that threatens Algerians is that the struggle for independence will only lead to a simple change in the regime of exploitation, consisting specifically in "the consolidation of a military regime,"[37] in the constitution of a military and political bureaucracy, in which Lyotard was right. The only solution to this constitution of new national exploiters was a class solution: the direct appropriation of land by the peasants.[38]

5. In accordance with the approach of SouB, the analysis of a situation and a turning back (*retournement*) of its opposition to a project of emancipation must lead Marxism to conceptual adjustments. If, as Lyotard writes of the Algerian war in 1958, "the French left can so easily lose its Marxism,"[39] it is because the terms of this Marxism require modification. In this case—and this is what makes Lyotard's analyses so original within the group—it is the *national* component of the war that must make us think. Lyotard tries to explain everything that prevented the formation of a class consciousness in Algeria. The economic and social weakness of the Algerian bourgeoisie plays a role and, above all, the fact that class divisions are covered by "ethnic" divisions, buried deep within national divisions, class antagonisms buried in colonial society.[40] The struggle is national in scope, targeting French imperialism and aiming at independence, which is instantiated as the opposite of exploitation:[41] the awareness of alienation can only be national in the first place.[42] In no way does this mean that the concept of class should be abandoned, but rather that the purpose of the analysis should be to understand what marks objective class relations, namely that a bourgeois leadership is capable of mobilizing all the Algerian classes in the struggle for independence. Why didn't the Algerian struggle find a manifest class content in the expression given to it by the FLN? Perhaps it was the result of a social vacuum, or the fact that Algerian society did not

have a working class that was able to be the sole supporter of nationalism and to take up arms.[43]

As early as 1958, Lyotard warned against the resistance and entrenchment of this national ideology, albeit vague, experienced by Algerian society as a unanimous response to French imperialism. The depth of this experience must defeat all his attempts at objectification: "We have to get rid of a certain kind of patronizing Marxism: an ideology has no less *reality* (even and above all if it is *false*) than the objective relations to which this Marxism wants to reduce it."[44] One feature of the Lyotardian method, particularly evident in his 1969 text against Althusser, is the requirement to start from the present social experience, taken seriously as it is, and only then to construct the theory.[45] It is a lesson he also learned from Merleau-Ponty; in "Marxism and Philosophy" (*Sense and Non-sense*, [1948] 1964), Merleau-Ponty defended the thesis of the reality of structures at their origin, to what gives them meaning, in the lived and felt experience of values. It is thus on the condition of recognizing the dimension not of reflection or representation of ideas but of experience that history can be understood, by also apprehending its meaning as the one that men give it by living—and they live it in various ways.[46]

Secondly, internationalism must be questioned by this other resistance to the national question that Lyotard pointed out in 1958: in recent years, we have never seen the French working class fight against the Algerian war. There is an obvious fact here that challenges the revolutionary Marxist scheme of spontaneous solidarity of the proletariat with the oppressed of all kinds, of an acute awareness of the convergence of the different struggles for liberation. However, the French proletariat showed no solidarity with the struggle of the Algerian people and, more generally, Lyotard writes, it must be noted that the proletariat of the old capitalist nations lacked solidarity with the movement of the young colonized nations.[47]

Taking into account the national dimension of the struggle does have a limit, however, and whilst Lyotard is able to manage this part of the question, Algerian nationalism is nevertheless reduced to a product of capitalist exploitation, explained socially and politically by the conditions of the exploitation of the peasantry, thus ruling out any analysis of culture, religion, etc. For Lyotard, this nationalism results from the different forms of alienation for which French colonization in Algeria is responsible (confiscation of the means of production, sabotage of the means of understanding, humiliation, etc.): "you do not create 70 percent profit margins innocently; you extract those profits from millions of dispossessed workers in the shape of sweat and death."[48] The nation is presented as offering a form of solidarity to these men crushed by French colonialism: "in colonized countries nationalism is the ultimate response of the population to the profound *desocialization* produced by imperialism."[49] And about the national character of the struggle:

> It is useless to look toward the spiritual heritage of the Arab tribes or the congenital bellicosity of the Muslim soul in order to understand them. These are hypotheses at once too crude and too light, refuted by the observation of any other peasantry placed in the same conditions of exploitation.[50]

6. The analysis is concerned with the singularity or specificity of the Algerian case. This is another feature of Lyotardian thought: welcoming the event, judging without criteria. Not only are the situations in Algeria and Russia shown to be incomparable,[51] Lyotard also presents all the structural differences between Algeria, Tunisia, and Morocco.[52] He looks at the history of Muslim Algeria and the history of colonization in order to set out the particularities of the Algerian situation each time. Listening to the singularity of the Algerian case implies leaving the perspective of the Algerian revolution open. At the same time, to use Lyotard's words, there is no alternative to exploitation other than socialism, and the perspective of the Algerian revolution cannot be defined as socialism in advance.[53]

Returning to his analysis of the Algerian war in *SouB* in the 1980s, Lyotard recalls the concern he already had not to anticipate the outcome in advance according to an already written Marxist scenario, not to resolve the contradictions of the present experience in advance. Contradictions there were, and the group was divided on what support should be given to the Algerian revolution. On the one hand, how could they support the National Liberation Front, which controlled the struggles of the Algerians, when the group tasked itself with critiquing all organizations which hindered the free development of class struggles, and encouraged spontaneity among the workers? There was also the need to distinguish their position from that of Sartre and his support for the FLN. On the other hand, how could they not support a liberation movement?

> Yes, the Algerians have the right, even the duty, to become free and to be recognized as a free community with its own name and equal to others—so we must support their struggle. Nevertheless, that struggle has no chance of instituting any of the principles of worker democracy, and it will not fail to produce a new class society under the control of a bureaucratic military leadership—so why should we give our support to the coming to power of new exploiters?[54]

Lyotard refused to resolve the contradiction. Uncertain, he already doubted that the liberation of Algeria could mean the resolution of the country's contradictions.

Conclusion

The uncertainty increases soon enough. Contemporary with his resignation from Pouvoir Ouvrier in 1966 is a monograph whose foreword bears the date "8 July 1966" and the title "The Threshold of History."[55] Here Lyotard indicates that the Marxist categories of analysis, beginning with that of the dialectic, must be abandoned in order to understand the movement of decolonization. The first part of the text, "The Peasant and History," seems to approach the Algerian liberation struggle within the framework of an analysis of the peasant uprisings which mark the history of imperialism. It is important not to impose a modern meaning on these, lending them the intention to transform society, by historicizing a traditional organization:

The longest and bloodiest wars of liberation can be followed by a dead calm. Algeria's deception after 1962 is a recent example of this . . . Fanon's mistake (1961) was to believe that a radical contestation of the colonial fact, like the Algerian uprising of 1954, could be extended into a radical contestation of all forms of domination; that the war of national liberation could thus lead to a process of total liberation. The truth is that the peasant can fight to the death against the foreigner and his associates without revising traditional social relations, no matter how deteriorated they are by colonization.[56]

It is the analysis of an opportunity missed between national struggle and revolution that Lyotard recounts in his Algerian chronicles. Certainly, the problem of colonial Algeria was the conquest of Algerian identity and not that of socialism as a movement towards a classless society. However, at the time, this observation was accompanied by the conviction that the hard-working Algerian masses would continue to be confronted with the crucial problem of exploitation, so that the revolution remained to be done.[57] It is this last conviction that will gradually leave Lyotard.

Notes

1. Thanks to the Bibliothèque Littéraire Jacques Doucet Library, Paris, where the J.-F. Lyotard archives were consulted for this work; also to the journal *Implications philosophiques* where the text appears in French as part of a dossier coordinated by Jean-Baptiste Vuillerod, for permission to translate, rework, and publish in English.
2. See Jean Amair et al., *Socialisme ou Barbarie: An Anthology*, tr. David Ames Curtis et al. (London: Eris, 2018).
3. See Claire Pagès, "To begin with," *Journal of the CIPH*, vol. 96, no. 2 (2019), 1–15. DOI: 10.3917/rdes.096.0001. Available online: https://www.cairn-int.info/journal-of-the-ciph-2019-2-page-1.htm
4. Jean-François Lyotard, *Peregrinations" Law, Form, Event* (New York: Columbia University Press, 1988), 25.
5. Jean-François Lyotard, "Manuscrit de 148 feuillets (1959–1961)," Bibliothèque Jacques Doucet, JFL 392–JFL 394.
6. Invited to give the conference paper "Le problème de l'histoire dans la perspective phénoménologique," in 1961, Lyotard was introduced as follows: "Connu des philosophes par son excellent petit livre, *La Phénoménologie*, plus que par sa collaboration à la Revue *Socialisme ou barbarie* . . ." (Known to philosophers more through his excellent short book *Phenomenology*, than through his contribution to the journal *Socialisme ou barbarie* . . .).
7. Jean-François Lyotard, *Pérégrinations: Loi, forme, événement* (Paris: Galilée, 1990), 40—translated from the French edition. See also Lyotard, *Peregrinations*: "A sense of how important my allegiance to the cause of combatting exploitation and alienation was can be gotten from the fact that for fifteen years I neglected all forms of activity and sensibility other than those directly connected to this cause" (17).
8. Lyotard, "A Memorial for Marxism," tr. Cecile Lindsay, in *Peregrinations*, 47.
9. Concerning the activities of Lyotard in helping Algerian militants to reach France, see Kiff Bamford, *Jean-François Lyotard* (London: Reaktion Books, 2017), 42–6.

10 Lyotard, *Peregrinations*, 17.
11 Ibid., 26. See Amparo Vega "Socialisme ou Barbarie et le militantisme de Lyotard," *Cité* 45, "Lyotard politique," (2011): 31–43 ; Marie Goupy, "Lyotard et la guerre d'Algérie. La guerre et la révolution," in Claire Pagès (ed.), *Lyotard à Nanterre* (Paris : Klincksieck, 2010), 225–37.
12 Lyotard, "Touches," *Peregrinations*, 16.
13 Cornelius Castoriadis, "Marxism and Revolutionary Theory," in *The Imaginary Institution of Society*, tr. Kathleen Blamey (Cambridge UK: Polity, 1997), 12. This text was first published in *Socialisme ou Barbarie* [*SouB*] issues 36–40 (April 1964–June 1965).
14 Miguel Abensour, *La Communauté politique des "tous uns," Entretien avec Michel Enaudeau* (Paris: Belles Lettres, 2014), 35.
15 Jean-François Lyotard, "The Name of Algeria" [1989], in *Political Writings*, tr. Bill Readings and Kevin Paul Geiman (Minneapolis MN: Minnesota University Press, 1993), 166.
16 Lyotard, "A Memorial for Marxism" [1982], in *Peregrinations*, 66.
17 Lyotard, *Peregrinations*, 2.
18 Lyotard, *Peregrinations*, 25–6.
19 Jean-François Lyotard, "La guerre des Algériens, suite," 4, Bibliothèque Jacques Doucet, JFL 287, typed manuscript (conference paper).
20 Lyotard, "A Memorial for Marxism," in *Peregrinations*, 75, n. 12.
21 Bibliothèque Jacques Doucet, JFL 437/1, "Questions coloniales" (folder 2, second set).
22 Bibliothèque Jacques Doucet, JFL 437.
23 Originally published in *Esprit* in January 1982 under the title "Pierre Souyri, le marxisme qui n'a pas fini." no. 61 (1982): 11–31.
24 Jean-François Lyotard, *The Postmodern Explained to Children: Correspondence 1982–1985*, tr. Julian Pefanis, Morgan Thomas et al. (London: Turnaround, [1986] 1992), 42.
25 Ibid., 46.
26 Lyotard, "La guerre des Algériens, suite," Bibliothèque Jacques Doucet, JFL 287, typed manuscript, 18–20 May 1995, 1–2; 8–9.
27 Lyotard, "Les comptes du "gérant loyal" (*SouB* 22, juillet–septembre 1957), in Jean-François Lyotard, *La Guerre des Algériens : Ecrits 1956–1963* (Paris : Galilée), 85. No English translation.
28 Lyotard, "La guerre des Algériens, suite," 3.
29 Lyotard, " La situation en Afrique du nord" (*SouB* 18, janvier–mars 1956), in *La Guerre des Algériens*, 48–49, translated in *Political Writings*, 176–7; "Nouvelle phase dans la question algérienne" (*SouB* 21, mars–mai 1957), in *La Guerre des Algériens*, 66–7, translated in *Political Writings*, 187–9; "Mise à nue des contradictions algériennes " (*SouB* 24, mai–juin 1958), in *La Guerre des Algériens*, 103, translated in *Political Writings*, 208–9.
30 Lyotard, "The Situation in North Africa," in *Political Writings*, 174.
31 Lyotard, "A New Phase in the Algerian Situation," in *Political Writings*, 187.
32 Lyotard, "The Social Content of the Algerian Struggle," in *Political Writings*, 225.
33 Ibid., 251.
34 Lyotard, *Political Writings*, 208–9.
35 Ibid., 194.
36 Ibid., 250–1.
37 Ibid., 186. ("La bourgeoisie nord-africaine," *SouB* 20, decembre 1956–février 1957).

38 Ibid., 178.
39 Ibid., 210.
40 Ibid., 235.
41 Lyotard, "The Situation in North Africa," in *Political Writings*, 171–8.
42 Lyotard, "Algerian Contradictions Exposed," in *Political Writings*, 211–12.
43 Lyotard, "The Social Content of the Algerian Struggle," in *Political Writings*, 239.
44 Lyotard, "Algerian Contradictions Exposed," in *Political Writings*, 199.
45 Jean-François Lyotard, "La Place de l'aliénation dans le retournement marxiste," *Les temps modernes* 277–8 (août–septembre 1969): 92–160, reprinted in *Dérive à partir de Marx et Freud* (1973). No English translation; for a summary see Matthew McLennan and T. Mars McDougall, "Adrift of Alienation: Mapping Lyotard's Critique of Althusser," *Décalages*, vol. 2, no. 2 (2018). Available online: https://paperity.org/p/156061970/adrift-of-alienation-mapping-lyotards-critique-of-althusser (accessed April 4, 2022).
46 Jean-François Lyotard, *Phenomenology*, tr. Brian Beakley (New York: State University of New York Press, [1954] 1991), 135–6.
47 Lyotard, "Algerian Contradictions Exposed," in *Political Writings*, 204.
48 Lyotard, "The Situation in North Africa," in *Political Writings,* 174.
49 Lyotard, "The Social Content of the Algerian Struggle," in *Political Writings*, 238.
50 Ibid., 245.
51 Lyotard, *Political Writings,* 207–8.
52 Ibid., 175–6.
53 Ibid., 251.
54 Lyotard, *Peregrinations*, 27.
55 In the Lyotard Archives we find the document JFL196 entitled "La raison de l'histoire: l'histoire et les signes" (in pencil on the title page: "Le seuil de l'histoire"), which bears the date "8 July 1966." The text was published in *Digraphe*, in two issues, May and September 1984, publications which are becoming almost impossible to find. In 1987, Lyotard republished the second part of "Le seuil de l'histoire" in a volume of studies offered to Jean-Pierre Vernant (École des Hautes Études en Sciences Sociales).
56 Jean-François Lyotard, "Le seuil de l'histoire (8 juillet 1966)," 15–16, Bibliothèque Jacques Doucet, JFL 196 [see n. 53].
57 Lyotard, "Algeria evacuated," in *Political Writings,* 326.

9

Lyotard and the Inhuman Mode of Production

Bartosz Kuźniarz

With one early exception, Lyotard never includes capitalism in the category of metanarratives.[1] His position on the question of capital—or *Kapital*, as he wrote in his ecstatic readings of Karl Marx in the early 1970s—changes several times. Between 1954 and 1964, as a member of the militant Marxist group Socialisme ou Barbarie, and for the next two years, with the splinter group Pouvoir Ouvrier, Lyotard saw in the working class the "authentic subject of modern human history."[2] After breaking with his former comrades and rejecting the thesis about the revolutionary role of the proletariat, his political radicalism erupted once more during the student protests in 1968. In the early 1970s, capitalism—with its multitude of flows, cathexes, and "pulsations of desire,"[3] foreshadowing Lyotard's paganism, as he named postmodernity after turning from a philosophy of desire to a philosophy of language at the end of the decade—unexpectedly becomes Lyotard's ally as a potentially disruptive force. In *Libidinal Economy* (1974), he writes against the "nostalgic idealization of archaic society"[4] of Jean Baudrillard: "There is as much libidinal intensity in capitalist exchange as in the alleged 'symbolic' exchange."[5]

This is not to say that Lyotard's relationship with the bearded patriarch came to a screeching halt; his ideas in this period are still partially "derived" from Marx, as suggested by the title of the collection of essays published a year earlier, *Dérive à partir de Marx et Freud*.[6] It is, however, a Marx who has undergone a thorough treatment with the Polyjuice Potion that emerges in a hard-to-recognize Little Girl Marx: "the Old Man is also a young woman to us, a strange bisexual assemblage."[7] Capitalism, for all its filth and violence, has its uncanny way of leading us into temptation. Thus, the old prosecutor tries to pass a harsh sentence, but his alter ego, Little Girl, is at the same time "offended by the perversity of the polymorphous body of capital"[8] and fascinated by it. So much so that she doesn't allow the prosecutor to complete the project.

The image of Marx, who, cheeks all flushed, goes through successive economic tables in the library of the British Museum, "finding a hundred thousand good reasons to prolong the study,"[9] who wants to staunchly reject capital while secretly trying to taste another portion of its pornographic intensities, is an image of the position of each and every capitalist subject. However, this is not a situation that critics of capitalism should simply deplore. Libido is a subversive force by definition: "The critique of political economy still unaccomplished, impossible to undertake perhaps, gives way to the affirmation of libidinal economics."[10] Outraged Marx, via fairly orthodox Freud, gives way to ecstatic Nietzsche.

Another important break comes at the turn of the 1980s and 1990s. When the global hegemony of capital becomes more and more evident—communism has just collapsed—Lyotard rejects his previous diagnoses. Libidinal economy was not only theoretically flawed, as he recognized as early as 1977–8.[11] Capitalism, the system, technoscience, or development—concepts Lyotard uses interchangeably from the mid-1980s onward—serve the inhuman, the logic of negentropy, something connected with man solely on the basis of contingent and temporary alliance. There are in fact two kinds of the inhuman: the good and the bad. The first provides the condition of humanization: only making commitments that exceed us transforms a human animal into a human being worthy of the name (in the words of another great French anti-humanist: "'to live' and 'to live for an idea' are one and the same thing"[12]). The second is a synonym of dehumanization. Capitalism serves only the second.

> The inhumanity of the system which is currently being consolidated under the name of development (among others) must not be confused with the infinitely secret one of which the soul is hostage. To believe, as happened to me, that the first can take over from the second, give it expression, is a mistake.[13]

In other words, contrary to what he wrote during the period of the "schizoanalysis" of libidinal economics, Lyotard now rejects the hope that a consolidated world-system of development, which is capitalism, will release the hidden potential of "heterotopic" or "paralogical" differences. Capitalism decodes reality, melts all solid structures into air, strips all earlier forms of their halos, and then recodes them according to the serial principle of performativity, alien to all that is human. What cannot be reterritorialized, coded by efficiency, the system simply omits. Therefore, the proper name of the system turns out to be the One and terror,[14] rather than the Multitude of polymorphic, polytheistic, or paralogical differends. But despite its global hegemony, and the even broader role played by capitalism in the system of solar energetics—which in the late 1980s replace Lyotard's libidinal energetics of two decades earlier—he still denies it the status of the grand narrative.

Perry Anderson, in a scathing criticism of Lyotard's intellectual path, argues that his troubled relation with capitalism faithfully reflects Lyotard's (regrettable) political trajectory. The author of *The Inhuman* started as "an outstandingly lucid commentator"[15] of the war in Algeria, where he worked as a teacher in the early 1950s. As a critic of capitalism, however, he quickly moved from "a revolutionary socialism towards a nihilist hedonism"[16] in order to, subsequently, land in intergalactic space and the world of astrophysics. What accounts for this change? Anderson points to Lyotard's "obsessive" anti-communism. It loomed large already in the milieu of Socialisme ou Barbarie which was premised on an anti-authoritarian Marxism, made manifest in the continual critique of the French Communist Party and its supporters. Later, in the 1970s, when communist parties in many European countries had proved likely candidates to participation in government, Lyotard became so alarmed that he recognized capitalism as the lesser evil when compared to the red monster of communism. After another ten years and the fall of the Soviet Bloc, Anderson continues, "the hegemony of capital became less palatable."¹⁷ Flirting with capitalism was perhaps acceptable when Big Brother was watching, as our advances could be presented as gestures of radicalism. However, with the disappearance of communism as a viable alternative to capitalism, such flattery would decidedly not be appropriate. And since the political path was closed for Lyotard—feasible anti-capitalist politics would spell the need to revive elements of the grand narrative of Marxism—he had no other choice but to transfer his considerations on capitalism to extraterrestrial regions.

Presumably, there are quite superficial, i.e., scholarly and political, reasons why Lyotard did not consider capitalism a metanarrative. I believe, however, that there is more to be gained by taking Lyotard at his word, as it were. He repeatedly gives consistent theoretical reasons why capitalism, despite its global reach and the triumph over ideological rivals, fails to meet the criteria for metanarratives. It is my main topic in this chapter's first section. In the second, I try to synthesize Lyotard's late reflection on capitalism. In the third, reading Lyotard slightly against the grain, I argue that the inhumanity of the capitalist mode of production is not exclusively negative, and that many of the broken threads of his philosophy add up to a surprisingly coherent diagnosis if we grant capitalism the status of a metanarrative. I believe that such rereading sheds light on the peculiar double mood of contemporary reflection on capitalism—stretched out schizophrenically between the visions of the Frankfurt and the Austrian schools—while simultaneously illuminating the tragic dilemma of the current ideal of infinite economic growth.

Why not a grand narrative?

The primary environment of the category of metanarrative in Lyotard is epistemology. Let us recall briefly: "scientific knowledge cannot know ... without resorting to the other, narrative, kind of knowledge, which from its point of view is no knowledge at all."¹⁸ Therefore, people *believe* in the discoveries of science not because the clarity of the scientific evidence convinces them, but because they are supported *a tergo* by the authority of historical narrative. In William Blake's words, "truth can never be told so as to be understood and not be believed."¹⁹ In Lyotard's view, the happy relationship of science and the grand narratives persisted in Europe until the nineteenth century, when the scientific demand for truth was applied to two grand narratives that had legitimized Western knowledge since the Enlightenment: the emancipation narrative, according to which the progress of knowledge would finally free humanity of all injustice, and the speculative narrative, which understood history as the gradual manifestation of rational Spirit within it.

The whole procedure turned out badly. The very thing that science could count on for support in its universalist claims to validity turned out not to meet the criteria of scientific objectivity. The grand narratives began to undergo a process of rapid deconstruction. As if this were not bad enough, by destroying the authority of the grand narratives, science indirectly undermined its own authority, which soon began to suffer even more from the discoveries made by scientists themselves, who began to visit the "catastrophic" realms of theoretical uncertainty. Lyotard claims that the result of all these processes was the disintegration of scientific language into isolated and incompatible sections, a set of "games" or local and ephemeral dialects. And in the wake of its fragmentation—this is the moment when metanarratives leave the field of epistemology—the social bond follows suit. Since no person, religion, ideology, or even modern science is able to tell us how things really are—universal legitimation has become impossible—the social universe turns fluid and begins to bear the hallmarks of transience. For Lyotard, this is obviously good news. The reverse would be to try to artificially fuse the incompatible elements, and thus create terror.

The Postmodern Condition was an incidental book, written on commission for the government of Quebec as a report on knowledge in developed societies. This circumstance weighed heavily on the way Lyotard constructed his argument. In his later texts, collected in *The Postmodern Explained: Correspondence 1982–1985*, Lyotard took up certain threads from *The Postmodern Condition* anew, this time giving them an entirely different shine. Crucially, in these texts metanarratives cease to be merely means of validating scientific knowledge, becoming stories that bear directly on the social imaginary. They are social myths shaping the course of entire cultures.

Accordingly, Lyotard no longer seeks the reasons for the disintegration of grand narratives—whose list at that time included, apart from the paradigmatic Marxism, socialism, enlightenment, capitalism, Christianity,[20] and was soon expanded to include imperialism, fascism, nazism, and communism[21]—in the internal dynamic of science. It is rather to be found in the influence of historical events: "'Auschwitz' can be taken as a paradigmatic name for the tragic 'incompletion' of modernity."[22] The horror of the Shoah cannot be presented as simply yet another stage on the way to universal emancipation. Lyotard asks rhetorically: "What kind of thought is capable of 'relieving' Auschwitz—relieving [*relever*] in the sense of *aufheben*—capable of situating it in a general, empirical, or even speculative process directed towards universal emancipation?"[23] Thus, it is Auschwitz, Gulag, and Laogai rather than Gödel's theorem or the uncertainty principle that constitute the peculiarity from which the contours of the postmodern world have emerged.

Despite certain similarities, metanarratives should not be identified with myths. It is true that they both share the function of "legitimating social and political institutions and practices." There are, however, two key differences. First, grand narratives, unlike myths, "look for legitimacy, not in an original founding act, but in a future to be accomplished, that is, in an Idea to be realized." Second, the Idea "(of freedom, 'enlightenment', socialism etc.) has legitimating value because it is universal."[24] Grand narratives, in other words, are projects, they are forward-oriented. Instead of looking for support for their postulates *in illo tempore*, in the founding gestures and deeds of legendary ancestors, they refer to the "to-come" (*l'à-venir*). Moreover, the idea constituting the telos of the grand narrative has a universal dimension and must be addressed to everyone. Myths can be rooted in local tribes or nature. Therefore, in more traditional parlance, the grand narrative is the promise of apocatastasis, or universal salvation. This, in turn, rules out capitalism.

Lyotard writes that the capitalist story of emancipation from poverty through technological and industrial progress was weakened by the crises of 1911 and 1929, but the final *coup de grâce* to the idea that the free play of supply and demand promotes the general enrichment of humanity came with the crises of 1974 to 1979. There are to be sure people who still get rich thanks to capitalism, but the belief that the economic path will eventually help us reach heaven on earth is now seen as a kind of ideological malaise.[25] Of course, Lyotard does not question the undeniable "victory of capitalist technoscience over the other candidates for the universal finality of human history."[26] He claims, however, that capitalism wins, as it were, unwittingly, without real legitimation. It is the universal purpose of our lives solely as a fact, but not as a value. Capitalism takes its toll on everything, yet its impetus comes not from an idea, but from striving for efficiency.[27] Projects have now been replaced by programs,[28] "-isms" have given way to "-ings" (mentoring, gaming, investing). While myth pointed to the past, and grand narrative to the future, the basic gesture of capitalism is to encourage contemplation of its present power.

The problem is that it is not clear who could take on this task. From around the mid-1980s, Lyotard returns to this thought repeatedly: the flipside of the lack of metanarratives is "the loss of the subject to whom this goal was promised."[29] Capitalism triumphs, but no one is happy about it. This in turn explains the melancholy mood of contemporary thought. By keeping capitalism within the *horizon* of the concept of metanarrative, while at the same time denying it a place among the most important modern projects, Lyotard draws attention to this particular feature of the postmodern condition. Whoever wants to keep the traditional subject of Western culture's emancipatory stories (humanity inhabiting the Earth) is doomed to tell children's fairy tales in a nostalgic retro style. Given such boundary conditions, we will always create something along the lines of a feast in the Shire or Bruegel's peasant wedding. Retrotopias. On the other hand, when we try to take into account what is intellectually stimulating and new around us, we quickly stop talking about the Earth and the psychophysical man (streaming platforms should urgently expand their offer by adding the category of "catastrophic family movies in post-apocalyptic scenery of the outer worlds," because their repertoire has been drifting in this direction for some time now).

It is no coincidence that the only contemporary scientific concept that resembles grand narratives, i.e., the geohumanist story of the Anthropocene, is in its ethical dimension a critical dystopia.[30] In other words, a lasting alliance of the technical power that legitimizes capitalism with the Earth-inhabiting, psychophysical human being is impossible. Either–or. For this reason, a wonderful fairy tale about capitalism, which—still in its early version—Lyotard tells for the first time in a text "working through" the destruction of the Berlin Wall, "represents the grand narrative that this world stubbornly tries to tell about itself"—"if it weren't for the fact that the hero is no longer Man."[31] Capitalism works like a grand narrative and has all the features of a grand narrative. However, it cannot be included in this category, because it is impossible to indicate the subject which the grand story of capital ultimately serves.

The tale of capital

The beginning of the fable of capital is not accidental. "The Sun is going to explode. The entire solar system, including the little planet Earth, will be transformed into a giant nova."³² Since the end of the 1980s, this theme has been a constant element of Lyotard's philosophy. The death of the sun is the place from which we ought to start thinking. "While we talk, the sun is getting older. It will explode in 4.5 billion years ... It's like a man in his early forties with a life expectancy of eighty."³³ Moreover, the explosion of the sun "is the sole serious question to face humanity today ... Wars, conflicts, political tension, shifts in philosophical debates, even passions—everything's dead already if this infinite reserve from which you now draw energy to defer answers ... dies out with the sun."³⁴

Establishing this vantage point for philosophy, Lyotard is overly optimistic. The deadline is much nearer. In about a billion years, the increased solar radiation will lead to evaporation of the oceans, which means that the Earth as a planet is in its sixty-first year of its eighty-year life. It is true, however, that faced with the necessity to leave the solar system, or at least our planet, we have two possibilities as thinking beings. On one hand, there is the complacent strategy of *après moi, le déluge*.³⁵ Let's dance and compose poems. What do I care about the sun's blast when liberal-democratic politics are colonized by populists who undermine the tripartite division of power? Let us organize our micro-matters first, take care of the here and now: health, love, friendship, and well-being. How much can we know about the future anyway? The second strategy takes the prospect of the end seriously. Challenge accepted. This is the tacit goal of economic growth and capitalism. Lyotard is very clear on this point: regardless of the current and not particularly sublime motivation of increasing surplus value,³⁶ the central project of capital is the attempt to provide "this software [our thought] with a hardware [material medium] that is independent of the conditions of life on earth." "Whatever the immediate stakes might appear to be: health, war, production, communication,"³⁷ the true point is (Lyotard tacitly assumes that human physical structure will never be able to hold outside the solar system) to "make thought without a body possible."³⁸ "Not without hardware, obviously."³⁹ Thought will need some kind of material medium.

From a broader perspective, therefore, the history of capital has little in common with man. It is an episode in a metaphysical war between the forces of chaos and the forces of information or negentropy. Does this mean that as humans we should support capitalist technoscience in its effort to detach thought from the body, because this is our best chance to save the *agalma* of human thought after a solar explosion? Lyotard is skeptical. The problem is that the thought, or the good inhuman, which is a guarantee of genuine complexity and the survival of negentropy after the death of the sun, is "inseparable from the phenomenological body."⁴⁰ Even if it was possible to program a silicon wafer so that it could perfectly simulate our mental operations (in practice, it is a well-known problem of a "comprehension of ordinary language by your machines"⁴¹), what will leave Earth "at the helm of spaceship Exodus will still be entropy."⁴² By programming the future, we will deprive ourselves of the possibility of creating authentically new things, and thus we will not save the most valuable element preserved by humanity. The cosmic war against entropy will have been lost. Lyotard argues that only embodiment—the fact of birth and childhood,⁴³ as well as the sex difference associated with it—is capable of inducing the desire necessary for the good inhuman, or negentropic thought, to emerge. Human desire—and the related anxiety or suffering[44]—is the only locus where resistance to the entropy process of the universe can effectively transpire.

Lyotard's reflection on capitalism may be summarized in six points.

First, capitalism or technological and scientific development is "the present-day form of a process of negentropy or complexification that has been underway since the earth began its existence."[45] Or quite simply: "Capital must be seen ... as the effect, observable on the earth, of a cosmic process of complexification."[46]

Second, the same, on a slightly lower level, applies to the people themselves: "human beings aren't and never have been the motor of this complexification, but an effect and carrier of this negentropy."[47] It means contingency and temporariness of the human form. "The formation called Human or Brain will have been nothing more than an episode in the conflict between differentiation and entropy. The pursuit of greater complexity asks not for the perfecting of the Human, but its mutation or its defeat for the benefit of a better performing system."[48] Thus, the spirit of complexity strides through history, and we are its temporary and replaceable workers. We cannot in any way affect the cunning process of information growth flowing through our existence: "The human race is, so to speak, 'pulled forward' by this process without possessing the slightest capacity for mastering it."[49]

Third—a repetition of the first and second points from the micro-perspective of human psychology—"it isn't any human desire to know or transform reality that propels this techno-science, but a cosmic circumstance."[50] Thus, even if we sense the living presence of desire in modern economics and in ourselves, it is still only a local, psychological manifestation of the process of negentropy. "One could go so far as to say that the desire for profit and wealth is no doubt no other than this process itself, working upon the nervous centers of the human brain and experienced directly by the human body."[51] There is nothing human about capitalism.

Fourth, the inhumanity of capitalism manifests itself not only in the uncontrolled development of technoscience, but also in exploitation and brutal political violence. Robots and toxic African landfills are two sides of the same coin. "When the point is to extend the capacities of the monad [the great monad is another of Lyotard's synonyms for capitalism] it seems reasonable to abandon, or even actively to destroy, those parts of the human race which appear superfluous, useless for that goal. For example, the populations of the Third World."[52]

Fifth, the artificial intelligence developed by contemporary capitalism or, in Lyotard's parlance, disembodied intelligence, "will make it possible to meet the challenge ... posed by ... the solar explosion to come,"[53] which also means that when leaving Earth, this intelligence will escape the doom that awaits any closed system in accordance with the second law of thermodynamics.

The problem, however, is—sixth—that, according to Lyotard, this intelligence will leave the Earth in a defective form: "the human body hinders the separability of this intelligence, hinders its exile and therefore survival."[54] Thus, the logic of capitalism will ultimately turn against itself.

Capitalism is the mechanism that will, at best, preserve thought in its present form. In the long run, this preservation of the present amounts to a triumph of entropy. Without the body, we will carry out of the solar system thought devoid of *élan vital*, internal causality, which is at best repetition. Could it be worse? For Lyotard, capitalism is something that we implement through our own actions and over which we have no influence. It's something we experience as our own desires, but which is completely alien to us. Moreover (a clear contradiction, or at least inconsistency in his narrative), if capitalism, or the earthly manifestation of the cosmic logic of the growth of information—which at the present stage translates into the development of artificial intelligence—will lead its project to the end, it will annihilate it. This is a Lyotardian or posthuman version of the fatal contradiction (Marx) or strategy (Baudrillard) inherent in capitalism. Detaching thought from the body will deprive it of its creative potential and therefore stop the process of negentropy.

Capitalism will sell itself the technology with which it will hang itself.

We are the curse

But capital is not a logic that is suicidal or as alien to human invention as Lyotard would have us believe. The fable in which "the Human and his/her Brain, or the Brain and its Human"[55] leave the solar system before the explosion of the sun is one step away from being a great and edifying story, as it tells about a process with a happy ending and involving everyone. The rub is that it lacks eschatology. What leaves Earth before the end is not the subject telling the fable, but an undefined energy formation—the Brain and its Human or something else—that will replace it. "The hero of the fable is not the human species, but energy."[56] We have already said that it is this lack of a happy ending, at least from a human perspective, that, according to Lyotard, is responsible for "the postmodern state of thought ... its crisis, its malaise, or its melancholia."[57] Postmodernity means despair resulting from the impossibility of writing an ending, which, on one hand, would be a logical consequence of the processes we are part of, and on the other, could be defended from the perspective of the needs and goals of the subject that we are.

Lyotard makes it clear: whether dehumanization results from the disembodiment of thought or the inclusion of individuals in some universal technological network, pulsating in accordance with the algorithm programed by machine intelligence ("new update is available," "you have 24 notifications"), it is impossible to continue from this place the story of human freedom as if nothing happened. The emancipation narrative halts at this point—as in the case of another "pure event" that is Auschwitz. Artificial intelligence will not bring freedom.

One can, however, add a logical ending to this story. Lyotard's postmodern fable can be turned into a full-fledged eschatological metanarrative in one step. We "just" have to allow for the possibility that the actual goal and beneficiary of our daily economic activity is an entity other than a human being. Capitalism is the grand narrative of a biotechnological or bioinformational superbeing, a posthuman form of existence that is created as the result of coupling of the world into a global information and economic network: "what appears to humanity as the history of capitalism is an invasion from the future by an artificial intelligent space that must assemble itself entirely from its enemy's resources."[58]

But does "posthuman" necessarily mean "antihuman" or "inhuman" in the first, negative, dehumanizing sense? If man and capital were *exclusively* enemies and we were playing a hilariously unconscious role in another subject's scenario, we would be in a comic realm. Our situation, however, is tragic. For, as Lyotard teaches, tragedy appears only when, following the example of Oedipus, we become aware that the most important problem is not external: "Oedipus resists his truth, until he also becomes aware that he is the virus."[59] Thus, in our case, we are the curse. Insofar as we are—and we are—desiring beings, we cannot but want capitalism. It is precisely for this reason that modernity is characterized by (Lauren Berlant's term) "cruel optimism"[60]. We desire what hurts our flourishing. The message of *Libidinal Economy* was similar. In the fragment that aroused the greatest (as predicted by Lyotard) disgust in many readers, including Anderson, the inhuman of capitalism takes on a double, simultaneously cruel and optimistic, character. Therefore, the English proletariat has become "the slave of the machine, the machine of the machine, fucker fucked by it, eight hours, twelve hours, a day, year after year." But contrary to appearances, it was not just necessity that forced it to do so:

> the English unemployed did not become workers to survive, they—hang on tight and spit on me—... enjoyed it, enjoyed the mad destruction of their organic body which was indeed imposed upon them, they enjoyed the decomposition of their personal identity, the identity that the peasant tradition had constructed for them, enjoyed the dissolution of their families and villages, and enjoyed the new monstrous anonymity of the suburbs and the pubs in the morning and evening.[61]

Thus, in the logic of capitalism—in its violent and dirty nature—lies an extraordinary power of attraction, which we often experience in the form of unwilling desire and enjoyment. And it is precisely in this way that the cunning process of negentropy steers our individual lives in the direction of some general, overarching destiny or, if you will, cruel capitalist enjoyment is the place where the true subject of human history transpassively enjoys itself.

Of course, the thirst for capital does not have to take on that morbid and ecstatic form described by Lyotard. Equally often, it is accompanied by a completely sober and straightforward enthusiasm—for example, when we are happy to hear that our children got a job in a genetics laboratory or are participating in some advanced IT project by Cambridge Analytica or Google. These are not simply David Graeber's bullshit jobs![62] Or let's take a scenario in which an outstandingly gifted student constructs a machine that answers the exam questions in philosophy in a fully human manner. The machine easily passes subsequent Turing tests, interacting with humans without raising suspicion about the artificial nature of its intelligence. Who of the radical contemporary critics of technoscience will prove luddite enough to delete from the student's account all files containing the technical diagrams of the device, instead of enthusiastically praising their ingenuity and inventive spirit? The late Lyotard also flirts with a similar idea, pointing to the kinship between the activities of capitalist scientists and the artistic avant-gardes he cherishes. It doesn't simply boil down to a paralogical, disruptive innovation. According to Lyotard, there is also a clearly perceptible sublime—or perfection[63]—of capitalist technoscience: "It is, in a sense, an economy regulated by an Idea—infinite wealth or power. It does not manage to present any example from reality to verify this Idea."[64]

This last point is crucial to my rereading of Lyotard's capitalism: the Idea that haunts and arouses a feeling of sublime among the participants and observers of the market game is the economy itself or, in other words, the "great monad"[65] of the inhuman subject that is the current stage of the metaphysical process of growth and thus the ultimate meaning of the mode of production we know as capitalism. Like many algorithms that are a product of machine learning, the Idea is unpresentable in the form of an object tangible to the human mind. That is why it can give us pleasure only by causing us pain.[66] The grand narrative of capitalism is the inner truth of our actions and the source of the accompanying enjoyment and enthusiasm, but the problem is that it is sublime: it can only be told in a language incomprehensible to us (likewise, oaks and polecat–ferret hybrids are not particularly known to rave about *On the Origin of Species*). Hence the dual nature of the descriptions of capitalist modernity. Cruel optimism. The Frankfurt School and the Austrian School. Utopophobia (we cannot imagine the future) and mass-produced apocalypse (yes, we can, but without corporeal humans as the crown of creation). A civilization of death and unprecedented subjective well-being. A euphoria of reality and a melancholy of thought. The modern deed and the postmodern hangover. Two kinds of the inhuman. The principle of performativity and Little Girl Marx. Late and early Lyotard.

To sum up, Lyotard changes his mind about capitalism at the end of the 1980s because he comes to the conclusion that there is no emancipatory element in it. But he withdraws too quickly. The inhuman at work in the structures of contemporary capital is not altogether alien—alas!—to that "transcendence in immanence … present deep inside, in the body, in the mind",[67] which "is the source of every invention, creation, and writing"[68] as well as the negentropy's best bet after the death of the sun. Little Girl Marx got it right. Capitalism implements one of the variants of what Lyotard termed the good inhuman. Therefore, when we prop up capitalism, we do not stand against man altogether. On the contrary, capitalism is the expansion of one of the possibilities inherent in our existence: the one that guarantees the survival, and perhaps also further growth of the physical order, of which we are a manifestation and a temporary historical carrier. The problem is that the inhuman of capital, though it may enable information to survive outside the solar system, at the same time will deprive people of biological bodies.

There are other Ideas and scenarios, however. One of them proclaims the truth of the Incarnation: the psychophysical human form as a place of revelation of the impassable horizon of all life and growth. Why should we not consider the corporeal man as a metaphysical and therefore *irreducible* whole? Lyotard, while defending the body, subordinates it to the imperative of preserving the creative potential of thought. Yet the psychophysical man, as we may argue, is the ultimate and indivisible synthesis of order and death, infinity and matter, growth and entropy. It is possible that by sticking to such outmoded notions we are condemning ourselves to thermonuclear apocalypse in a few billion years. The body will never leave the solar system, and the last sight to be seen by the last man will be a blinding wave of radioactive light. But is this an obvious reason—and here comes the tragic part, or perhaps just a ritual, belated, and powerless gesture of dissent—to reject this scenario? Lyotard put it succinctly: mere survival "is not very interesting." In fact, it is not interesting at all.[69]

Notes

1. See Jean-François Lyotard, "Lessons in Paganism" [1977], tr. David Macey, in Andrew Benjamin (ed.), *The Lyotard Reader* (Oxford, UK and Cambridge MA: Blackwell, 1989), 153.
2. Jean-François Lyotard, "The Wall, the Gulf, and the Sun" [1990], in Jean-François Lyotard, *Political Writings*, tr. Bill Readings with Kevin Paul Geiman (Minneapolis MN: University of Minnesota Press, 1993), 115.
3. Jean-François Lyotard, *Libidinal Economy*, tr. Iain Hamilton Grant (Bloomington and Indianapolis IN: Indiana University Press, [1974] 1993), 82.
4. Steven Best and Douglas Kellner, *Postmodern Theory: Critical Interrogations* (New York: The Guilford Press, 1991), 156.
5. Lyotard, *Libidinal Economy*, 109.
6. Jean-François Lyotard, *Dérive à partir de Marx et Freud* (UGE: Paris, 1973). *Dérive* is most usually translated as "drift" but with the sense of a connection maintained, as in "drifting from" or "drifting with." See Lyotard *Driftworks*, ed. Roger McKeon (Semiotext(e): New York, 1984).
7. Lyotard, *Libidinal Economy*, 96.
8. Ibid., 97.
9. Ibid., 97.
10. Jean-François Lyotard, "Notes on the Return and Kapital," tr. Roger McKeon, *Semiotexte(e)*, vol. 3, no. 1 (1978), 53.
11. See Best and Kellner, *Postmodern Theory*, 158.
12. Alain Badiou, *Logics of Worlds. Being and Event, 2*, tr. Alberto Toscano (London and New York: Continuum, [2006] 2009), 510.
13. Jean-François Lyotard, *The Inhuman: Reflections on Time*, tr. Geoffrey Bennington and Rachel Bowlby (Cambridge UK: Polity, 1991), 2.
14. See Jean-François Lyotard, *The Postmodern Condition: A Report on Knowledge*, tr. Geoff Bennington and Brian Massumi (Minneapolis MN: University of Minnesota Press, [1979] 1984), 63.
15. Perry Anderson, *The Origins of Postmodernity* (London and New York: Verso, 1998), 27.
16. Ibid., 28.
17. Ibid., 35.
18. Jean-François Lyotard, *The Postmodern Condition*, 29.
19. William Blake, "The Marriage of Heaven and Hell," in *Collected Poems* (London and New York: Routledge, 2002), 168.
20. See Jean-François Lyotard, *The Postmodern Explained: Correspondence 1982–1985*, tr. Julian Pefanis, Morgan Thomas et al. (London: Turnaround, 1992), 29–30.
21. See Jean-François Lyotard, "Oikos" [1988], in Lyotard, *Political Writings*, 114.
22. Lyotard, *The Postmodern Explained*, 30.
23. Ibid., 91.
24. Ibid., 29–30.

25 See Robert H. Nelson, *Reaching for Heaven on Earth: The Theological Meaning of Economics* (Savage, MD: Rowman & Littlefield, 1991).
26 Lyotard, *The Postmodern Explained*, 30.
27 See Lyotard, *The Inhuman*, 7.
28 Ibid., 68–9.
29 Lyotard, *The Postmodern Explained*, 39.
30 See Fredric Jameson, *Archaeologies of the Future: The Desire Called Utopia and Other Science Fictions* (London and New York: Verso, 2007), 198.
31 Lyotard, "The Wall, the Gulf, and the Sun," in *Political Writings*, 120.
32 Jean-François Lyotard, *Postmodern Fables*, tr. Georges Van Den Abbeele (Minneapolis MN and London: University of Minnesota Press, [1993] 1997), 83.
33 Lyotard, *The Inhuman*, 8.
34 Ibid., 9.
35 Ibid., 11.
36 Ibid., 71.
37 Ibid., 12.
38 Ibid., 13.
39 Ibid., 14.
40 Ibid., 23.
41 Ibid., 18.
42 Ibid., 23.
43 See Lyotard, "Oikos," in *Political Writings*, 103–7.
44 See Lyotard, *The Inhuman*, 19.
45 Ibid., 22.
46 Ibid., 67.
47 Ibid., 22.
48 Ibid., 99.
49 Ibid., 64.
50 Ibid., 22.
51 Ibid., 71.
52 See Ibid., 76–7. Internal comment is mine.
53 Ibid., 22.
54 Ibid., 22.
55 Lyotard, *Postmodern Fables*, 84.
56 Ibid., 92.
57 Ibid., 100.
58 Nick Land, "Machinic desire," *Textual Practice*, vol. 7, no. 3 (1993), 479.
59 Jean-François Lyotard and Sergio Benvenuto, "Resistances. A Conversation," tr. Gianmaria Senia, *European Journal of Psychoanalysis*, no. 2 (Fall 1995–Winter 1996). Available online: https://www.journal-psychoanalysis.eu/resistances-a-conversation/ (accessed January 31, 2021).
60 Lauren Berlant, *Cruel Optimism* (Durham NC: Duke University Press, 2011), 1.
61 Lyotard, *Libidinal Economy*, 111.
62 See David Graeber, *Bullshit Jobs: A Theory* (New York and London: Simon & Schuster, 2018).
63 *Die Perfektion der Technik* is the German title of an essay written by Friedrich Georg Jünger, published in English as *The Failure of Technology: Perfection Without Purpose*, tr. Fred D. Wieck (Hinsdale IL: Henry Regnery, 1949).
64 Lyotard, *The Inhuman*, 105.

65 Ibid., 69.
66 See Lyotard, *The Postmodern Explained*, 19.
67 Lyotard, *The Inhuman*, 21–2.
68 Lyotard, "Oikos," in *Political Writings*, 107.
69 Ibid.

10

Lyotard, After Us[1]

Yuk Hui

In November 2019, I organized a symposium titled "40 Years after *The Postmodern Condition*" at the China Academy of Art in Hangzhou, and earlier I also initiated and organized another symposium related to Jean-François Lyotard's exhibition "30 Years after *Les Immatériaux*" in 2015 at the Leuphana University in Lüneburg.[2] It is not simply because I want to take these anniversary opportunities for academic activities, rather I believe deeply that the work of Lyotard has to be reread beyond all the misunderstanding around the concept of the postmodern and in light of the technological condition that we are in today. Lyotard is not an unfamiliar figure to many audiences, since his name is closely related to the buzzword "postmodern"—a term that has rather different provenances and meanings in Europe, the United States, China, and perhaps Japan. This symposium dedicated to his inaugural *The Postmodern Condition* aimed to present a Lyotard who is not only pertinent to us, but also crucial and critical to the understanding of our contemporary situation.

Without providing too much of Lyotard's biography, which readers are presumed to know already, I want to focus firstly on the concept of the postmodern and take it in rather unconventional directions. There are certain confusions and misunderstandings of Lyotard's concept of postmodern in different cultural contexts, because the postmodern is relative to the modern. Firstly, to take China as an example, in the past decades the question of modernity in China has never been a problem, but rather a desirable objective, while the postmodern is antagonistic to the modern in the discourse of Lyotard. Secondly, Chinese readers were more influenced by the reading of Lyotard in the United States, for example texts by Fredric Jameson, Susan Sontag, etc. This obscures some of Lyotard's own ideas and his genius view on the epistemic transition from the modern to the postmodern. This symposium on the occasion of the fortieth anniversary of Lyotard's book was a weak attempt to bring back Lyotard's concept of the postmodern and explore some important subjects that were previously ignored. Today, it is widely known that the postmodern is associated with the rejection of grand narratives such as Marxism, but why? Maybe we can start from here to unfold our inquiry into the postmodern.

Myths concerning grand narratives

Is it because the postmodern is an indication of the collapse of all ideals and theories? Or is it because the postmodern is a description of such a condition in which every theoretical attempt and every resistance could be subversively turned into its object of criticism, e.g., commodities, which the American theorist Fredric Jameson described as the logic of "late capitalism"? If we understand Lyotard in this way, we never arrive at understanding the significance of what he calls postmodern. Even though in the first page of *The Postmodern Condition*, Lyotard referred this term postmodern to its use in North American sociology, where it is used to describe developed industrial cities in North America, Lyotard's take is not only sociological; he also constructs a genealogy of the concept of the modern which is fundamental to his philosophical inquiries.

The postmodern describes a condition which we call here *episteme* (though Lyotard never used this word[3]), and under this condition, the form of knowledge production has greatly changed; these changes are directly reflected in knowledge itself, because knowledge is not separable from its forms and means of production. The concept of the postmodern is based on an observation and interpretation of the epistemological rupture taking place in science and technology, which consequently constitutes a new episteme. This new episteme in turn conditions the discursive nature of knowledge and knowledge itself.

The understanding of the world and its history is always conditioned—which also means limited—by an episteme, or a paradigm, as it is termed in the social sciences. In *The Order of Things*, Michel Foucault has shown that since the sixteenth century one could generalize three epistemes in the West: namely, renaissance, classical, and modern. These epistemes are themselves conditions—in the sense of Immanuel Kant—of knowledge. This is also the reason why I reinterpret episteme as *the sensible condition under which knowledge is produced*. I emphasize the question of sensibility because it is also that which makes the coexistence of different epistemes possible.[4] Philosophy is no exception to being conditioned by such epistemes. Therefore, in early modern times we see that mechanism is the theoretical ground of understanding existence, including plants, animals, humans, and God. The rejection of mechanism, especially by Kant, and later the Jena Romantics and the post-Kantians produced a new paradigm, which we can call organicism. The organic was the lens through which the universe, world politics, world history were reconstructed. Georg W. F. Hegel is probably the most rigorous thinker of his time who has systematically formulated a dialectical method that at the same time assimilates the dynamic of organism, which he calls logic, and a concept of progress not being measured by speed or volume but rather by the march towards the Absolute—the most concrete form of the self-knowing of the spirit. There is so much to be said about Hegel and his continuation in Marx, who has analyzed capitalism according to the Hegelian method, as well as projecting the dialectical method to the idea of revolution—namely by opposing the bourgeois society to the proletariat, and sublating this antagonism with a third, the Communist Party. These are grand narratives, or historicism, made possible by a certain episteme, and assured by the latter to be practically possible.

Lyotard was very attached to the resistance and revolution movement in the 1950s, when he was a teacher of philosophy in a lycée in eastern Algeria, and as a member of the editorial committee of the journal *Socialisme ou Barbarie*. Later Lyotard broke with the group Socialisme ou Barbarie, and abandoned the metanarratives of Marxism. Lyotard's break from Marxism is not a matter of belief, but rather he sees the limit of the Marxist metanarrative: as a product of the Enlightenment and German idealism, it repeats the Hegelian logic in a new guise. What makes the metanarratives ineffective? For sure it comes partially from the resistance against totalitarianism and the tendency intrinsic to metanarratives which necessarily exclude other narratives; however, what is more significant is Lyotard's formulation of the concept of system, which maintains an intimacy with Hegelian philosophy but at the same time constantly attacks it. This could be seen as one form of paralogy, which we will explain later.

System as episteme

What makes the metanarratives possible is the concept of the system, but it is also that which makes it impossible. Lyotard never expressed it so explicitly, but we can attempt to explain why it is so. The concept of system is first of all the *credo* of eighteenth- and nineteenth-century philosophy, be it Romantics, Kantians, or Post-Kantian idealists. It is beyond our capacity here to reintroduce this history,[5] but we can briefly recapture the importance of this theme. If since the seventeenth century mechanism has become the dominant episteme, which produces Descartes's concept of the human, encyclopedist concept of progress and the Hobbesian concept of the mechanical state, then towards the end of the eighteenth century this mechanical view was largely challenged by the research in natural sciences, especially biology, which was only formally recognized as a scientific discipline in the early nineteenth century. The concept of organism immediately challenges the mechanical explanation, for the question "how is an animal body possible?" cannot be fully explained by mechanical causes. The later thinking of Kant, especially the *Critique of Judgement*, was born out of this context, which directly influenced Johann Gottlieb Fichte, Friedrich Schelling, Hegel, and the Romantics. A philosophical system is no longer one that is mechanical, but rather for it to be, it has to be organic, in which reason is endowed with autonomy. The autonomy of reason is regulative, namely that it has to be regulated by a heuristic, which is not mechanical in nature. If we look at Kant's exposition of the limit of human cognitive power in the *Critique of Pure Reason*, it was still largely mechanistic; it was not until *Critique of Judgement* that an organismic operation was introduced to expose the complexity of both aesthetic judgment and teleological judgment. What is central to the aforementioned judgments is reflective judgment, which has to be distinguished from determinative judgment. The rules of reflective judgment are not given universally *a priori*, as in the case of determinative judgment; instead of applying the universal to the particular, it starts from the particular and recursively arrives at the universal. We may be able to distinguish two images of thinking in Kant's philosophy across theoretical, practical philosophy and aesthetics: in one group we have constitutive principle, hypothetical imperative, and determinate judgment; in the other we have regulative principle, categorical imperative, and reflective judgment. In *Recursivity and Contingency*, I have tried to reconstruct this history from Kant, via Schelling and Hegel, to cybernetics, and how such organismic thinking took its concrete form in the conceptualization of nature and technology. This logic of auto-legitimation for Lyotard is paralogy, a term which has multiple meanings for him.

Firstly, in philosophical language, paralogy means fallacious inference or fallacy and error in reasoning[6]—for example, Kant's well-known paralogisms of pure reason. It would be a paralogy to say that fallacy is the logic of auto-legitimation. Paralogy here means differences or, more precisely, contradictions, so it demands a reflection as an attempt of self-correction, a coming back to itself, to resolve the seeming contradiction. And if paralogy is capable of auto-legitimation, it is because it is analogous to a reflective judgment instead of a determinative judgment.

Secondly, in biological terms, paralogy, or paralog, means a relationship of two characters arising from a duplication of the gene for that character.[7] When Lyotard refers to the terms paralogy and homology in *The Postmodern Condition*, it is not clear how much he takes from the sense of these terms in biology. He opposes homology and paralogy (and if he took biology seriously, he would recognize that a paralog is also homologous, i.e., coming from the same ancestor), and derivatively, the expert's homology and the inventor's paralogy, or *consensus* and *dissensus*.

We can generalize here the meaning of the term "paralogy" in terms of paradox and dissensus. As paradox, it serves as the driving force of the auto-legitimation of the system, since it implies a non-linear or reflective or recursive form of operation; as dissensus, it produces differences and therefore it also resists the totalizing tendency of the system.

> The problem is therefore to determine whether it is possible to have a form of legitimation based solely on paralogy. Paralogy must be distinguished from innovation: the latter is under the command of the system, or at least used by it to improve its efficiency; the former is a move (the importance of which is often not recognized until later) played in the pragmatics of knowledge.[8]

Therefore we must recognize that the collapse of grand narratives is the refusal of a specific kind of narratives which are homological, for example based on consensus. This rejection is not a mere opposition between determinative judgment and reflective judgment, mechanism and organism, evil and good.

Lyotard was finely examining the historical, social, political, and aesthetic transformation of the new situation brought about by industrialized society; to what extent might certain discourses not be legitimated and to what extent must a new philosophical framework be set up for cultural and political analysis. Let's reiterate the points that we have attempted to make. Firstly, the rejection of metanarratives is not the rejection of the systemic dynamic within the metanarratives of Hegel and Marx, but rather the systemic nature of these metanarratives has simply been falsely taken in mechanistic ways, namely dogmas. The evolution of a system is subject to contingency, and that which one calls "progress" is governed by necessity, while such necessity cannot be fully captured by a single logic, namely the grand narrative. Secondly, the later development of the concept of system seems to be rendered by such necessity which is contingent on governing progress; in other words, the necessity of the logic that drives the evolution of the system is only a special or particular case among many others. Thirdly, the system ceases to be a mere philosophical question, rather, through modern science and technology, it has pervaded every aspect of urban lives. As a result we moved from a conceptual system to what Jacques Ellul calls the technical system (or literally technician system, *système technicien*), and to what is widely discussed as digital earth and artificial earth. This process has also radically influenced our understanding of the world and its evolution. Maybe we can draw from it the following conclusion: the opposition between communism and capitalism maintained by a grand narrative, as was the case between the bourgeoisie and the proletariat, no longer confers the legitimacy that they used to enjoy as the truth of human history; the system is in favor of an auto-legitimation not according to authority but performativity.

The notion of performativity has replaced the previous criterion for truth; it is because performativity presents itself to be a more flexible criterion endowed with a temporal dimension. It rejects the mechanical mode of proof according to pre-established standards, or the universal *a priori*. The early moderns desire order and regularity, which perfectly coincide with mechanical presentations. For example, Descartes during his sojourn in Amsterdam was impressed by the regularity of the grids divided by the canals; later, he commented on the urban design of Paris and mocked it as something coming out of a child's hands.[9] The postmodern, on the contrary, originates from a different episteme, which no longer sees certainty and security as the necessary ground of knowledge, but rather recognizes the instability and insecurity of knowledge. Therefore, performativity, which is sometimes called reflexivity or resilience, can better capture the formation of knowledge in the scientific discipline, in both research and education.

The system itself, being capable of auto-legitimation and auto-organization, is the paradigm of the postmodern. This is also the reason why the metanarrative, conceived as a guidance of historical progress, is rendered inefficient. Of course, if we go back to the root, we can also say that the Hegelian system is based on reason's capacity of auto-legitimation, a notion shared by the other post-Kantians, and which Lyotard knows very well: "Hegel's *Encyclopedia* (1817–27) attempts to realize this project of totalization, which was already present in Fichte and Schelling in the form of the idea of the System."[10]

Lyotard didn't go further to explicitly establish the relation between the Hegelian system and the cybernetic system, or the systems theory of Niklas Luhmann. In *The Postmodern Condition* and elsewhere, he reproached Luhmann, and criticized the latter's systems theory as being cynical. However, we have reason to believe that Lyotard was aware of this intimate relation between the idealists' idea of the system and Luhmann's system, which best characterizes the postmodern condition. The totalizing capacity of the Hegelian system and the totalizing tendency of cybernetics—especially systems theory—are close to each other, and it is also because of the danger of totalization that Lyotard gives his preference to Kant's sublime rather than to Hegel's absolute. This passage from Hegel to Luhmann via Gotthard Günther[11] was elaborated in *Recursivity and Contingency*, which I don't want to repeat here. We simply want to add that this passage from Hegel to Luhmann in a way confirms what Martin Heidegger says—that metaphysics ended in Hegel—and that cybernetics is the realization of such an end (end in the sense of completion and accomplishment). It was through Luhmann's systems theory that Lyotard confirms the central role of performativity:

> The performativity criterion has its "advantages." It excludes in principle adherence to a metaphysical discourse; it requires the renunciation of fables; it demands clear minds and cold wills; it replaces the definition of essences with the calculation of interactions; it makes the "players" assume responsibility not only for the statements they propose, but also for the rules to which they submit those statements in order to render them acceptable.[12]

There are for sure conceptual differences between Hegel and Luhmann's concepts of system, but what is more significant is that in Luhmann's time, the system doesn't only exist as a method or a logic, but rather it exists in full material terms. This could be read as the externalization as well as alienation [*Entäusserung*][13] of the Hegelian Idea, as Günther claims. That is to say, the systemic thinking since Leibniz, passing by idealism, is realized in a "general physics," a term that Lyotard used to describe Luhmann's systems theory:

> This monadology was still a philosophical system that presupposed a finality, particularly that of a benevolent God ensuring the harmony of the whole. However, systems theory is not a philosophical system but a description of reality, "a so-called reality" ["*die sogenannte Wirklichkeit*"] that has become entirely describable in terms of general physics, which stretches from astrophysics to particle physics (electronics, information technology, and cybernetics are only aspects of this general physics) and of course also in economic terms.[14]

Whether systems theory is a philosophical system or not is not easily discernible and also beyond the scope of our arguments. If there is an agreement between Lyotard and myself, it is that the concept of system is gradually realized in modern computational machines, which are no longer based on mere mechanical rules but also exhibit a certain reflexivity in their operation, as is the case with robotics and machine learning. Lyotard has observed this sharply, and probably much less vaguely than his contemporaries:

> We are finally in a position to understand how the computerization of society affects this problematic. It could become the "dream" instrument for controlling and regulating the market system, extended to include knowledge itself and governed exclusively by the performativity principle.[15]

Postmodern and the thermodynamic ideology

What Lyotard had seen was the triumph of system, or more precisely a certain model, the open system, whose success could be explained by thermodynamics. In 1979, when *The Postmodern Condition* was published, it was meant to be a "report on knowledge," and Lyotard probably hadn't yet developed the implication of his genealogy of the modern from global perspectives. We will not be able to comprehend this if we simply take the postmodern as the collapse of grand narratives as a literal question of style. The central idea of the postmodern in all senses is the triumph of the open system as episteme. It is therefore not justified to say that Lyotard pays no attention to entropy; more than anyone else, Lyotard observes that this physical-biological model and its use in social and political analysis lead to a dominant view on the transformation of the world politics. In the text titled "The Wall, the Gulf and the Sun," written in 1990, eleven years after *The Postmodern Condition*, this identification of the postmodern with the open system is even clearer:

> Given the increased self-control of the open system, it was likely that it would be the winner in the competition among the systems all over Earth. Nothing seemed able to stop it, or even to direct it in ways other than contributing to its development. Incidents like the collapse of the communist societies and the Gulf crisis were, on the one hand, the opportunity for the system to increase its influence while preventing it from reducing its "blank" internal space as bureaucratic regimes had already done, and, on the other hand, the occasion for the system to improve its control over other sources of energy. Moreover, the system had also started to moderate its victory over other terrestrial systems by extending its ability to regulate the ecosystem so as to ensure its survival.[16]

The open system has invaded into all domains: free market economy, liberal democratic ideology, social sciences research, astrophysics, etc. The human as a species is struggling against the entropic becoming of its own society in order to maintain an open system, any closed system is regarded as a road to serfdom, and namely self-destruction. Maybe we can call it a thermodynamic ideology, in the sense that it is the scientific principle or guidance for politics and research. For sure, no one wants to be called an ideologist today, since it has such a bad name. Habermas discredited Luhmann's systems theory as ideology, and today on the outer wall of Luhmann's family house in Lüneberg we can find an acrylic plaque saying that Luhmann developed an ideology-free social theory.[17] In an article titled "Can thought go on without a body?" included in *The Inhuman* published in 1988, Lyotard ironically describes that all technological and scientific research is preparation for the collapse of the solar system, to develop a strategy for the survival of the human being—to maintain the existence of the mind without an organic body. It continues today when we think of the transhumanists' quest for immortality through human enhancement. During the 1980s, this thermodynamic ideology was recognized after the historical events that prepared for the unification of Europe. This observation was confirmed in the later political writings of Lyotard, especially those dedicated to the fall of the Berlin Wall and the Gulf Crisis, which for Lyotard means the triumph of the open system and its liberal democracy:

> Marxism, the last shoot stemming from both the Enlightenment and Christianity, seems to have lost all of its critical power. When the Berlin Wall fell, it failed definitively. By invading the shops in West Berlin, the East German crowds gave

evidence that the ideal of freedom, at least of the free market, had already invaded Eastern European minds.[18]

The fall of the Berlin Wall and the Gulf War marked the culmination of the end of the crisis of Western political philosophy as conceived in the twentieth century: Nazism and Communism. Lyotard is no neoliberal thinker; what he was aiming to do is explore the limits of the postmodern and the forms of resistance against certain aspects of the system. The fall of the Berlin Wall was the moment when two opposed ideologies confronted each other, and such confrontation ended up in an unhappy consciousness in the Hegelian sense, meaning that one is aware of the impossibility to overcome such contradiction:

> Having been in East Berlin in June and December 1989, I was able to observe how anxious and concerned the East German intellectuals were (even if they had been more or less compromised with the communist bureaucracy) to save, maintain, or elaborate a view enabling all of us to criticize both Eastern totalitarianism and Western liberalism. For somebody coming from the tradition of radical Marxism, this request sounded like an appeal to go backward and start again with the double-edged criticism, directed against both "late capitalism" and so-called "communist" society, that we had undertaken in the fifties and sixties. Although it's attractive, the purpose is vain.[19]

Lyotard anticipated the unresolvable ideological conflicts and the failure to sublate such contradiction. One may wonder, were Lyotard still alive today, what would he make of the development of China? After the financial crisis of 2008, there is a consensus in the West concerning the end of neoliberal economy, promoted by the Thatcher and Reagan governments in the 1980s. Is this the indicator of the system's failure? I have reservations in arriving at such a conclusion, since according to our earlier analysis, the system is even more pervasive through technological development. And if it were true that the "open system" fails, will closed systems in the new guise of data economy and national security be the only candidate? This is a question that has been imposed on us by the COVID-19 pandemic: the potential social transformations, which could arise from within it, might unfortunately be subordinated to the revival of closed or semi-closed systems, in the guise of a "social credit system" or simply "digitization." In view of this polemic, we have to ask what would be the significance of going back to the concept of "entropy" to develop a new politics without falling back on the thermodynamic ideology?

Art within the paralogy of the system

Art might not provide us with a solution, but it offers some conceptual tools or even prototypes to look into the question (of the system and its aftermaths) from different perspectives. Lyotard rejected the idea that he has a system, or more generally that there is a system of thinking and of art at all. This anti-system gesture is a reminder of the philosopher's critical stance towards the discourse of the open system. What was Lyotard's strategy to resist this thermodynamic ideology at the same time without being cynical of it? It is true that Lyotard belongs to a movement called the "linguistic turn," and he was fascinated by a parallel reading of both Ludwig Wittgenstein and Immanuel Kant, later published as *Le Différend* (1983) [*The Differend*, 1988], which Lyotard claims to be his proper philosophy. However, this doesn't mean that Lyotard's analysis was limited to the language game. Criticisms against the linguistic turn have been made by the movement known as "new materialism" today for the ignorance of materiality, but it doesn't follow that new materialism is theoretically more advanced. The significance of Lyotard's thought is that he never sets up easy oppositions, choosing the good and abandoning the evil. In fact we can try at this moment to articulate Lyotard's own paralogy concerning the postmodern as an antisystem working through the system.

Around this time Lyotard was in dispute with Jürgen Habermas concerning the project of modernity. Habermas was longing for a transparent, communicative, noise-free society of consensus as the project of modernity and therefore argued that modernity has not yet come to an end. Habermas's defense of the Enlightenment and modernity is for Lyotard out of order, as he stated in *The Postmodern Condition*:

> Is the aim of the project of modernity the constitution of sociocultural unity within which all the elements of daily life and of thought would take their places as in an organic whole? Or does the passage that has to be charted between heterogeneous language games—those of cognition, of ethics, of politics—belong to a different order from that? And if so, would it be capable of effecting a real synthesis between them?
>
> The first hypothesis, of a Hegelian inspiration, does not challenge the notion of a dialectically totalizing *experience*; the second is closer to the spirit of Kant's *Critique of Judgment*; but must be submitted, like the *Critique*, to that severe reexamination which postmodernity imposes on the thought of the Enlightenment, on the idea of a unitary end of history and of a subject.[20]

We may be able to draw from the above statement that Lyotard opposes Kant to Hegel, even though Hegel's system borrowed a lot from Kant's. If Habermas's defense is problematic for Lyotard, it is because it legitimates a totalizing system, which includes both open systems and closed systems; while Lyotard, especially with his reading of Kant's "Analytics of the Sublime" in the *Critique of Judgement*, sees the possibility of the sublime as an anti-system approach. To put in in a nutshell, for Kant, the sublime indicates a moment when the cognitive system (understanding and imagination) is not able to arrive at a definite concept after a long process of heuristic operation. It is also the moment when reason has to intervene in order to impose violence on imagination, namely to violently put a halt to the system. For Lyotard, the sublime is something which cannot be assimilated by the system, since it is the unpresentable. Thus, when he comments on the Schlegels' reading of Denis Diderot, we understand that:

They knew that the problem was precisely not that of consensus (of Habermasian *Diskurs*), but that of the *unpresentable*, of the unexpected force of the Idea, of the event as the presentation of an unknown phrase, initially unacceptable and then accepted because tried out.[21]

This unpresentable is something recognized by the system, but which the system cannot fully grasp. It stands as a possibility to transform the system, as was done in the domain of art, for example, with the Dadaists and the Surrealists. In an article titled "Après le sublime, état de l'esthétique," Lyotard claims that "for the last century, the arts have not had the beautiful as their main concern, but something which has to do with the sublime,"[22] which leads Jacques Rancière to claim that, though without citing Hegel, Lyotard followed Hegel by attributing the sublime form to symbolic art.[23] The pyramid for Hegel is an example of symbolic art, in contrast to what he calls classical and romantic art, but identifying Hegel's pyramid and Kant's pyramid doesn't seem to be a strong argument to align Lyotard with Hegel. Lyotard asked what can art be without being sacrificed to the expression of morality, as when nature was considered as such a utility (*Gebrauch*). It is the reason why the unpresentable (*undarstellbar*) constitutes the core idea of the avant-garde; for example, in the timbre and the nuance in music and in painting it "introduces a kind of infinity, the indeterminacy of the harmonics within the frame determined by this identity," or the "here and now" in the painting of Barnett Newman,[24] since the unpresentable is that which activates the confrontation between reason and imagination, and that finally leads to the unrepresentable (*Unvorstellbar*).

Lyotard's writing on aesthetics is fascinating and sometimes even constitutes a tension with philosophy, a tension which at the same time prevents it from becoming merely a footnote or illustration of philosophy; it introduces a practical dimension to philosophy. But beyond his writing on individual artists, Lyotard's thinking on art and philosophy culminated in his 1985 exhibition at the Centre Georges Pompidou titled *Les Immatériaux*, which without exaggeration is the first postmodern exhibition.[25] The exhibition, or better a manifestation, wanted to demonstrate a postmodern episteme—a term that Lyotard didn't use—which expresses uncertainty, the insecurity of the information society.

Instead of refusing insecurity and uncertainty, which destructs the concept of the human and its mode of existence in modern time, Lyotard wants to take this as a chance to subvert the modern, and in certain sense he even pushes it further to implant the Kantian sublime in every station of the exhibition. The sublime implies both shock and, at the same time, respect [*Achtung*]. There is both openness and criticality in Lyotard's approach to the postmodern. Lyotard introduced a liberal idea of paralogy, of dissensus, and the necessity to invent new games, but also new audiences. This advocation for diversity, for difference is also the agenda of the thermodynamic ideology of open systems, but Lyotard refuses to simply subsume differences into one single, totalizing system; he intended to explore that which is not reducible to the assimilation of the system and that which always escapes the system, not as a line of flight, but as new acts in the existing games and new games that didn't exist before.[26] This is how we should understand Lyotard's interest in Adorno's notion of *Kunstfremd*, "acinema," and on the question of art; this is also how, on the question of technology, we should understand the concept of technodiversity or multiple cosmotechnics that I have proposed elsewhere.[27]

The death of Lyotard in 1998 prevented him from seeing the development of the twenty-first century, which more than ever realizes his concerns in the postmodern discourse, now unfortunately neutralized as a buzzword or literary genre. The reason is that the term modern or modernity has different meanings in China and in the United States, because modernization means first of all progress. The West, especially Europe, has experienced critical moments of modernity—of its values and epistemologies—and has tried to overcome modernity for more than a century. However, this awareness of overcoming modernity was probably only found in Japan before the Second World War among the thinkers of the Kyoto School. For some European thinkers, China is a country which has modernization without modernity, namely without the same cultural process of the transformation of values, of world views. Then how can the non-European countries talk about postmodernity while not having modernity? In Japan, the postmodern was associated with Otaku culture, with the super flat theory of Takashi Murakami, and even to Alexandre Kojève's reading of Hegel's end of history (for example, via the work of Hiroki Azuma); the postmodern in China is often associated with a specific genre of literature and movies.[28] The concept of the postmodern is still buried in an excitement towards technological modernization, towards the realization of a digital earth and its data economy. The thermodynamic ideology continues, preparing for the collapse of political regimes, and the collapse of the solar system. More than ever, we need paralogy, paralogy of technology, paralogy of thinking.

Notes

1. An earlier version of this chapter appeared in the *Journal of China Academy of Art*, as an introduction to the proceedings of the 2019 conference dedicated to the fortieth anniversary of the publication of Jean-François Lyotard's *The Postmodern Condition. A Report on Knowledge*, with the participation of Bernard Stiegler, Philippe Parreno, Sarah Wilson, Ashley Woodward, Hiroki Azuma and others.
2. Yuk Hui and Andreas Broeckmann (eds), *30 Years after* Les Immatériaux: *Art, Science and Theory* (Lüneburg: Meson Press, 2015).
3. The postmodern as episteme was instead elaborated by Jean-Louis Déotte; see Jean-Louis Déotte, "Ce que je dois à Foucault," *Appareil*, 4 (2010). Available online: http://journals.openedition.org/appareil/913 (accessed February 1, 2021).
4. For example Michel Foucault even describes modernity as "a way of thinking and feeling"; see Michel Foucault, "What is Enlightenment?," in Paul Rabinow (ed.), *The Foucault Reader* (New York: Pantheon Books, 1984), 39.
5. See Yuk Hui, *Recursivity and Contingency* (London: Rowman & Littlefield, 2019).
6. Simon Blackburn (ed.), *The Oxford Dictionary of Philosophy* (Oxford: Oxford University Press, 2008), 267–8.
7. Original definition of orthology and paralogy by Walter Fitch, "Distinguishing Homologous from Analogous Proteins," *Systematic Biology*, vol. 19, no. 2 (June 1970): 99–113: "Where the homology is the result of gene duplication so that both copies

have descended side by side during the history of an organism (for example, alpha and beta hemoglobin) the genes should be called paralogous (para = in parallel)"; "Where the homology is the result of speciation so that the history of the gene reflects the history of the species (for example alpha hemoglobin in man and mouse) the genes should be called orthologous (ortho = exact)."

8   Jean-François Lyotard, *The Postmodern Condition: A Report on Knowledge*, tr. Geoff Bennington and Brian Massumi (Minneapolis MN: University of Minnesota Press, [1979] 1984), 61.
9   Jean-François Lyotard, "After 6 months of work . . ." in *30 Years after* Les Immatériaux, 34–5.
10 Lyotard, *The Postmodern Condition*, 33–4.
11 See Gotthard Günther, *Beiträge zur Grundlegung einer operationsfähigen Dialektik*, vol. 1. (Hamburg: Felix Meiner Verlag, 1976); see also Hui, *Recursivity and Contingency*, Chapter 2.
12 Lyotard, *The Postmodern Condition*, 62.
13 The term *Entäusserung* is translated by T. M. Knox into English as "alienation" in the context where Hegel talks about the legal aspects of private properties in his *Outlines of the Philosophy of Right*, e.g., to give away or exchange one's own possession; the term is equally translated as *extériorization* by Roger Garaudys in his *Dieu est mort, étude sur Hegel*.
14 Jean-François Lyotard, *Political Writings*, tr. Bill Readings and Kevin Paul Geiman (Minneapolis MN: University of Minnesota Press, 1993), 98.
15 Lyotard, *The Postmodern Condition*, 67.
16 Lyotard, *Political Writings*, 123.
17 The plaque reads: "In dem zugehörenden Anwesen verbrachte der Soziologe Niklas Luhmann (geb. 1927) seine Kindheit und Jugend. Er entwickelte eine weltweit anerkannte, soziale Systeme übergreifend analysierende, ideologiefreie Gesellschaftstheorie." (The sociologist Niklas Luhmann (born 1927) spent his childhood and youth in this place. He developed a globally recognized ideology-free theory of society for a comprehensive analysis of social system.)
18 Lyotard, "The Wall, the Gulf, and the Sun," in *Political Writings*, 114.
19 Ibid.
20 Lyotard, *The Postmodern Condition*, 72–3.
21 Lyotard, *Political Writings*, 27, my italics.
22 Jean-François Lyotard, "After the Sublime, the State of Aesthetics," in *The Inhuman: Reflections on Time,* tr. Geoffrey Bennington and Rachel Bowlby (Cambridge UK: Polity, [1988] 1991), 135.
23 Jacques Rancière, "The sublime from Lyotard to Schiller: Two readings of Kant and their political significance," *Radical Philosophy* 126 (Jul/Aug 2004): 8–15. This article forms the basis for a chapter in *Malaise dans l'esthétique* (Paris: Galilée, 2004), tr. Stephen Corcoran as *Aesthetics and its Discontents* (Cambridge UK and Malden MA: Polity, 2009): chapter titled "Lyotard and the Aesthetics of the Sublime: a Counter-reading of Kant," 88–105.
24 Ibid., 140; 89.
25 See Yuk Hui, "Exhibiting and Sensibilizing: Recontextualizing 'Les Immatériaux,'" in Tristan Garcia and Vincent Normand (eds), *Theater, Garden, Bestiary: A Materialist History of Exhibitions* (Berlin: Sternberg Press, 2019): 235–45.
26 Jean-François Lyotard, "Le jeu de l'informatique et du savoir," interview with Yannick Blanc, *Dialectiques* 29 (1980): 4.

27 See Yuk Hui, *The Question Concerning Technology in China. An Essay in Cosmotechnics* (Falmouth: Urbanomic / MIT Press, 2016/2019); also Yuk Hui, *Art and Cosmotechnics* (Minneapolis MN: University of Minnesota Press, 2021).
28 See Hiroki Azuma, *Otaku: Japan's Database Animals*, tr. Jonathan E. Abel and Shion Kono (Minneapolis MN: University of Minnesota Press, [2001] 2009).

Lyotard Supplement II

11

Apathy in Theory[1]

Jean-François Lyotard, 1977
Translated by Roger McKeon

"I think the moment has come for breaking off . . ." The moment has come to break off theoretical terror. This matter is a very big one, that we will have on our hands for quite a while. The desire for truth, which feeds everyone's terrorism, is inscribed in our most uncontrolled use of language, so much so that any discourse appears naturally to deploy its pretension to speak the truth, by some sort of hopeless vulgarity. Well, the time has now come to remedy this vulgarity, to introduce into ideological or philosophical discourse the same refinement, the same force of lightness obtaining in works of painting, music, "experimental" cinema, as well, obviously, as in those of the sciences. In no way is the idea to invent one or more new theories, nor interpretations either; what we lack is a diablerie or an apathy such that the theoretical genre itself suffer subversions that its pretension does not recover from; that it turn into merely a genre again and be dislodged from the position of mastery or domination that it has held at least since Plato: that truth become a question of style.

The text that Freud published in 1920, *Beyond the Pleasure Principle*, contains an outline of this attitude. It is not a bad thing to examine it whilst Freudian scholasticism strives to make the pathos of knowledge—conviction—, rule everywhere.

Advocatus diaboli

Freud: "I think the moment has come for breaking off.

Not, however, without the addition of a few words of critical reflection [*Besinnung*: reverting to the sense]. It may be asked whether and how far I am myself convinced [*überzeugt*: in the sense that a testimony, a *Zeugnis* convinces one, as in "conviction piece"] of the truth of the hypotheses that have been set out in these pages. My answer would be that [*würde lauten*: would sound something like] I am not convinced myself and that I do not seek to persuade [*werben*: as would a recruiting agent] other people to believe in them. Or, more precisely, that I do not know how far I believe in them. There is no reason, as it seems to me, why the emotional factor [*das affecktive Moment*] of conviction should enter into this question at all. It is surely possible to throw oneself [surrender oneself: *sich hingeben*, as in "to yield oneself up" to pleasure, to debauchery] into a line of thought [*Gedankengang*] and to follow it wherever it leads out of simple scientific curiosity [*Neugierde*: desire for the new and news], or, if the reader prefers, as an *advocatus diaboli*, who is not on that account himself sold [*verschreibt*] to the devil. I do not dispute the fact that the third step in the theory of the instincts [*in der Trieblehre*], which I have taken here, cannot lay claim to the same degree of certainty [*Sicherheit*] as the two earlier ones—the extension of the concept of sexuality and the hypothesis of narcissism [...]. And in any case it is impossible to pursue an idea of this kind [*die Durchführung dieser Idee*: i.e., the idea that a drive is always "regressive" in the sense that it brings the "organism" back to an earlier state] except by repeatedly combining factual material with what is purely speculative [*mit bloss Erdachten*] and thus diverging widely from empirical observation. The more frequently this is done in the course of constructing a theory, the more untrustworthy, as we know, must be the final result. But the degree of uncertainty is not assignable. One may have made a lucky hit or one may have gone shamefully astray. I do not think a large part is played by what is called "intuition" [*Intuition*] in work of this kind. From what I have seen of intuition, it seems to me to be the product of a kind of intellectual impartiality [*Unparteilichkeit des Intellekts*]. Unfortunately, however, people are seldom impartial where ultimate things, the great problems of science and life, are concerned. Each of us is governed [*beherrscht*] in such cases by deep-rooted [*tief begründeten*] internal prejudices [*Vorliebene*], into whose hands our speculation unwittingly plays [*denen er mit seiner Spekulation unwissentlich in die Hände arbeitet*: to suit someone, serve someone's purpose]. Since we have such good grounds for being distrustful, our attitude towards the results of our own deliberations [*der eigenen Denkbemühungen*] cannot well be other than one of cool benevolence. I hasten to add, however, that self-criticism such as this is far from binding one to any special tolerance [*zu besonderer Toleranz*] towards dissentient opinions. It is perfectly legitimate to reject remorselessly theories which are contradicted by the very first steps in the analysis of observed facts [*in der Analyse der Beobachtung*], while yet being aware at the same time that the validity of one's own theory is only a provisional one. We need not feel greatly disturbed in judging our speculation [*Spekulation*] upon the life and death instincts by the fact [*würde es uns wenig stören*] that so many bewildering and obscure [*unanschauliche*] processes occur in it—such as one instinct being driven out by another or an instinct turning from the ego to an object, and so on. This is merely due to our being obliged to operate with the scientific terms, that is to say with the figurative language, peculiar [*der eigenen Bildersprache*] to psychology (or, more precisely, to depth psychology). We could not otherwise describe the processes in question at all, and indeed we could not have become aware of them [*ja, würden sie gar nicht wahrgenommen haben*]. The deficiencies in our description would probably vanish if we were already in a position to replace the psychological terms by physiological or chemical ones. It is true that they too are only part of a figurative language; but it is one with which we have long been familiar and which is perhaps a simpler one as well."[2]

The important event

The reference shifts all along this text. The theory of drives in its third state is indeed what is at issue throughout. But the idea to be "pursued" is, in this theory, that of the repetition compulsion as a fundamental law of drive processes; the impassibility [*würde es uns wenig stören*] before a potential accusation of thinking fantastically, as a free wanderer, is asserted, at the end of this text, with reference to the speculations on life and death drives.

We are at the end of section VI of *Beyond the Pleasure Principle*, Freud has just borrowed, most fantastically, to be sure, from philosophers, poets and biologists, in order to support his hypothesis of drive regression. What is this hypothesis? That all drives are *repetitive*, have no other purpose than reestablishing a prior, lost state, a state approximately *devoid of tension*. And that thus it is not the accomplishment of desire which constitutes the end of drive activity, but the return to this state, even though the process might be painful. Freud based himself on, or made a pretext of, four "examples" of repetition: transference in the analytical cure, dreams in traumatic neuroses, children's play, compulsions of destiny.

But another concern grafted itself onto this theoretical outline: if all drives are repetitive, then the doctrine of drives must be *monist* (as is Jung's and are those of all philosophers) and that is out of the question: whence and how would neurosis proceed if all drives aimed to reestablish one and only one type of state? It will thus be necessary to imagine two state qualities: one, death, is the total elimination of tension; the other, on the contrary, is the state of a living organism at rest, not devoid of tension, but expending a minimal or optimal amount of energy to maintain itself. In truth, Freud is not all that clear in the attribution of functions to the two drive principles.

What, in fact, did Freud's incredulity or his lack of conviction have to do with? The repetition hypothesis or that of duality? Rather the latter. Again, one can produce observations of facts of repetition exceeding the pleasure principle and therefore implying a power of recurrence independent of this principle (and, in Freud's view, more archaic than it). Drive duality, by contrast, is not and cannot be observed (and perhaps even not understood, *unanschauliche*): life activity always covers that of the death drives; the only thing one ever hears is "the rumor of Eros." Death drives must therefore be invented without the support of observable facts. An enigma must accordingly be invented as well, and accepted: it is not only that two types of states repeat themselves, but also the event of their difference. The name that event bears is sexuality: gap, cam lift that would bring the index of tensions not to the zero of death, but to the energetic level of life, thus delaying death, a matter of speed.

Things are quite clear, except that the lift itself remains unexplained: "But what is the important event [*welches wichtige Ereignis*] in the development of living substance which is being repeated [*wiederholt*] in sexual reproduction, or in its forerunner, the conjugation of two protista? We cannot say; and we should consequently feel relieved if the whole structure of our argument [*Gedankenaufbau*] turned out to be mistaken. The opposition between the ego or death instincts and the sexual or life instincts would then cease to hold [*entfallen*] and the compulsion to repeat would no longer possess the *importance* [*Bedeutung*] we have ascribed to it."[3] The enigmatic event takes over in the 1920 discourse from that which in the 1890's had been identified as what was called the seduction of children by adults: this initial "narration," this first "edifice of ideas" already pointed to the effect of an *excess* of excitations, and thus of tension to link these, supervening in the peace of innocence or, rather, in the inertia of what is not "ripe."

Epistemologically speaking, we have here a scarcely credible theory: one of the entities it produces not only has no fact whatsoever to support it, but also requires that an *event* be postulated, the event of a dissociation, a departure. Now, what can an event be in theoretical discourse? Its blind spot, that which its function is precisely to reabsorb. The event belongs to narrative discourse; no matter what the narratologists say, it is its mainspring, its beginning and thus its end: the "once upon a time" of the event bars the "universally valid" of theory. Freud says: "We cannot say [*das sagen*] this event," and thus he says the event, he maintains it outside theoretical discourse, as a referent the meaning of which cannot be produced internally, in the closure of this discourse, or as a partition (life and death) that precedes reasons and posits them. Properly speaking, there is no *opposition*, *Gegensatz*, between life and death drives, opposition being the thinkable and, above all, the mainspring of thought *par excellence*, the thinking; there is the event, which belongs to the *Wanderung*, the voyage.

Let us recall Freud's prefatory remarks to the English edition of Varendonck's *The Psychology of Day-Dreams* (1921): "For that reason I think it is advisable, when establishing a distinction between the different modes of thought-activity, not to utilize the relation to consciousness in the first instance, and to designate the day-dream, as well as the chains of thought studied by Varendonck, as freely wandering or phantastic thinking, in opposition to intentionally directed reflection."[4] The final state of the doctrine of drives, could it not itself be a *freely wandering or fantastic thinking, a Gedankengang*, a march of ideas wholly different from "scientificity"? From a theoretical standpoint, it does little to convince, says Freud, but the affect of conviction is of little importance here, he adds. That is the point. This wanderer is an apathetic.

Indiscernable effects

Thus the epistemological inconsistency does not stop Freud. He does not even write his way out of it with the usual trick, i.e., time will tell if I was right or wrong; or, as he does at the end with the description of drive processes [*Vorgänge*]: one is condemned to provisional uncertainty by the language employed, that most colorful language of depth psychology. No, when it comes to the new duality of drives, he does not extirpate himself from his inconsistency at all, he remains with it, he intends to go on with it, to persist in it. On what basis, according to what *Stimmung*?

Normally, a theory is accompanied by a specific affect: conviction. There are testimonies, attestations, backed up by observations, allowing for the constitution of a kind of discourse (a narrative, for instance) inducing credence, on the part not only of the addressee, but also on that of the addressor, which implies not that this discourse is universally valid, but at least that it pertains to the domain in which the question of its validity can and must be raised. Conviction is the affect corresponding to the closure of the enquiry, to the filing of conclusions. Vocabulary of the court. (Very different from that used by a Husserl at that time). One produces the exhibits, one pleads. The theoretician is an attorney. There is a rhetoric of scholarly discourse; its economic principle is the effect of conviction, which, unlike the effect of persuasion (the age-old Peitho), cannot be obtained by working "directly" on the affectivity of the addressee. To convince, himself to start with, the theoretician-attorney must endow his discourse with certain properties, including the formal properties of internal consistency and completeness in relation to the field of reference. There will thus be at least figures or turns of rigorousness, others of exactness. And many more yet,[5] that in principle have nothing to do with knowledge and probably remain unconscious for the users. The affect of conviction is obtained on condition that this battery of *loci* be used.

When Freud ponders the hypothesis of the two drive principles, he begins by questioning his *Stimmung*: am I affectively convinced? The affect that signals, if not the *validity* of the hypothesis, at least its *existence* as a theoretical hypothesis subject to discussion, is it present? After replying no, he corrects himself: I don't know whether I am convinced.

Is this tepidity in certainty? It is very much something else. The new drive theory includes an *effect of uncertainty*, insuppressible, some of the practical implications of which must appear to be redoubtable to any therapeutics. In its two previous states, the doctrine of drives revolved around the opposition between two *instances*: need/sexuality (or reality/pleasure), then I/object. Symptoms could be read as so many conflicts and compromises between the two functions fulfilled respectively by the two instances. Dream analysis as a whole had been predicated on this opposition. To each instance pertained a function, e.g., accomplishment of desire *versus* satisfaction of needs. (Other formulations were possible). Those dualisms gave one, or so one believed, a *principle for deciphering* symptoms.

But if the dualism becomes that of *principles* of functioning and not of instances, how can the effects of these principles be discerned in the symptoms, how can this or that established fact be assigned to the former rather than to the latter? The conflict between life and death drives is not a war between two instances, it does not generate contradictions; the effects of the principle named death drive are always dissimulated within the others, those of Eros. What does this *dissimulation* consist in? In that the effects of each principle are indiscernible from the effects of the other.

Take Dora's respiratory symptom. Is it due to life or death drives? Undecidable within the last doctrine. If it spoke, what would it say? First of all, undoubtedly *I live*, because the symptom is well, like a microorganism resistant to all "external" aggression, including that which can emanate from the "organic body" of Dora. It would also say I kill, I kill it, the "organic body" that I threaten with asphyxia and mutism. If one objects that the discourse's reference has shifted from one statement to the other (hysterical microorganism in the first, "organic body" in the second), one will continue: the respiratory symptom still says *I am dying* or *I live dead* and it is the death drives that, referring then to the microorganism as the inviable, disclose in it nevertheless a kind of monstrous regulation; and finally *I revive it*, the organism, by forcing it to increase its metabolism in order to meet the challenge I put it up against: Dora, will she not go to see Freud? The "cure" is it not a reactivation of the exchanges of the "body" with its environment? Now it is Eros that disrupts the body of reference, but for the purposes of more life, more differentiation. Thus *four* statements blocked together, such that it is undecidable whether the symptom is governed by one principle of drive functioning or the other. Tonsillitis, aphonia, hoarseness, asthma, all "signify" both life and death.

Yet is this not to say enough, for it would lead to concluding quite simply: they are ambivalent. But it is not a matter of ambivalence. Life and death, as drive principles, fulfill *respectively* the *two same functions*, let us say regulating and deregulating, for instance. Life is self-regulating when the symptom "says" *I live*, but when it "says" *I revive it*, while it is what is at it again, since the effect is "erotic," said effect is disruptive, hetero-deregulating nonetheless; and conversely, death drives disrupt the organism (*I kill it*), but also have the strange regulating effect that is the monstrosity of the *I live dead*, of the inviable live. Exchange of the "functions" or, if one prefers, of the effects, of one principle with those of the other. This is something altogether different from ambivalence; it precludes any conviction, for it makes it impossible to plead *a cause*, i.e., an established and stable relation between an effect and an instance.

If the hypothesis of the two drive principles cannot bring about belief, that of Freud himself, it is because it is in obvious contravention with an axiom indispensable to the discourse of knowledge, at least such as Freud and his time imagined it, that of the decidability of causes. Economic dualism in its ultimate form is not a dualism; the two drive functionings, identical in nature (repetition), overlap in their effects; their difference, which is, in principle, a difference in regime, cannot be circumscribed. Freud himself bears witness to this when he remains uncertain as to the designation he should give to the *level* at which the *index* of tension brings the "body" back: is it zero, the minimum, the optimum? His entire text hesitates on this decisive point. At the beginning: "The mental apparatus endeavors [*Bestreben*] to keep the quantity of excitation present in it as low as possible *or at least* to keep it constant." (emphasis mine).[6] In the middle: "The dominating tendency of mental life [*als die herrschende Tendenz des Seelenlebens*], and perhaps of nervous life in general, is the effort [*das Streben*] to *reduce* [*Herabsetzung*], to *keep constant* [Konstanterhaltung], or *remove* [*Aufhebung*] internal tension due to stimuli [*der inneren Reizspannung*]" (emphasis mine);[7] here the three indices are given in a jumble, not as identical, although the level this push is effectively meant to establish is a matter indifferent, possibly even undecidable; now, the acknowledgment of this *Streben*, Freud adds, is "one of our strongest reasons for believing [*glauben*] in the existence of death instincts." At the very end, again: "The pleasure principle, then, is a tendency [*Tendenz*] operating in the service of a function whose business is to free the mental apparatus entirely from excitation [*erregungslos*] or to keep the amount of excitation [*den Betrag des Erregung*] in it constant or to keep it as low as possible" (emphasis mine).[8]

One could only be surprised by all these "oder," by the absence of determinacy, if one did not appreciate the significance of this last theory of drives in the theoretical "field" itself: hesitation in the discourse of knowledge merely parallels the dissimulation of principles in the economic reference of the discourse. It is thus not a "want" or a lack of conviction that the 1920 economist experiences, but an undecidability of affect, a positive potency of not knowing whether he believes in his theory or not, a potency of affirmation alien to the question of belief. From the outset, Freud declared the domain of tensions and relaxations (the economic) "[...] the most obscure and inaccessible region of the mind, and, since we cannot avoid contact with it, the least rigid hypothesis, it seems to me, will be the best [*die lockerste Annahme*]." *Lockerheit*, laxity is the property of psychic energy that Freud put forward in the *Introductory Lectures* (1917) and again in *The Ego and the Id* (1923), to account for artistic activity as a correlate of the malleability of repressions; in the latter text, he associates it with the *Verschiebbarkeit* of energy, its displaceability, the fact that it is not cathected. The distinctive features required here for the theory of drives are thus the same as those Freud describes for the "psychic apparatus" of the artist.

One could be tempted to declare the laxity of the economic theory to be second, seeing that it accompanies a return on the theoretical "body" of the same dissimulation as that which the theory points to on the drive "body." But that would be an impropriety: this return is not one; the fact is that this theoretical discourse makes its appearance here, taken initially according to its specific affect, as one of the surfaces of a vast drive "body" and that the epistemological uncertainty obtaining within it is none other than the undecidability of the effects on this "body" in general. In these few lines of Freud's, theory all of a sudden ceases to have anything to do with the true and the false; what concerns it above all is how much pathos it comprises or not. The difference invoked at the end of *Beyond the Pleasure Principle*, under the guise of a poet, between *flying* and *limping*, is not of method but of passion: claudication[9] is an affection relating to space and time, it is the wobbling extension and the stuttering duration; the limper does not know *whether he believes* in space and time, whereas the flyer does: he is *convinced*.

Passionate apathy

A theory of the indiscernibles takes shape only according to an undecidable affect. Far from being able to elicit conviction, it opens up a new affective region: that of *apathy*. Freud couldn't *convince* anyone, to begin with himself, that there are death drives infiltrated in life drives. He appeals rather to irresponsibility, to the potency of disregarding the demand for conviction. If he pleads a case, it is thus in another court than that of the community of savants. *Beyond the Pleasure Principle* does not belong to the genre of scientific discourse. The third theory of drive "duality" eludes the theoretical and practical requisites of the savant genre. It is a *fiction-theory*. Its specific affect is *impassivity*, and not conviction. Impassivity must be understood to mean the impossibility of being affected by the yes or the no of conviction.

Diablerie in matters of theory (most remote from *diabolism*) would consist in one's preferring to let loose the potency of inventing rather than to consolidate by way of proofs the innovations one proposes. Yet is that not saying enough: one prefers to put oneself in the situation of having to invent rather than to remain in the position of having to present proof. One thus "decides" to cease to reply, one makes oneself irresponsible, one excludes oneself from savant society. Theoretical intelligence makes itself *insensitive* to arguments, to *sic et nons*, to the values of knowledge, to mathemes. It desires the new, *nur aus wissenschaftlicher Neugierde*; but then what a singular "scientificity" it is, which yields (*sich hingeben*) to this lust (the radical *gierde* is very strong: *Du sollsts nicht begehren deines Nächsten Weib*), which indulges in this lust for the new, as in debauchery! Debauchery in matters of knowledge is to pursue the idea *soweit er führt*, as far as it leads, to desire the *soweit*, the very space where the idea pays out insofar as that space does not stop opening up, the thread of the idea, its *Gang*, unfolding before it new surfaces of thought, possibilities of unprecedented statements. Scientificity is parodied thus: the discourse one holds, that Freud holds, continues to have a reference (the drive economy), statements appear to keep complying with the precepts of the denotative function, but the reference—namely the death drives, and thus the drive dualism itself—can no longer be opposed to any statement for the "reason" that it cannot be exhibited in observations, nor give rise to counter statements. Scientific discourse lacking an attestable reference, which at one go sweeps away the privilege that observation arrogates to itself in the statute of science. And the internal consistency of this discourse is, as was seen, no less solicited than its referential function. In the place of this "seriousness," a passion for the new.

But an apathetic passion. Apathy is a Sadian word that Klossowski comments on magnificently in *The Philosopher-Villain*. If Freud speaks of "diablerie," if he admits to "surrendering himself" to curiosity for ideas, if he confesses a desire to go along with them and follow their course (as though with young ladies strolling by), and if he declares at the same time not at all to have sold his soul to the devil and only to adventure in fiction-theory out of curiosity (already at the beginning of section IV: "What follows is speculation, often far-fetched speculation, which the reader will consider or dismiss according to their individual predilection. It is further an attempt to follow out an idea, consistently, out of curiosity [*aus Neugierde*] to see where it will lead [*wohin dies führen wird*]"[10]), it is because this parody of science resembles Sadian "libertinism." The latter also requires impassivity in the most excessive desires and in their most adventurous exploration. Freud deals here with the surfaces of language of knowledge as Sade deals with those of skins: to follow a train of thoughts is more than following the course of drives: it is to extend it, and coldly. Sade said that anyone endowed with singular tastes is sick, and Freud that any theoretician without proof, without *Zeugnis*, has found his master (*beherrscht*) in deep predilections (*Vorliebene*). Hence Sadian libertinism of skins and Freudian libertinism of words do indeed want coldness, but also the most incommunicable pathos in coldness: singularity. The Sadian is a monster, not so much on account of his tastes, for there is no universality of tastes, no norm to appraise, condemn, and possibly correct such singularity; he is a monster in that he adds to the affirmation of his singular tastes an encyclopedic curiosity for what the systematically complete irritation of voluptuous surfaces (*eine Versuch zur konsequenten Ausbeutung einer Idee*) can allow one to experience. Blocked thus inside his libidinal apparatus by his tastes, but running way *beyond* it by his will to *Aufklärung* of drives. Both devil, owing to pathos, and *advocatus diaboli*, by parody, *or the reverse*. In any case, it is in the nature of the devil to have an advocate: diabolism masquerading as diablerie. *Or the reverse*. Likewise, this Freud of the pseudo-theory (the third drive "dualism") is stuck in an apparatus known as the desire for truth, which doesn't keep him from clearing off, while phlegmatically plundering ideas. Repetitive preferences work within the apparatus from the moment that it is no longer restrained, tested, corrected by observation; encounters and inventions play their part in the adventure of "curiosity"; compliance and non-compliance with the rules of savant discourse, occurring together, fiction-theory dissimulates itself in theory, which it dissimulates in return.

Was that but a moment in the theoretical destiny of Freudianism? Is it in general only an epistemological moment, that of imagination in the work of inventing hypotheses? Is this apathy ephemeral, must it give way to a return of conviction? The fate that the final drive "dualism" will suffer in Freud's later works, most notably in *Civilization and its Discontents*, i.e., the reconstitution of a scarcely dissimilating opposition, quite simply ambivalent, between love and aggressiveness, seems to validate a "dialectical" reading of this apathy: it led Freud back to convictions, or so they say. Too bad for this Freud and his epigones.

The parody

The big thing for us at this point is to destroy theory, and that cannot be done with a vow to silence. On the contrary: silence marches in step with theoretical terror, it is its accomplice and guarantor. They always say to us: if you do not speak to tell the truth, be quiet. In this passage from *Beyond the Pleasure Principle*, Freud does not tell himself for an instant: since I don't have what I would need to make a theory fit to be presented (consistent and saturated), then I will keep quiet. He does not give in at all to the intimidation of the "What cannot be said must be passed over in silence;" he intends, on the contrary, to speak all the same and that his speech be not a derision but a parody of theory. The destruction of theory can be brought about solely according to this parody; it in no way consists in *criticizing* theory, since critique itself is a theoretical *Moment* that one cannot expect to instigate the destruction of theory. To destroy theory is to make one, several pseudo-theories; the theoretical crime is to fabricate fiction-theories.

Freud desires *Lockerheit*, or laxity, as well for his discourse as for the unconscious of artists: does he mean to shirk the *responsibilities* of knowledge? No, not to dodge them, but to play and get round them as a devil and devil's advocate. Get round them by playing them. Is it requested of artists that they carry the weight of the world on their shoulders, the burden of problems that those in charge are confronted with but know not how to solve? That has happened and happens yet; they themselves sometimes ask for it. Let us wail. Not in the name of a conception of gratuitous, disinterested art, for art (which was in many respects Freud's); but on the contrary because art, like science, is only another name for displaceability and voyage.

Fictitious-theoretical activity will carry into philosophical discourse the same potency of *wandering* as that operating in the arts and sciences. The real priests are the theoreticians, they are the ones who *curb* this potency, demand its sedentarization and see to it that it blames itself when it errs beyond the norms. Even in the Freud of 1920 can you detect this *remorse*. Let us listen to Sade: "[. . . do] immediately, in cold blood, that very thing which, done in the throes of passion, has been able to cause you remorse [. . .]" One has to reaccomplish apathetically the Freudian crime, too timid yet, committed against theoretical terrorism. That is what is at stake from now on, not only against the petty doctors who believe they exercise their prestige over the intellectual world with theoreticity, but against all that, in this world, intimidates and kills in the name of the great mathemes: these are but the fruit of *deeply anchored predilections*, hiding behind the alibi of a capital name.

One last word: if one exiles oneself from the society of savants, must one renounce intervening in it, criticizing and arguing? Not at all. Theoretical apathy is not a depressive state, it goes together with the greatest intransigence towards the discourses that submit to the law of true and false. No tolerance for that which, in this field, does not fulfill the demands that define it. Freud sees this very clearly. Do not hope, therefore, that the artists of fiction-theory will leave the stage clear for truth-theory: on the contrary, they will *also* be present in this old battle and they will joust. Thus the dissimulation will be complete, the parody not allowing itself to be distinguished (in terms of true or false) from its pretended "model." The only ones who will not lose their heads and hearts in this are those who are cured of theoretical pathos, the apathetics.

Notes

1 [Published as "Apathie dans la théorie" in Jean-François Lyotard *Rudiments païens : Genre dissertatif* (Paris: UGE, 10/18, 1977; republished Paris: Klincksieck, 2011), 19–49. Reproduced in English translation with permission of Éditions Klincksieck, Paris. Copyright 2011.—Eds.]
2 [Sigmund Freud] *Jenseits des Lustprinzips*, G. W. XIII, 63–5. [Sigmund Freud, "Beyond the Pleasure Principle," in James Strachey (tr. and ed.), *The Standard Edition of the Complete Psychological Works of Sigmund Freud*, vol. XVIII (London: Hogarth, 1955; London: Vintage, 2001), 58–60.—Trans.; interpolations in brackets are Lyotard's own commentary on extracts from the German text.—Eds.]
3 Ibid., 46. [Freud, "Beyond the Pleasure Principle," 44.]
4 [Sigmund Freud] G. W., XIII, 440. ["Introduction to J. Varendonck's *The Psychology of Day-Dreams*" in James Strachey (tr. and ed.), *The Standard Edition of the Complete Psychological Works of Sigmund Freud*, vol. XVIII, 272.]
5 See Bruno Latour and Paolo Fabbri, "La rhétorique du discours scientifique" [La rhétorique de la science. Pouvoir et devoir dans un article de science exacte], *Actes de la recherche en sciences sociales*, 13 (February 1977), 81–95. [Bruno Latour and Paolo Fabbri "The Rhetoric of Science: Authority and Duty in an Article from the Exact Sciences," tr. Sarah Cummins, *Technostyle*, vol. 16, no. 1 (Winter 2000): 115–34.—Eds.]
6 Freud, "Beyond the Pleasure Principle," 9.
7 Ibid., 55.
8 Ibid., 62.
9 [Whilst the French term *la claudication* has some current usage as a medical term, the equivalent in English is less familiar: "claudication" is a condition which can cause limping.—Eds.]
10 Freud, "Beyond the Pleasure Principle," 24, trans. modified.

12

"What we cannot reach flying we must reach limping..."
Art Présent: Interview with Jean-François Lyotard by Alain Pomarède, late 1978[1]

Translated by Kiff Bamford and Roger McKeon

The difference invoked at the end of Beyond the Pleasure Principle, under the guise of a poet, between flying and limping, is not of method but of passion: claudication[2] is an affection relating to space and time, it is the wobbling extension and the stuttering duration; the limper does not know whether he believes in space and time, whereas the flyer does: he is convinced.

—J.-F. Lyotard, "Apathy in Theory"[3]

Jean-François Lyotard: I believe it is a passage that concerns the pathos of truth, certainty. The one who is certain takes flight. As a result, certainty is dominated. Light with one's own certainty, one dominates everything one doesn't yet have, and will try to make it rise: there is an ascending process which implies a verticality...

In *limping*, what interested me was to show that in effect this very crazy thing that is claudication[4] is in reality wisdom itself. Someone with claudication is someone who doesn't know exactly where the ground is. I would almost say: who distrusts the ground. And this mistrust is wise, not full of resentment, since one walks nonetheless and can move forward, asking oneself, whilst walking, about verticality, horizontality.

It was only much later that I reread Beckett's text, which I wasn't thinking about at all, in *Watt*, I believe, at the beginning, where Beckett describes the gait: "Fling out the left foot to the South, then lean on the left foot, throw the right foot towards the North, bring it back towards the left foot and then pull on the left foot to get it in alignment with the right foot."[5] So there is this description which is exactly that of a limper, one who limps badly.

To put it differently, I thought that this was what was missing in the *Phenomenology of Perception*, for example: there is this idea of a relationship to the world, to things, and thus at the same time to the realm of truth which, as it happens, is the relationship of the right body caught up in the right matrix of the world or in the right matrix of words, in which it feels like a fish in water.[6] A fish that doesn't limp since it flies—an aero-aquatic element—and so it goes where it needs to. It doesn't question things. It thinks that the world is well made and that it is made for the world and that truth is well made and that it is made for the truth.

I believe that the limper flies in precisely the right sense of the word. When Beckett says: "You must throw your right foot to the North," what is that? At that moment the right foot flies, all the while exploring a half-horizon, a whole part of the world, a whole system of polarized coordinates. But these are short flights, sorts of jumps that come back to earth, that are never definitive, that one doesn't get the hang of either, for that matter. Each step is a problem.

Art Présent: In claudication, a series not of stops but of repeated explorations, somewhat like certain approaches in experimental cinema...

J.-F. L. Ultimately it is Zeno who is at issue here. Zeno and Diogenes: the paradox of the arrow in flight, which Zeno shows cannot fly; and in a way he is right. It is absolutely impossible to conceive of flying. If one sticks to cold logic, one who believes an arrow to fly is deluded.

Similarly, I think that two-thirds of experimental cinema works against the very notion of cinema; that is, of a movement considered as the serendipitous, natural synthesis of the different states of a body in space, of the different positions through which it passes. And the whole ensemble of experimental cinema either accelerates it or stops it. Either by excess or by defect, it tries to battle against what ideology in cinema writes as a synthesis of the different positions of a body in space.

If one wants to be serious about it, actually, if one wants to go with a thought like Zeno's—a thought of singularity, really—there are as many bodies as there are positions of the body and the synthesis between each of them will never be made, unless by delusion. In the notion of *cinema*, there is already the process of constructing a totality from a series of singularities. That is Zeno. And when Zeno's argument is repeated to Diogenes, the Cynic: "There is no movement, movement cannot be demonstrated," what does Diogenes do? He gets up and walks. Now, everything we know about Diogenes suggests that he limped; Diogenes Laertes, who recounts the story doesn't say so, but I am sure that Diogenes must have walked in an absolutely scandalous way.

I believe that what *limps* par excellence, in the proper sense of the term, is dance inasmuch as it makes the relationship between body and space as paradoxical as possible—and it is what announces itself in claudication, it is that paradox we have to question. When one starts to think in the field that is called *the theoretical*, the discourse of truth, it is not true to say that one flies, one limps. Which is to say that, in fact, one can move forward only by paradoxizing as much as possible what one thinks in relation to what one has to think about.

The arrow in flight, that's theoretical terror: "You see that it makes a unit, it is going somewhere; I'll tell you where it's going and where it comes from." It is the unity constituted from the non-existence of unity; it was Merleau-Ponty's madness to want to recover a given unity. If you descend beneath the constituted units, you can only go with Hume: *no unity*. Terror begins when you want unity, that's to say at the level of cinema.

A.P. Is cinema not made to produce flight?

J.-F. L. You can say that cinema is made for that, very broadly. But perhaps, not only for that. There is indeed all the rhetoric of the image, of the sound, which is definitely intended to produce flight. At the same time, it seems to me that something else can occur, even in a narrative film on general release, something like a claudication, a hesitation for the spectator, an uncertainty that can be a certainty over the image, a turning point in the narrative, unexpected, an ending which wasn't what you expected, a character who becomes dubious, etc. It is extremely frequent, even if on a small scale, even if it seems to experimental cinema-makers completely insufficient, ridiculous ... even then, it really makes the spectator limp.

I remember seeing some films in New York in a movie theater that was open all the time: *The Kitchen*.[7] You could just breeze in and out of it. On request, you could see all the experimental films there; and already, that changed a lot. It didn't feel like being in a cinema at all. You were in another position.

What interests me and makes experimental cinema tiring and often unbearable in the long run is that it is very often meta-cinema: cinema that speaks about and shows off the processes of cinema. I remember Tony Conrad's films ... very simple systems where you have light and sound synchronized on the same tape. So you have passages of black and white synchronized with sound clicks of variable intensity. Claudication thus reaches its lowest or highest level, as you wish—but it's amazingly interesting. You get a meta-pleasure. You get a pleasure of pleasure.

It decorporates, or, let's say dehumanizes or inhumanizes the body. It undoes this kind of beautiful harmony in which we live, which is the "silence of the organs" and it makes some noise, that's for sure. I can also see the extreme dangers of it all. "White Noise," for example, a torture developed at the Cologne-Ossendorf prison.[8] "White Noise" is also experimental psychology, studied by someone like Cage, for example. So I see very well that it is extremely dangerous but I also believe that we have to explore it.

A.P. There is another form of torture, the "snuff movie": torture to death filmed as a sequence for the privilege of a few "amateurs."

J.-F. L. That's possible only in conditions of impunity, but it's not enough to say that. There is a tremendous misconception in that direction: an anchoring, in fact, always a reference made to the organic body as a living body. One thinks that what is essential in all these operations is that they consist precisely in deconstructing the body. When it comes down to it, in effect, the absolute deconstruction of the body is Chinese torture as it is photographed, well ... taken up by Bataille; and it is actually Bataille's error to have believed that the intensity was in proportion to the cutting-up of the living human body and that this was necessary to go far. That's his reading of Sade and basically what remains of humanism in Bataille.

In experimental cinema, it is not a question of that at all. And when I said: the body must be decorporized or dehumanized, what is at stake in experimental cinema means in no way torturing it, lacerating it to death. It means transforming it, in the "Duchamp" sense, let's say, of transforming, in other words *making it conductive*—not for the audience, but for itself—*making it conductive* of unheard-of intensities, well, unseen, unpalpated, and so on. Burst the body by making—I'm thinking of music—by making the ear capable of receiving and transmitting to whom it may concern—but we don't know who that is, I mean: inside an organic body—sounds or sonic arrangements for which it isn't made. It's about making the eye capable of effectively recording and recomposing at will a material which it has never seen before and which in a certain way is invisible, and so on. It's not even a question of maximalization, it's a question of actually altering these kinds of small transformers, well connected both physiologically and culturally, which are, for example, the sensory organs; and when I say a work of decorporization, of alteration of the body; that's what I'm thinking of. Which is to say, really, how can I put it, to *extend* ... but the metaphor is very weak.

If we look then at the receiver of experimental cinema, the body of the receiver ... there is no *body*—and if we compare this to the receiver of the "snuff movie," the gap is enormous. What's happening with this person, either present at the shooting of this torture, or watching the film shot in these conditions? Nothing more and nothing less, in fact, than what a Western body is capable of perceiving. Both to endure and not to endure these things. It is not at all a true exteriority in relation to the Western body and what it touches. Whilst in this kind of experimental work, much more modest, more severe, more ascetic, there is really a work to de-Westernize the body. Of course, the body immediately becomes a Western body again: all that has come from experimental cinema, the difference in the nature of the images, of lighting, colors, framing, editing, assembling and which has been integrated for thirty years. But anyhow, that's the way it works, there is no doubt that it refines to an extraordinary extent, that it spreads out this body of sorts. The emotions of the "snuff movie," that's much more elementary, more gross, it's porn.

A.P. Experimental cinema uses an extraordinary profusion of documents, through which it squanders History for its own benefit. A very different stance from those of Vertov and Medvedkin, for instance. Does it not retreat from social conflicts in doing so?

J.-F. L. I know plenty of experimental works of cinema that are punctual explorations. Perhaps they don't display an obvious social character, in the sense of Vertov and his train's journey, but I believe it is there nonetheless.[9] I am thinking, for instance, of a film by Snow: *Wavelength*, that interminable camera movement which advances in an empty room and finally ends on an image hanging in the bedroom, which one wasn't even paying any attention to, an image of a wave.[10] It is an extraordinarily punctual work on the social fabric of that room. Because in spite of its being empty, it is incredible—that zoom, extremely slow and long that lasts I don't know, three quarters of an hour, populates the room.

A.P. These movements don't seem very compatible with the filmic work of production processes, of ideological antagonisms, within the social bond.

J.-F. L. There is an incompatibility here, simply because what is privileged in this case is the production process, as if it were of the very nature of the social bond, as if it were there that everything happens.

I have nothing against that, I am not in any way saying that it is false pure and simple, it is much more complicated than that. If the process of production is really the social bond itself, the place where it is woven, why should one have to come to it with everything gathered in the form of explorations, harvested from experimental cinema? Why would that be what makes the social bond visible? If the social bond is in the place of production, the only approach is the simplest.

A.P. A plus, that experimental cinema desires, is really a plus of attention, a presence.

J.-F. L. Precisely, it wants that plus of attention because it doesn't really know what the social bond is. What it is made of. And that perhaps, after all, the social bond is made up of a relationship between the value of this grey telephone and that of this grey typewriter and that, as a result, this little bit of something will have to be filmed with the utmost care, modifying the lighting, the shots, the focusing and so on. Personally, I think that the social bond is absolutely everything and absolutely nothing. In this relationship between the phone and the typewriter, there is at least as much social bond as if I were to photograph a worker on an assembly line...

The attention in question is a free-floating attention in Freud's sense. It can take an ideological aspect but in fact, I believe that that isn't the true function of experimental cinema. To the extent that it is didactic, it is bloody boring—like everything didactic. It takes you by the hand, it says, "Did you see, huh? Understood? OK!" Well that, no!... I'm thinking of those films on the windows and doors of a mountain chalet, made by Werner Nekes: it's not didactic in the least, simply the guy shoots whilst letting his attention hover.[11] There, at that moment, something happened. He notes it. He records it. He doesn't give us his image, his film, to teach us to see. I think it's a question for him. Let's say "OK, something is going on there." It's a very simple thing to say, but it's not more than that. Neither is it "Here is what's essential in the relation of people to things and with one another." And precisely, because it is very modest, very small, it is important! You said "presence," and I would rather say "absence," in a very positive, affirmative sense. As long as there is going to be presence—presence is like theft—, we will be reassured. We will say "OK, then, see, it's like a well framed image. I have there, in my sights, that telephone and that typewriter, truly an admirable grid system, suitable lighting, I can make you a great picture." But that is not what is at issue because what it is really going to do is give us presence, the presence of the social bond. It is going to give us the presence of the moment, the presence of men. As will the beautiful images of *The Family of Man*,[12] for instance, extraordinarily pedagogical, psychological. The images that will work in experimental cinema go instead in search of absence—of gaps. Not at all absence, in the sense of "we miss meaning, we are poor wretches, we have lost everything, etc."... the great romantic nostalgia of modernity; it is not that, but the impalpability of this bond.

A.P. The interest of experimental cinema is nonetheless this freedom given to reading...

J.-F. L.   Yes... maybe so. That's what was valued for a while. That was Butor's thesis on music, for instance, when he worked with Pousseur.[13] I'm not really convinced—and I believe that Butor isn't convinced at all any more—by the fact that the interesting thing is that one can draw one's way through a work... function somewhat like a computer that will open and close paths. It is not so much that which is interesting. What is interesting, is that one is going to be bored stiff all through the reading. And in the best cases, but that doesn't happen so often, this predicament of the reader will be compensated, so to speak. There will be extraordinary secondary benefits. All of a sudden, functions of words, chunks of sentences, bits of spaces, of the book or of the play one is dealing with, will effectively become very intense. So, it's more the aspect of adventure; rather what this gives you, what you can do with it. One is in a situation not of passivity but precisely of wavering, of limping [*claudication*].

A.P.   Why is it that there is no series with Duchamp?

J.-F. L.   Duchamp, it's very simple... what is it that he always wanted to represent? He wanted to "represent" the unrepresentable par excellence, the thing that is never there. That is, he wants to represent the bride stripped bare. The bride stripped bare is always too early or too late. She is still dressed or already naked. If she is still dressed it's too early, if she is already naked it's too late. So, he knows in advance that he will never be able to represent her. And that's what he's interested in. And in the end there are but two works *The Bride Stripped Bare* and *Given* which are in relation to one another, in a transformative relationship, and which speak of the same thing.[14] In *The Bride Stripped Bare*—well, in the *Large Glass* you never get to see the naked woman, so it's too early... and in *Given*, it's too late: she couldn't be any more naked and that's all you can see through the hole in the door.

Everything else in Duchamp is a work of research. Of true research. Whether in language, three-dimensional or two-dimensional objects or in music, all go in the same direction: trying to capture the instant and knowing all too well that it cannot be caught since that instant will always be missed. So, it completely corrects the idea of a series. If there is anything that reinforces the idea of a series, it is precisely the idea of the instant. It follows from the composition of the two ensembles that there will never be a present. So there will never be a re/presentation either, in the strict sense of *reproduction*. And, in the case of Duchamp, there will be no re/presentation because there is no presentation.

What he wants is to multiply—and this is where he is brilliant, obviously—to multiply the paradoxes. As with the moment of stripping taken as a function, as a model—it's not a model, actually: it's the horizon, the vanishing point of the whole work, the stripping—that instant, you can't even say that it's a one-off, as it's never there. In the temporalist ideology of presence, that instant doesn't exist. What this means, actually, is that operators and transformations that are as paradoxical as possible must be found, which, each in its own sphere, in its field, gives the equivalent of the paradox of the instant: of the not yet which is already past... which is the temporal paradox itself.

All the wordplay, all the puns, all the linguistic research, it's the same thing. They are linguistic paradoxes. Through disconnection of language level, for instance: phonemes are said in places where they shouldn't be in order to obtain paradoxical alterations of semantemes. The same thing is true, of course, for his work on perspective, which must be conceived, in keeping with his spirit, as a particular case of anamorphosis, and anamorphosis is also part of the transformations, and so on ... At the end of the day, perspective is an anamorphosis. It is always said that "anamorphoses are weird cases of perspective," but it is clear that, with Duchamp, things must be reversed and that he thinks of everything as anamorphosis, and thus of perspective itself as a special case.

A.P. The duration of a work depends on the elements involved, including the audience.

J.-F. L. There is no duration in the strict sense of the word *duration*, because he is in an overlap of sorts. On the side of the past, he's no longer there, so he's already gone and the future isn't here yet, so it's still to come, and the instant is effectively—that's in Aristotle—that impossible thing.

A.P. Yet the different elements of the work are indeed what, you could say, count/tell time.

J.-F. L. Let's take the *Large Glass*. I have tried several times to make a reading of it. That makes no sense, because it just doesn't end. There is the way of getting to the moment targeted by this composition, that of the stripping, the path which goes through the narratives that accompany the *Large Glass* ... because the *Large Glass* does tell something all the same: there is the bachelors' apparatus, there is the bride machine. There is a grand narrative that is subdivided into two, the bride's narrative and that of the bachelors. And then, on the side of the bachelors, there are other small narratives which don't enter into the grand narrative at all and whose purpose is completely unclear. All of this tells a story, a number of stories even. There are some very worrying little stories in there. One wonders what they are doing there. The story of the chocolate grinder ... one doesn't see very well how this connects to the whole ensemble ... because there is no chocolate ascending in the bride's part ... there is only gas ...

... So you take this route to enter the work, you are going to see that it very quickly becomes a kind of endless labyrinth. Next you take a route which would be a more plastic approach, a plastic analysis of the painting, same thing: there is an abundance, a profusion of plastic paradoxes. I don't say that it is inexhaustible, because that has no sense, but I believe that it isn't finished showing more yet.

These are only paradoxes. Some are obvious, one jumps on them with glee, but others are completely hidden, very subtle. What this means is that the reader of the picture, whether they take the narrative route or the plastic route—there are others, actually—is doomed to the not yet. It is not finished yet and, there, the work perfectly fulfils the function about which Duchamp says: "it's a delay." What is delayed is obvious: the moment of stripping. It's the stripping of the picture, it's the stripping of the woman by the eye and the stripping of the picture by the commentator, which is not done yet, nor will ever be, never.

You can talk about a duration of the reading, but that duration will stretch out, will become very long, and, in the eyes of Duchamp I assume that is the point of "painting." It is, indeed, to defy all commentary.

In the case of *Given*, i.e., the second room in Philadelphia, the procedure is reversed. You walk in. There's a hidden recess. You enter into the recess, there is nothing. There is some kind of old wooden door, Spanish. You don't know that it's Spanish. It's a wooden door. I've seen people pass by, they see a door, they say "OK, it's a room that's not finished..." and they leave. And those who are a little better informed know that there are two holes in the door and that you have to put your eyes to the holes and there you discover the completely shaven vulva of a woman exposed through a broken brick wall set against a landscape background (... mill, waterfall, woods, gaslight). And there, it is too late. You are trapped. There, that's it, you have seen. Not the *stripping* but the stripped. It's the same thing, the same operation as in the previous case: paradox in a case that is the not yet and, in the second, the already over.

A.P. "Not yet," "already over," it's a question of speed...

J.-F. L. One is never in sync with the thing one speaks about, thinks about, paints, looks at. And precisely, the point of doing all this is not to get synchronized but on the contrary to multiply the paradoxes in order to render the speed. The speed of the stripping, for instance. So you see, one can accelerate, decelerate...

A.P. To use one of your expressions, does the "belly laugh" a lot with Duchamp?

J.-F. L. I don't know why I said *belly*. It was about paintings by René Guiffrey. But I think there was a connotation of ventriloquism, of dissociation. It is in the very nature of this kind of work to fascinate you. At the level of "OK, so this has to be commented on," and seriousness takes over, you start your little semiotic, psychoanalytic analyses ... But, at the same time it makes the belly laugh. If your belly doesn't laugh, truth be told, you have missed everything. Any work is always an attempt to solve a tiny problem—which is always an enormous problem—of messing with materials, color, etc. and that you can understand, it's intelligible, and then you have your working notes. But, at the same time, there is always something else that makes you say "Ah, the bastard, son of a bitch!" Our claudication has thus begun already. I don't say that the belly is always right, but I do say that if there isn't this kind of a gap, of limping, the commentary will be poor. It's quite obvious with Klee.

Do you know that Klee danced? A musician, I can't remember who, lived underneath his studio. He heard a tremendous commotion in Klee's studio. He walked up and said: "What's going on, I heard noise which sounded as though someone were pacing your studio." Klee replied: "Please forgive me, but when I paint, I sometimes dance," and he added: "I never dance otherwise." Lame dancing, the works' humor.

A.P. What do you mean by asceticism?

J.-F. L. For someone like Duchamp, asceticism is an absolutely constant and systematic effort to dehumanize oneself against the cultural profile that one has been imprinted with. If the objective is to refine and multiply transformations, someone who sets themselves this task clearly has as a counter-condition a terrible asceticism.

Because if they content themselves with less, they are obviously going to give only what they have, and they really have nothing to give, only to give back. They have been on the receiving end. So they are not going to experiment with anything.

Example of asceticism: Cézanne puts his little pack on his back, goes into the mountains and sits for three hours, gazing at Mont Sainte-Victoire. Peasants who pass by say to him "Monsieur Cézanne, are you all right, is there anything wrong?" Three hours without moving. So that is an explicit, obvious asceticism. That's what I think of when I am told of asceticism. Or in the sense that there is a Sadean asceticism, it's the same thing.

A.P. But staying still doesn't imply "clearing the mind" here, does it?

J.-F. L. Not at all. He is looking for transformation. In other words, the disruption of vision. "Derangement" in relation to the "good view" of the Western eye,[15] focused, ordered, framed, derangement such as it can give the lines, values and colors of something entirely transformed starting from the good image of Sainte-Victoire.

A.P. So you find the Buddhist notion of clearing the mind to be limited, for a Westerner.

J.-F. L. It seems borderline to me. What they mean by that is understandable. Because actually it's to make oneself a *conductive body*.

A.P. Clear the mind, to see what impresses the body.

J.-F. L. Yes, in that sense, I see very well that we need something like that, like emptiness. But I abhor all the mystical salad that Westerners dress up around it. What concerns us more is to identify social connections, between objects, which escape our usual perceptions, precisely not obvious and not present.

A.P. Today, in the field of criticism, this usage of eastern ideas thus seems to you a palliative for the disappearance of theory...

J.-F. L. But theory has not disappeared. On the contrary, theories must be multiplied. If we say "let's destroy theory," we go back to being as terrorist as the theorists. Theory is a genre, or a language game, I don't see why it shouldn't exist like the others.

A.P. There is, however, one aspect of theory which means that as soon as it is developed...

J.-F. L. ... we believe in it. That's where, first of all, the plural is important. It's also where Cézanne's three hours of posture in front of his mountain are very important. Eagerness to believe is clearly what we are dealing with. Eagerness to believe or eagerness to convince. To believe on the side of the addressee, to convince on the side of the addresser. That must be overcome. We have to be able to take theories as language games.

A. P.   In Wittgenstein's sense?

J.-F. L.   Absolutely, in fact Wittgenstein mentions it among the language games.
... Furthermore, as far as I know, no artist has ever presented anything to a public with the idea that the purpose of their work was to make artists of those who would look at them. It is in the nature of theory to ensure that those who hear, read, receive it, subsequently broadcast it. The disciple must become a master. And there I find the Buddhists again, because on this the Buddhists are positive: certainly not! You know ... old story.

A. P.   Can you conceive of a self-directed communication?

J.-F. L.   It seems to me that I am very much in favor of self-directed communication, since that is what I do, three hours a week at Vincennes.[16] They give me the floor and for three hours I declare everything I think. The important thing is that the conveyance of these messages, be they linguistic or plastic or whatever, is always accompanied by the language game clause. That is all I ask. In other words, basically, that the theorist or politicist know that they speak like an artist, that they do it like an artist. I don't know whether it's possible, but I believe that it's an issue which is now being raised.

A. P.   What about representativity, in the sense of the State?

J.-F. L.   Representativity, in the sense of the State, belongs absolutely to the plastic, geometric, classical sphere. The question is: can you conceive of modern societies that would not be mediated by a representative which is the State or anything of that sort ... Whether this State appears as a kind of monster controlling all civil authority, or whether it is internalized by everyone, as would be the case, in my opinion, for self-governance, which in fact requires that each one of us be citizen, minister and judge at the same time: that would really be torture. Can we conceive of a shift to minorities. A general state of civil society where minorities would be in fluctuating relations to one another in the sense of a fluctuating rate of currency. That's to say subject to permanent negotiations. Exchanges and contracts, plural, not singular, and contracts which could always be revised, and never the Social Contract once and for all.

No need for politics as a separate activity. For example, the people who make alternative radio in Italy or France, for instance, are politicists in this sense. They broadcast and disclose information.

A. P.   Isn't it inevitable that, at some point, this institutionalization of exchanges would reappear?

J.-F. L.   Disrespect theorists and belly laugh when you see theory. Use humor. It is our protection against terror. Humor is pagan because it knows very well that the hunter is at any moment also the hunted. When Actaeon chases Diana, until he sees her naked— what a mistake—he is transformed into a stag. In other words, the hunter becomes the hunted. Well, this reversal of the point of view carries a Pascalian name, it's humor. That's what makes all pagans laugh.

A.P. The exchange system assumes that we are able to give ourselves the materials we need anytime we need them.

J.-F. L. We have to get to that. We have to be artists.

A.P. Two situations: At the International Conference on Psychoanalysis, Winter '77, Conference on Dissent, it seemed obvious that the set-up, the place and the papers, made any dissent impossible, whether of language, gestures, or research. One could have made an immediate, "pre-analytic" critique, merely by looking at the staging of the theoretical institutions.

And the second one, the occupation of *Libération*. Occupation caused by the fact, among others, that they had printed "*Bande à Baader*" [Baader gang] instead of "*Fraction Armée Rouge*" [Red Army Faction]. A lack of distanciation that made them reproduce the information delivered by teletypewriters...

J.-F. L. There is a problem of composure in speed. That's where you need this asceticism and equanimity. Where you have to create habits that are very complex. Cohn-Bendit at Nanterre, in '68, was prodigious on that account.[17] He was brilliantly composed in the speed of interpreting situations. In other words, he received information similar to that and if the equivalent of "*Bande à Baader*" had been submitted to him, it would not have worked. And there you could see that the transformer was intact in weariness, in noise, always clear as crystal.

A.P. Which implies that I know my place as well as yours.

J.-F. L. Yes, that's true. In particular, there is that aspect. Among the transformations, the fact that you and I cannot be substituted is very important. Fundamental, even. That's one of the things that is forgotten in the themes of democracy, autonomy, equality ... While non-substitutability is also one of the things to rediscover.

A.P. Doesn't the devil's advocate run the risk of no longer being believed?

J.-F. L. Absolutely, that's what is at risk. Still, perhaps that's precisely what is needed, to no longer bring about conviction but to arouse a secondary interest, or I know not what, which consists in appreciating the beauty or the strength of one's production, one's commentary if one is a writer or a critic, of a pictorial oeuvre if one is a painter ... instead of eliciting conviction. So, by playing the devil's advocate, one is doing a good job because one doesn't aim to convince those who are listening or watching, but rather to enter into a pagan relationship with the object that the devil's advocate proposes. That is, a relationship of both aesthetic or ethical appreciation and a dissembling relationship. Both of agreement and mistrust, and that it elicits in those who hear the devil's advocate's proposal the question "What am I going to do with it" rather than "Do I believe it or don't I?"

Or, finally, will we side to the end with the little people, living and thinking day by day, assured of nothing because mastering nothing, yet invoking no higher authority, be it Law or Name, to relinquish the "insignificant" realities, to devalue them by representing other more noble, more real things or turning them into pure voids of sense? Shall we concern ourselves only with affirming forces where there is no sign to point to them, where there is no master to establish these signs? Shall we neither say that the representation is insincere, the scenario pure fiction, the actors buffoons, nor that the spectators are asleep, chained up, lunatic; that we have come to announce what the one and the others are lacking, making marks with whatever we have at hand, distinctive marks each time like so many proper names, distracted, neglected tensions. The weapon on the side of little people is ruse, the only machine capable of making the weakest the strongest. Ruse has humor as its accomplice.[18]

—Lyotard, "Humor in Semiotheology"

I can never judge of the same thing exactly in the same way. I cannot judge of my work, while doing it. I must do as the artists, stand at a distance, but not too far. How far, then? Guess.[19]

—Pascal, *Pensée* 114, 1670

Notes

1 ['Interview with Jean-François Lyotard" *Art Présent*, no. 8 (Spring 1979), 3–11. The present title is taken from Sigmund Freud, "Beyond the Pleasure Principle," *The Standard Edition of the Complete Psychological Works of Sigmund Freud*, tr. and ed. James Strachey, XVIII (London: Hogarth, 1955; London: Vintage, 2001), 64; this title was used for the German publication of the interview in *Jean-François Lyotard Philosophie und Malerei im Zeitalter iheres Experimentierens* (Berlin: Merve Verlag, 1986), 25–49.—Trans.]

2 [Whilst the French term *la claudication* has some current usage as a medical term, the equivalent in English is less familiar: "claudication" is a condition which can cause limping. "Intermittent claudication is a cramping pain that limits walking ability. It may be neurogenic or vascular ... Claudication most commonly affects the calf muscle." Michael Kent, *The Oxford Dictionary of Sports Science & Medicine*, 3rd ed. (Oxford: Oxford University Press, 2006), 116.—Trans.]

3 Jean François Lyotard, "Apathy in Theory," *Rudiments païens* (Paris, UGE, 10/18, 1977), [tr. Roger McKeon, in this volume, 147—Eds.]

4 [See n. 2 above—Eds.]

5 [Not an exact transcription from Beckett; see Samuel Beckett, *Watt* (New York: Grove, 1953), 30, and the French edition *Watt*, tr. Ludovic and Agnès Janvier (Paris: Minuit, 1968), 31–2.—Trans.]

6 [*Phenomenology of Perception* by Maurice Merleau-Ponty was first published in French in 1945; it has been commented on by Lyotard in several works, including *Phenomenology* [1954] (1991) and *Discourse, Figure* [1971] (2011).—Trans.]

7 [Founded by a group of artists including Steina and Woody Vasulka in 1971 as part of the Mercer Arts Centre, *The Kitchen* moved to SoHo in 1973 where its program of

experimental film and video, performance, music, and dance was accompanied by a video distribution network from 1974.—Trans.]
8 [Members of the armed left-wing guerrilla group Red Army Faction, including co-founder Ulrike Meinhof, were incarcerated in solitary confinement at Cologne-Ossendorf Prison from 1971; in the "dead wing" sounds and external visual stimuli were minimized or removed, to create a site of sensory deprivation including acoustic isolation, known as the "silent section."—Trans.]
9 [*Man with a Movie Camera* directed by Dzirga Vertov (VUFKU, 1929), 35 mm, black and white, silent, 1 hr 8 min.—Trans.]
10 [*Wavelength* directed by Michael Snow (1967), 16 mm, color, 45 min.—Trans.]
11 [*Diwan* (Part 5: Hynningen) directed by Werner Nekes, 1973, 16 mm, color, 85 min.—Trans.]
12 [*The Family of Man* was a photography exhibition organized by Edward Steichen at New York's Museum of Modern Art in 1955. Taking the form of a photo essay comprised of 503 photo panels and 50 text panels, it toured the world for eight years.—Trans.]
13 [The writer Michel Butor collaborated with composer Henri Pousseur from 1960 to 1968, resulting in the experimental opera *Votre Faust*, first performed in 1969. Determined in part by audience involvement, *Votre Faust* consists of a variable, aleatory structure with reflexive commentary on the traditions of the genre, incorporating elements of collage and quotation.—Trans.]
14 [Marcel Duchamp *La mariée mise à nu par ses célibataires, même* (Le Grand Verre) [*The Bride Stripped Bare by Her Bachelors, Even* (The Large Glass)], 1915–23, oil, varnish, lead foil, lead wire, and dust on two glass panels, 277.5 × 177.8 × 8.6 cm. *Étant donnés: 1° la chute d'eau, 2° le gaz d'éclairage . . .* [*Given: 1. The Waterfall, 2. The Illuminating Gas . . .*] 1946–66, mixed media assemblage, 242 x 1778 x 124 cm. Both works are in the Philadelphia Museum of Art.—Trans.]
15 [See Arthur Rimbaud, "Lettre à Paul Demeny" [15 mai 1871], *Œuvres Complètes* (Paris, Gallimard, La pléiade, 1972), 251. "*Je dis qu'il faut être voyant, se faire voyant. Le poète se fait voyant par un long, immense et raisonné dérèglement de tous les sens.*"
  Arthur Rimbaud, "Letter to Paul Demeny" in *"I Promise to be Good: The letters of Arthur Rimbaud, Volume II*, tr. and ed. Wyatt Mason (New York: Random House, 2007), 33. "I mean that you have to be a *seer*, mold oneself into a seer. The Poet makes himself a *seer* by a long, involved, and logical *derangement of all the senses.*"—Trans.]
16 [Vincennes refers to the University of Paris 8, where Lyotard taught in the philosophy department from 1970 to 1987; the university was relocated from the site at Vincennes to St-Denis in 1980.—Trans.]
17 [Daniel Cohn-Bendit was an influential, unofficial student leader during the uprising, strikes, and protests of 1968, which began in March at the University of Paris campus at Nanterre, where Lyotard was teaching at the time. Known as "Danny le Rouge," Cohn-Bendit featured prominently in the media as a voice of the activists and his expulsion from France, as a West German national, in late May led to further media attention.—Trans.]
18 Jean-François Lyotard, "Humour in Semiotheology," *Rudiments païens* (Paris: UGE, 10/18, 1977; Paris: Klincksieck, 2001), 42. [Translation by Roger McKeon.—Eds.]
19 Blaise Pascal, *Pensées*, "Thought 114" [1670], tr. W. F. Trotter (New York: Dutton, 1958).

Part Three

Why Art Practice?

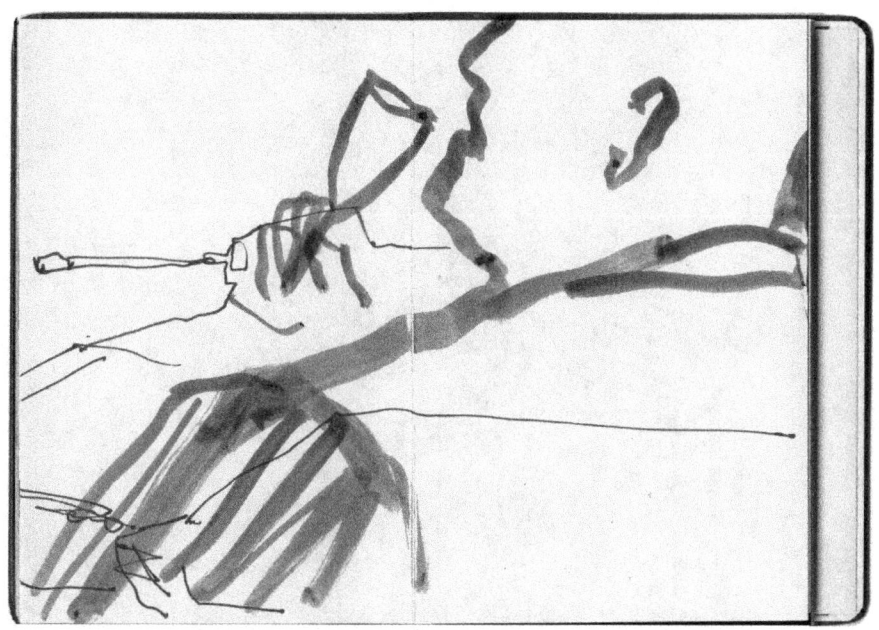

Figure 13.1 Jill Gibbon, Eurosatory, Paris, 2018, ink on paper, 140 mm × 192 mm.

Figure 13.2 Jill Gibbon, DSEI, London, 2017, ink on paper, 140 mm × 192 mm.

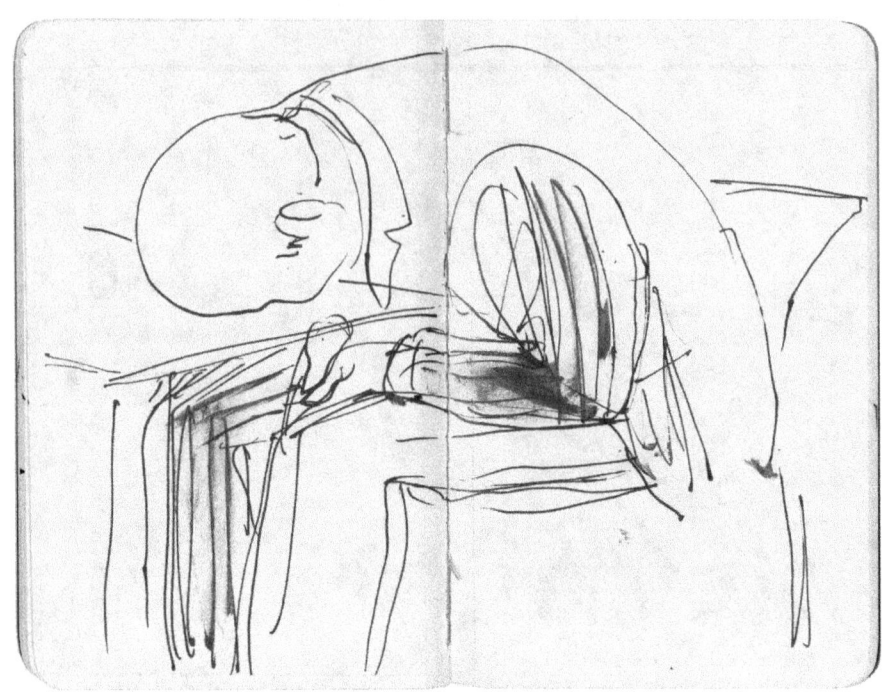

Figure 13.3 Jill Gibbon, Milipol, Paris, 2019, ink on paper, 140 mm × 180 mm.

Figure 13.4 Jill Gibbon, DSEI, London, 2017, ink on paper, 140 mm × 180 mm.

13

Mute Communication: Drawing the Military-Industrial Complex

Jill Gibbon

We buried them the same day because they had turned into severed limbs. There were no corpses left to examine. The flesh of this person was mixed with that person. They were wrapped up [with blankets] and taken away.
—A relative of the al-Kindi family[1]

You are informed that human beings endowed with language were placed in a situation such that none of them is now able to tell about it. Most of them disappeared then, and the survivors rarely speak about it. When they do speak about it, their testimony bears only upon a minute part of this situation. How can you know that the situation itself existed?
—Lyotard, The Differend §1[2]

It is a warm September morning in London, Docklands. I am wearing a suit, pearls, paint peeling off in places, heels, and a lanyard bearing a fake company name. I am sweating, whether from fear or the heat I am not sure. The badge allows me into DSEI, the Defence and Security Equipment International, the world's largest arms fair. In the distance, on the other side of the railway lines, someone is shouting about Saudi airstrikes on Yemen but they are held back by police barricades. A line of security guards bow as I arrive. DSEI is a polite event.

DSEI takes place every two years, offering an international meeting place for the globalized military-industrial complex. Inside are ballistic missiles, cruise missiles, air to surface missiles, surface to air missiles, guided bombs, unguided bombs, bombers, fighter jets, attack helicopters, stealth helicopters, pistols, assault rifles, sniper weapons, machine guns, submachine guns, bullets, tanks, tank ammunition, anti-tank ammunition, rocket launchers, armored personnel carriers, infantry fighting vehicles, surveillance cameras, surveillance drones, attack drones, grenades, grenade launchers, tear gas, gas masks, pepper spray, batons, boots, gloves, helmets, daggers, and more. All of the multinational arms corporations are here—BAE Systems, Boeing, General Dynamics, L3 Harris Technologies, Leonardo, Lockheed Martin, MBDA, Northrop Grumman, Raytheon, and Thales—each taking up a vast section of the event. There are also multinationals not known for arms production like Rolls Royce, Land Rover, and Du Pont who produce components of weapons—engines, gears, fabrics, nuts, bolts, computers, and cameras. And there are smaller companies with their own ranges of guns and tear gas. Here, sales staff mingle with government ministers, contractors, brokers, dictators, and despots.

President Eisenhower coined the phrase "military-industrial complex" in 1961 to describe a network of alliances between the arms industry, military, and state with a vested interest in weapons production, and growing influence over government policy. Since then the military-industrial complex has grown as part of wider processes of globalization becoming "more varied, more internationally linked and less visible."[3] Arms companies have merged into multinationals, diversified into security, and focused on international sales often to repressive regimes, undermining Western justifications for arms production as defending abstract values of freedom, justice, and democracy. BAE Systems, Raytheon, and MBDA have sold bombs, missiles, and fighter jets to Saudi Arabia which have been used in the war in Yemen where thousands of civilians have been killed in Saudi airstrikes.[4] Meanwhile UK-made tear gas, pepper spray, and surveillance equipment has been used around the world to suppress pro-democracy movements.[5] Instead of containing the global expansion of the arms industry, the UK and US governments have facilitated it, brokering international deals, encouraging permissive use of export regulations, and protecting arms companies from legal scrutiny.[6] John Berger summed up the role of the state in this new setting:

> National states in general have been politically downsized and reduced to the role of vassals serving the new world economic order. The visionary political vocabulary of three centuries has been garbaged. In short, the economic and military global tyranny of today has been established.[7]

I started visiting DSEI to draw the military-industrial complex, in an attempt to make visible the "economic and military global tyranny" that Berger describes.[8] I soon realized this was impossible: the military-industrial complex may meet at DSEI, but it is hidden behind a polite corporate façade. The word corporation stems from *corpus*, the Latin for body. With a lanyard around their necks and logo glowing overhead, arms company executives, supervisors, managers, and sales reps speak, act, and dress as part of the body of the corporation. Biological bodies are coiffured, sculpted, powdered, and choreographed. They wear immaculate suits, point to weapons with manicured hands, adopt amenable expressions, and speak phrases from the sales catalog.

> The organic body is a *body-politic*, in the sense of the term within political economy. It is endowed with limits which circumscribe the *propriety* of its own body; it is affected by a *regime* or a *ruling* (*régie*) which is its constitutional system. Every investment of a zone of this body that does not conform to this rule is registered as a rebellion, a sickness, as anarchy and threatens the death of the whole. The interest of the whole serves to authorise its repression. In fact, the organic body is the incessant product (a product which must be constantly produced) of operations,

manipulations, excisions, separations and conflation, grafts, occlusions and derivations, running across the labyrinthine libidinal band.[9]

Ideals previously used to justify imperialist wars are used here as attributes of brands, available to any regime who is a client. MBDA has a string of slogans running around its stand promising progress and mastery: "turning innovation into reality," "mastering technology," "championing customer sovereignty."[10] These values are also conveyed through the design of the stand, with missiles presented like sculpture—dramatically lit against white walls and standing on plush carpet. A bomb is split open to show a perfectly crafted interior. There are white orchids on the reception desk, and waiting staff offering trays of avocado, prosciutto, and brie on small slices of artisan bread.

Aesthetics is the mode taken by a civilization that has been deserted by its ideals. It cultivates the pleasure of representing them. And so it calls itself culture.[11]

On a neighboring stand, a Paveway laser-guided bomb is suspended beneath a red Raytheon sign, the logo the same color as the tip of the bomb. A video screen shows the skylines of London and San Francisco at sunset. A rep explains that the Paveway project is the result of UK and US cooperation: it has "revolutionised tactical air-to-ground warfare, converting 'dumb' bombs into precision-guided munitions." He opens a catalog showing a bomb dropping through a pure blue sky. There are no images of what happens next when the bomb hits homes and flesh.

We have many words to gloss the aestheticization inherent to culture: staging, spectacularization, mediatization, simulation, hegemony of artifacts, generalized mimesis, hedonism, narcissism, self-referentialism, auto-affection, auto-construction, and others. They all speak to the loss of objects and the ascendancy of the imaginary over reality. You can take an inventory of this gentle deception in every field of activity and thought: the "human sciences" can speak forever on this subject.[12]

Three months earlier a 500-pound Raytheon Paveway II bomb was used in a Saudi Arabian airstrike on Warzan, a village in Yemen, killing six members of the al-Kindi family. The testimony which opened this chapter was given by a relative of these victims. The attack killed Abdelqawi Abdu Ahmed al-Kindi (aged 62), his wife Hayat Abdu Seif Mohamed (50), their two children—Ahmed Abdelqawi Abdu Ahmed al-Kindi (28) and Hussein Abdelqawi Abdu Ahmed al-Kindi (12), and their grandchildren—Hamza Abdelqawi Abdu Ahmed al-Kindi (9) and Ayman Ali Abdelqawi Abdu Ahmed al-Kindi (6). Abdelqawi and his son Ahmed had worked as construction contractors; according to neighbors, the family had no military involvement.[13] But this cannot be spoken of here. At DSEI, a bomb is a clean, new product, its eventual use irrelevant. Even so, the marketing does not quite disguise the material properties of the weapons. The missiles loom over the aisles, throwing the carpets, flowers, and napkins into shadow. Guns are available to lift, aim, and to try for weight and size. Tank tracks tower overhead. Weapons may be presented as products, but the power to stalk, aim, hit, crush, and annihilate is everywhere.

It is as difficult to draw the weapons as it is to draw the military-industrial complex. How to draw a bulldozer with a shovel so large it can demolish a house, a drone so small it resembles an insect? How to convey the destructive power of a missile, or a bullet? It is not possible, but I keep coming back. There is something seductive about this place, on the clean side of weapons, courted with wine and avocado. Yet it is my body that gives away the conflict—I smile when I am offered a drink, but feel too nauseous to finish it. I have no reason to be here: my suit and business are a sham. My hands shake when a security guard approaches. I draw to appear busy and as I draw, I notice similar reactions around me. Sales staff may be employed to act as the body of the corporation, but their own bodies rebel. The corporate choreography is undercut by gestures conveying unease, duplicity, despair. A rep slumps his head on a desk. A manager staggers, anesthetized with wine. At times there is something stronger—an undercurrent of violence stirred and validated by the weapons. A client surveys waiting staff like merchandise. They flinch as he advances.

"Feeling is a phrase. I call it the affect-phrase. It is distinct in that it is *unarticulated*."[14] Impolite feelings cannot be spoken at DSEI but they are communicated, mutely. The body sweats, blushes, sickens, it shudders, swells, and shrinks. "This mute communication is made up of non-discrete inspirations and expirations of air: growlings, pantings, sighs. It spreads over the face and it spreads through the whole body which thus 'signals' like a face."[15] Such expressions of feeling disrupt the polite veneer of the event: "within the order of discourse the affect-phrase is inopportune, unseemly, and even disquieting."[16] What is repressed here—the brute violence of the weapons, the horror of their effects—haunts the bodies of the attendees. A sales rep tenses his jaw and shuts his eyes, as if to banish an unwelcome thought. An arms trader bows to a client, but his expression is deadened. Can drawing convey symptoms of repression, before they are also repressed? Drawing is itself a form of mute communication. It is gestural, visceral, guided by the hand, guts, eye, and pen as much as the mind. When I despair at the impossibility of drawing at DSEI, the lines seem to take over the process of drawing themselves, tracking the movements of people around me. The drawings also record my own unease; they are smudged, awkward, and interrupted. Produced by the body, drawing hovers on the border between the cultural and animal. Like the gestures they record, the marks are both learned and spontaneous. As Lyotard writes of the act of drawing, in a section of *Postmodern Fables* under the title "Crypts":

> By drawing the line of a threshold, art distinguishes itself from symptom. The eye that paints by the sooty torchlight in Lascaux removes the colors from the bright daylight in which they give themselves straightforwardly. He banishes them and calls on them to return transmuted. This refractive gesture traces a bordering.[17]

Both drawing and the military-industrial complex are based on observation, but of very different kinds. Modern weapons use cameras, telescopic sight systems, video, infrared optical sensors, radar, laser gyroscopes, and GPS to see with scientific precision. Raytheon promises "Technologies that see further, process data faster and precisely guide interceptors to targets."[18] A military drone hovers like the invisible eye of God, seeing everything below it, while remaining itself unseen.[19] Drawing is much more rudimentary, constrained by the limits of the human body. Whereas a weaponized drone records everything, a drawing begins with a blank page, the hand picking out fragments of a scene. The process of editing is sensed rather than reasoned. Whereas a weaponized drone focuses outside itself, identifying targets (in the ultimate act of othering), a drawing is entangled with what is drawn. It is a "refractive gesture," interpreted and performed by the body.[20] A drawing is always tentative, a sketchbook drawing particularly so, a fleeting record, with earlier drawings from previous pages dimly showing through. "What is played out is the mutation of sight into vision and appearance into apparition. Apparition is appearance stamped with the seal of its disappearance. Art puts death's insignia on the sensible."[21]

The corporate façade is soon restored. The rep rearranges his tie; the manager regains her balance. I accept a catalog, wince at my complicity, and walk on.

You can't make a political "program" with it, but you can bear witness to it.
—Lyotard, *The Differend* §264.[22]

Notes

1   Quoted in Amnesty International (2019), Press Release, September 26, 2019. Available online: https://www.amnesty.org.uk/press-releases/yemen-entire-family-killed-us-supplied-bomb-new-findings (accessed September 15, 2020).

2   Jean-François Lyotard, *The Differend*, tr. Georges Van Den Abbeele (Minneapolis MN: University of Minnesota Press, [1983] 1988), 3. Copyright 1988 by the Regents of the University of Minnesota. Originally published in *Le Différend*. Copyright 1983 by Les Éditions de Minuit.

3   J. Paul Dunne, and Elisabeth Sköns, "The Military Industrial Complex," in Andrew T. H. Tan (ed.), *The Global Arms Trade Handbook* (London and New York: Routledge, 2010), 291.

4   See Rob Evans, "BAE Systems Secretly Sold Mass Surveillance Technology to Repressive Regimes," *The Guardian*, June 5, 2017. Available online: https://www.theguardian.com/business/2017/jun/15/bae-mass-surveillance-technology-repressive-regimes (accessed September 15, 2020); Dan Sabbagh, "BAE Systems Sold £15 Billion Worth of Arms to Saudis During Yemen Assault," *The Guardian*, April 14, 2020. Available online: https://www.theguardian.com/business/2020/apr/14/bae-systems-sold-15bn-arms-to-saudis-during-yemen-assault (accessed September 15, 2020); Ruhan Nagra and Brynne O'Neal, "Day of Judgement: The Role of the US and Europe in Civilian Death, Destruction, and Trauma in Yemen," ed. James L. Cavallaro (Mwatana for Human Rights, University Network for Human Rights, and Pax for Peace, 2019). Available online: https://mwatana.org/en/day-of-judgment/ (accessed December 10, 2020).

5   See Lloyd Russell-Moyle, "Our Government's sale of powerful surveillance equipment to repressive regimes jeopardises more than human rights" *The Guardian*, March 7, 2018. Available online: https://www.independent.co.uk/voices/uk-government-surveillance-equipment-repressive-saudi-arabia-bahrain-egypt-a8240981.html (accessed September 15, 2020); Jon Stone, "UK supplies human rights abusers with

tear gas, rubber bullets and riot gear" *The Independent*, June 21, 2020. Available online: https://www.independent.co.uk/news/uk/politics/uk-rubber-bullets-tear-gas-protests-saudi-arabia-uae-a9574091.html (accessed September 15, 2020).
6 Sam Perlo-Freeman, "The United Kingdom arms industry in a globalized world," in Andrew T. H. Tan (ed.), *The Global Arms Trade Handbook* (London and New York: Routledge, 2010), 261.
7 John Berger, *Hold Everything Dear: Dispatches on Survival* (London and New York: Verso, 2016), 1.
8 Ibid.
9 Jean-François Lyotard, "A Short Libidinal Economy of a Narrative Set-up: The Renault Corporation Relates the Death of Pierre Overney" [1973], tr. Keith Crome and Mark Sinclair in James Williams and Keith Crome (eds), *The Lyotard Reader and Guide* (Edinburgh University Press: Edinburgh, 2006), 205–6.
10 MBDA. (2020), *About Us*, [online] https://www.mbda-systems.com/about-us/ (accessed September 15, 2020).
11 Jean-François Lyotard, *Postmodern Fables*, tr. Georges Van Den Abbeele (Minneapolis MN: University of Minnesota Press, [1993] 1997), 235.
12 Ibid., 236.
13 Amnesty International (2019), Press Release, September 26, 2019
14 Jean-François Lyotard, "The Affect-phrase" in this volume, 67.
15 Ibid, 71.
16 Ibid, 69.
17 Lyotard, *Postmodern Fables*, 246–7.
18 Raytheon, "Missile Defense." Available online: https://www.raytheonmissilesanddefense.com
19 See Grégoire Chamayou, *Drone Theory*, tr. Janet Lloyd (London: Penguin, 2015).
20 Lyotard, *Postmodern Fables*, 247.
21 Ibid., 246.
22 Lyotard, *The Differend*, 181.

Mute Communication: Drawing the Military-Industrial Complex 175

Figure 13.5 Jill Gibbon, Eurosatory, Paris, 2018, ink on paper, 140 mm × 192 mm

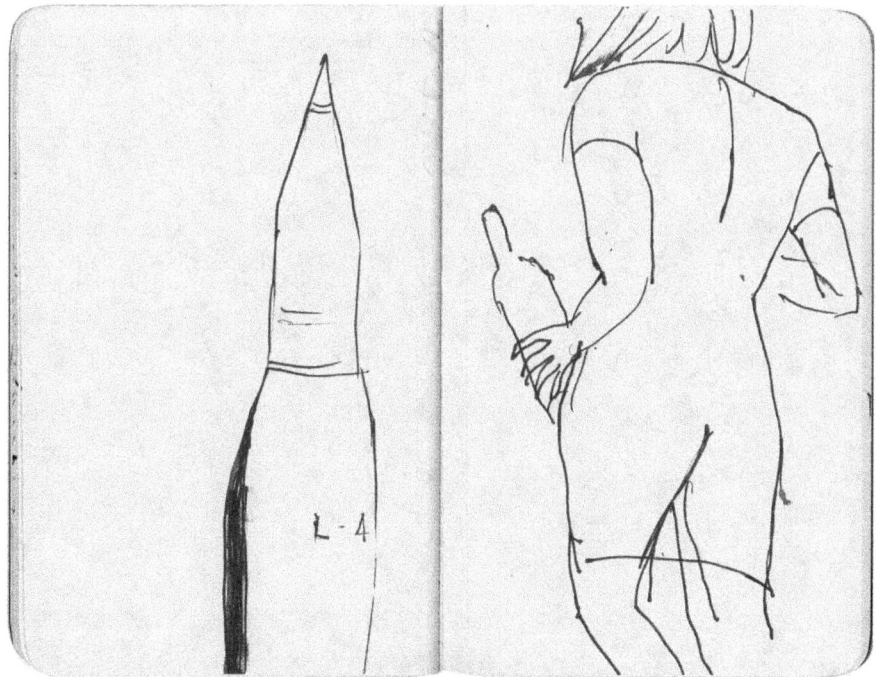

Figure 13.6 Jill Gibbon, Eurosatory, Paris, 2018, ink on paper, 140 mm × 180 mm

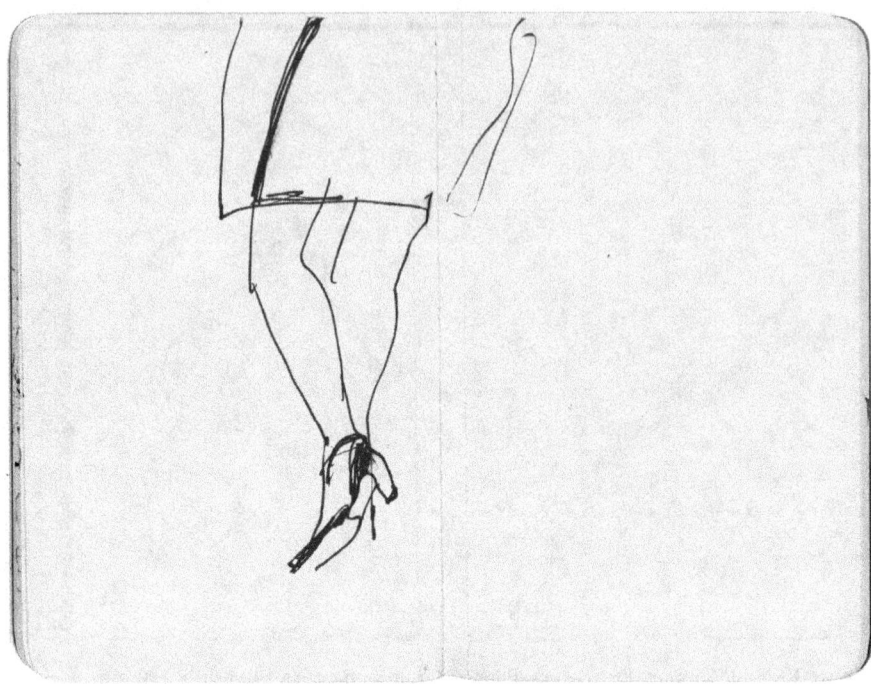

Figure 13.7 Jill Gibbon, Milipol, Paris, 2019, ink on paper, 140 mm × 180 mm.

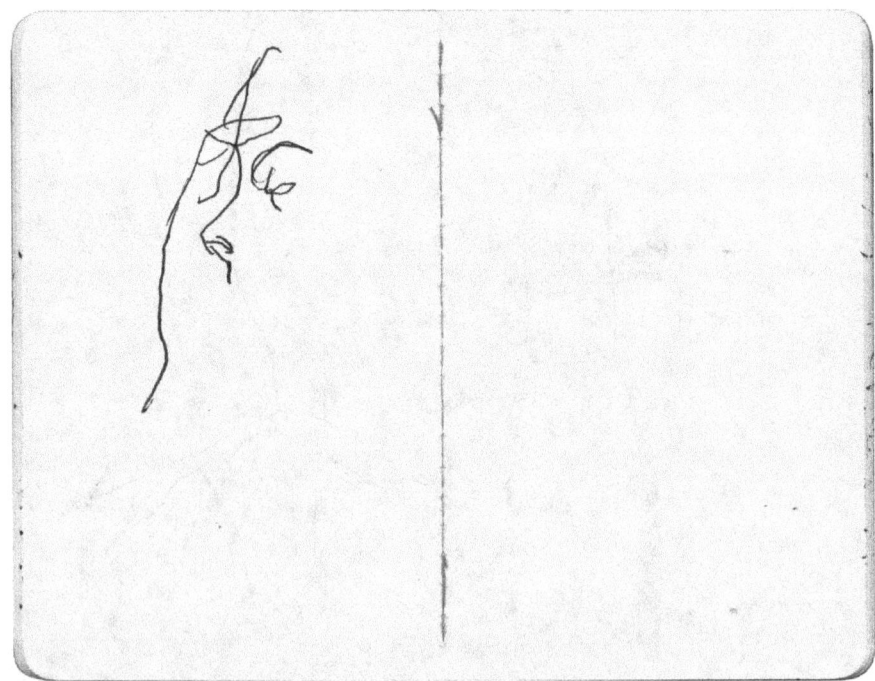

Figure 13.8 Jill Gibbon, Milipol, Paris, 2019, ink on paper, 140 mm × 180 mm.

14

Critical Practice and Affirmative Aesthetics

Ashley Woodward

Negating Lyotard

A number of contemporary scholars have attempted to negate Lyotard's philosophy of art and its potential legacy today. Of those who have managed to do so with some success, the most prominent is Jacques Rancière.[1] Through many writings, Rancière has constructed an image of Lyotard as a melancholy thinker who makes of art nothing but a perpetual mourning for the failed dreams of emancipation, a testimony to the impossibility of such hopes and a reminder and warning against it. Lyotard's philosophy of art is thus construed as a kind of reversal of earlier avant-garde traditions. According to Rancière, Lyotard thereby undermines all art's positive political potential. Yet this image is precisely that: a *construct*, which depends upon a very *selective* reading of Lyotard's texts.[2]

As such a construction, Rancière's Lyotard is not without its brilliance, not without some insight, but it is a fantastic distortion. I do not, however, wish to dwell on his interpretation and its problems here.[3] Instead, I want to construct an alternative image of Lyotard, by selecting different texts and ideas—ones which are not reconcilable with Rancière's image, and which invite a radically different assessment of Lyotard's contemporary relevance.

In contrast to Rancière's Lyotard, for whom art can only *negate* the dreams of emancipation, this Lyotard understands art as entirely *affirmative*. This Lyotard develops a deep reflection on how art practice—understood as a positive practice of invention and transformation—continues to be politically efficacious, and vitally relevant to the social good.

Affirmation and critique

This volume is framed in terms of *critical* practice, but I want to say something about *affirmative* art and aesthetics. Is there a conflict here? Lyotard marked a distinction between critique, or the "critical function," of works of art, and an understanding of art as *affirmative* in his own transition from the former to the later point of view in the early 1970s:

> By putting forward the idea of transformation or transformance, that is to say the result of this path away from the notion of critique, my intention was to arrive at conceiving the artistic activity in a way that is affirmative, not negative.[4]

The idea of "critical" art understands it as existing in a dialectical relation to past artforms, which it challenges. It is related to a certain understanding of the history and vocation of avant-garde art, where the point is to move things forward by reacting against past trends, producing the new through the negation of the old. For example, the Impressionists critiqued academic assumptions about light, but maintained the perspectival space intact; Cézanne then attacked these assumptions, distorting the space of the picture plane, but continuing to paint recognizable objects; abstract art did away with objects ... and so on. What Lyotard calls affirmative art, however, simply invents something new without a negative relation to the past of the art-historical tradition. Art conceived as affirmative is additive, without being subtractive. It adds to and expands the realm of art's possibilities, without delegitimizing old forms.

Despite this distinction, there is good reason to say that affirmative art is still, in a sense, "critical": it continues to have a critical relation to all codes, social or artistic, which would deny it. The unusual logic at work here is found in Nietzsche's analysis of the difference between noble and slave morality, and was influentially clarified by Gilles Deleuze. The eagle, exemplar of noble morality, affirms himself, and only as a secondary effect is the lamb, exemplar of slave morality, negated. This secondary negation is in fact only due to the lamb's own negation of the eagle: the eagle's self-affirmation only comes into conflict with the lamb because the lamb chooses to negate the eagle.[5] Critique then may be understood as involving just such a secondary negation which results from a primary affirmation. Affirmative art simply affirms itself, but an effect of this affirmation is the negation of anything which would negate *it*. The production of works of pop art, for example, while seeming only to affirm the culture in which they appear, negates any suggestion that such forms cannot be art. In short, this means that Lyotard's affirmative art can be understood as consonant with the idea of a critical practice, insofar as it has a critical political function: it invents new possibilities denied by existing practices, discourses, and arrangements of power of all kinds. Most significantly, affirmative art, like "critical" art, can be understood as a critical practice insofar as it is not content to conform to existing norms, but seeks to transform them and invent new possibilities.

Resistance and invention

A further challenge to Lyotard's contemporary relevance is posed by Bernard Stiegler, who completed his Master's degree under Lyotard's supervision. While insisting that we must continue to read and reread Lyotard, Stiegler has framed his dissatisfaction with the politics of the "post-structuralist" generation—and of Lyotard in particular—in terms of a distinction between *resistance* and *invention*.[6] Resistance sees no hope of a transformation of social reality; all it hopes for is the saving of something of value from its complete destruction. Lyotard's politics of resistance, according to Stiegler, suggests "that it is in principle impossible to imagine an alternative," and that it is impossible to invent new solutions to social and political problems, leaving invention entirely up to the technocrats.[7]

While "resistance" is a complex notion in Lyotard's work, encompassing psychoanalytic, aesthetic, and communicational aspects,[8] all these are reducible, in a broad perspective, to the idea that "the Thing" might hold out a resistance against the threatened total hegemony of development.[9] To the extent that this seems to be largely a private affair, Stiegler's critique is fair. However, I want to argue that if we look at the way Lyotard frames what he calls "affirmative art" in the 1970s, it can and must be understood as invention. It does not take a negative, critical bearing on past forms of art, or simply deconstruct the norms of social reality, but experiments and positively adds something new to the existing store of sensations and plastic forms. Insofar as Lyotard continued to see the role of art as one of creating the new, despite his adoption of a politics of "resistance" in his later thought, he never stopped asserting a certain role for invention in the arts. In an interview dating from the 1990s, he says: "I want to make new possibilities appear with words, colours, ideas, sounds, to bear witness to the powers, the gestural meanings of language, of acoustic and chromatic space."[10] Understood as invention, art can and must be considered to have a transformative effect on the political conditions of "being together" beyond what Lyotard himself was often willing to hope for in his later life.

The argument I shall pursue in this chapter follows the logic of affirmation outlined above. It is not my intention to directly critique Rancière's and Stiegler's readings of Lyotard, but to positively construct an alternative image. If their readings are thereby critiqued, it is because the negation is on their side, in being unable to incorporate such an affirmative image.

Art and politics

What is the "use" of practicing art? There are of course many possible ways of answering this question. One way of justifying art, common in the art world today, is to cite its political relevance in terms of specific social problems in which it might intervene: problems of justice and injustice, of inclusion and exclusion, of remembrance and forgetting, and so on. While Lyotard's philosophy of art is not without relevance for such issues, I wish to focus here on another modality of his work, which has received less attention: the role of art in responding to the effects of science and technology. There is some truth in Rancière's and Stiegler's images of Lyotard: in the 1990s, at the end of his life, Lyotard held out little hope for any substantive transformation of society; the liberal-democratic-capitalist System was here to stay, threatened only by the impending death of the sun in 4.5 billion years. In such a context, politics became for him a minimal practice of resistance, and his privileged model was Winston writing privately in his diary in Orwell's *Nineteen-Eighty-Four*.[11]

Yet today, we are no longer in a situation where this image of a stable world System is plausible.[12] Given that Lyotard was such a restless thinker, always modifying his thought in line with his assessment of the contemporary situation, one thing is sure: if he were alive today, he would not have the same views on art and politics he held in the 1990s. This change of situation licenses us, I believe, to sift through Lyotard's hydra-headed, protean *oeuvre*, and to construct a Lyotardian philosophy of art which Lyotard himself would never have held at any particular time in his life. This is a matter of connecting points between diverse aspects of his work, in different periods. There are three main points I wish to connect here: Lyotard's work on Duchamp in the mid-1970s, his work as director of the exhibition *Les Immatériaux* in the mid-1980s, and his reflections on the crisis of foundations in both the arts and sciences in the later 1980s. We will proceed, however, in the reverse direction, laying out first the theoretical coordinates of the crisis Lyotard believed beset postmodernity, then examining how his work on the arts demonstrates how art responds to this crisis in an affirmative manner. We will see how, despite an apparent opposition, there is in fact a confluence discernible in Lyotard's thought between critical practice and affirmative aesthetics.

The crisis of foundations

The idea that there has been a "crisis of foundations" in the sciences since the early twentieth century is a common one. This is associated with developments such as relativity theory, which put paid to the late nineteenth-century view that physics was practically finished, and Gödel's incompleteness theorem, which proved that mathematics can never be a foundational system. Lyotard's distinctiveness is in understanding this crisis as bearing on the relations between the faculties of sensibility and understanding.[13] In short, the sciences, accomplishments of abstract reason, have challenged the evidence of sensory experience. This means that the sciences cannot match up "the given"—that is, the data of our senses, our bodily sensations—with the conclusions of rationality, leading to debates regarding which of these provides the required foundation for all knowledge. The proposed solutions to this crisis are then split between tendencies Lyotard calls the "intuitive" and the "axiomatic": the intuitive insists that knowledge requires space and time to be grounded in bodily perceptions, while the axiomatic insists that all the requirements for knowledge can be met by a consistent rational formalization.

On Lyotard's account, the crisis of the sciences is not, however, limited to abstract knowledge. Especially through the developments of technologies, this crisis has come to bear on everyday experience and postmodern culture. All of the ways that technologies have changed our experiences of time and space—through the telephone, the internet, cars, high-speed rail and airplanes—have disrupted our "groundedness" in the here and now. This theme has been influentially explored by Heidegger in his critique of the essence of technology. This essence is *Ge-Stell*, the "enframing" which reveals all beings as *Bestand*, resources to be used in accordance with determined needs. For him, technology is a *realization* of metaphysics, and its highest point of development, where "metaphysics" is understood in his pejorative sense as that which occludes Being in its own manifestation and temporal unfolding. That is, metaphysics gives primacy to what the subject tries to think, occluding the world of objects (and at deeper level, the given in general) it might otherwise be "open" to. Heidegger links this decline of Being with what Nietzsche called nihilism: it marks the deepest crisis of meaning, because it reduces all meaning to a narrow technological criterion of effective usefulness.

Many have followed the general thrust of Heidegger's thought, seeing sciences and technologies as having *alienating* effects. Lyotard, however—while recognizing such dangers—also sees a more positive modality of the "crisis of foundations" in a parallel movement in the arts. Lyotard sees the arts themselves as also responding to such a crisis, from the beginnings of the avant-garde traditions. Such arts, in becoming abstract, minimal, and in other ways experimenting with the norms of the artistic tradition, have broken with the "common sense" way of representing the world, and explored sensibility in multiple directions. The link Lyotard makes between developments in the arts and the sciences is that both concern a deregulation of the relationship between sensibility and the understanding. He writes (for example):

> The avant-gardes in painting fulfil romanticism, i.e., modernity, which, in its strong and recurrent sense, is the failure of stable regulation between the sensible and the intelligible.[14]

The crisis of foundations manifested through sciences and technologies produces a crisis in our very grasp of time and space, the basic coordinates of sensory experience, and a subsequent feeling of disorientation. According to Lyotard, the avant-gardes have rigorously and searchingly interrogated these conditions of time and space. He sees avant-garde arts as exploring new ways of "meaning-making"—not in the sense of signification or conceptual meaning, but of aesthetic feeling in response to sensation.

Immaterials

The crisis of perception, of sensibility, of space and time, was explored in the dramaturgy of *Les Immatériaux* ("Immaterials"), the major exhibition at the Pompidou Centre in 1985 that Lyotard directed.[15] The exhibition sought to provoke a questioning, sensibly as well as theoretically, regarding the profound changes new sciences and technologies were bringing about in human life, through heightening a feeling of anxiety towards these transformations. The many artworks, scientific displays, and technological artifacts the exhibition housed were organized along an overall route which stretched from one end of the fifth floor of the building to the other. The beginning of the exhibition drew attention to the body, disrupting our habitual sense of it: first with amplified sounds of pumping blood in the entry vestibule, then the site with which it opened, the "Theatre of the Non-Body," which presented five dioramas representing the themes according to which the exhibition was organized. The catalog states that "This vast site suggests the resistance of the body (me, here, now) to the dematerialisation of its contexts in mediatised life."[16] At the other end of the exhibition was the "Labyrinth of Language," which collected multiple computers and displayed some of the cutting-edge applications of the day, such as a poetry-generating program ("Rambaudelaire") and a networked collective discussion ("épreuve d'écriture"). This zone demonstrated the power of automated reasoning—the ability of materialized objects to take over functions that had previously been thought to be exclusive to the human mind.

In its overall organization, its route from the body to language-processing machines, *Les Immatériaux* can be seen as displaying the "crisis of space and time": it demonstrated the disinheritance of the body, in its sensuous materiality and groundedness in the here and now, and its usurpation by the sciences and technologies we have constructed. These sciences and technologies have extended our knowledges beyond the body's capacities to synthesize its experience, and which are beginning to replace even the most prized of our features, our subjective rationality.

The painter of postmodern life

Yet as well as technological artifacts, *Les Immatériaux* displayed the works of artists, especially works which also seem to have an effect of "dematerialization." Two notable examples were extremely important in Lyotard's *oeuvre* in general: Jacques Monory and Marcel Duchamp. Monory was represented in the site called "Painter without Body" ("Peintre sans corps"), in a series of paintings, *Explosion*, created through the projection of photographic slides onto photosensitive material. According to the exhibition catalog, the result is "[m]ore than gesture, more than 'craftsmanship.' The style will be photographic. You put the painting body outside the circuit of the painting. And you can multiply the product."[17] This example of Monory's painting demonstrates how industrial techniques not only destroy the habits of the body and its sensibility (in this case, traditional painting techniques), but expand its possibilities. This then begins to indicate how Lyotard construes arts as having an inventive capacity which transforms the effects of sciences and technologies on human life.

In her introduction to Lyotard's book on the French painter, Sarah Wilson has noted that Lyotard interprets Monory "under the sign of Baudelaire."[18] We might understand this by saying that Lyotard sees Monory as responding to the conditions of postmodernity, just as Baudelaire saw Constantin Guys responding to the conditions of modernity: Monory would thus be "The Painter of Postmodern Life."[19] Baudelaire himself responded to such conditions, in his case through writing. Jonathan Culler explains the distinctive modernity of Baudelaire's poetry as follows:

> Baudelaire produces dissonant combinations, which can be seen as reflecting the dissociated character of modern experience, where consciousness is confronted by objects, sensations and experiences that do not go together. Dissonant images may also be seen, though, as models for combining or synthesizing disparate sensations, offering moderns a way of appreciating and thus dealing with inchoate experience, encouraging a poetic attitude to the alienation said to characterize modern life.[20]

This indicates the capacity of art to "poetically" or aesthetically transform conditions which might otherwise appear to threaten only alienation. Such transformative capacities receive a more precise analysis with Lyotard's work on Duchamp.

The great sophist

Lyotard entitled a review "Marcel Duchamp, or the Great Sophist."[21] An insult for nearly all philosophers since Socrates, Lyotard revalued what "sophistry" might mean. He found in the sophists a weapon called "retorsion": it is the art of turning an opponent's argument back against them. Retorsion has the general form of saying: Let us accept the premises, and show how they can be seen to lead to a different conclusion.[22] Art can be affirmative by effectuating a sophistical retorsion in relation to the technoscientific developments of (post)modernity, transforming the mutations of time and space, of bodily and intellectual experience, into something more than alienation. Art positively *experiments* with sensible conditions, and invents new forms of meaning, new ways of making the sensible significant (not in the sense of giving it a signification, but of eliciting aesthetic feeling).

Lyotard's work on Duchamp is his first great foray into the *retorsional* capacities of art. On his interpretation, Duchamp does not simply pave the way for art's becoming-conceptual, but demonstrates how this becoming-conceptual has an effect *in sensibility*. As such, the work on Duchamp can be seen as setting the coordinates for the retorsions of *Les Immatériaux*, and of showing how art can respond to the technoscientific crisis of foundations.

The transformer

Lyotard's book *Duchamp's TRANS/formers* collects a number of essays he devoted to the artist from 1974 to 1977. As the book's title suggests, Lyotard understands the affirmative function in Duchamp as a kind of transformation. Lyotard thus proposes that as well as being a great sophist, Duchamp is a great transformer, and the problematic of transformation governs all his works.[23]

Duchamp transformed the possibilities of art itself. Exactly how to understand his works' significance remains a matter of interpretation and debate, but it is well known that he railed against what he called "retinal" art—art which is made primarily to appeal to the eye (or to the senses in general), and in so doing he inaugurated what became known as conceptual art. Duchamp emphasized what can be thought but not seen; what can be rationalized but not intuited. The interpretation of his many notes on his works, for example, are just as important to the works themselves as what strikes the viewers' eye in looking at them. Moreover, his work with fourth-dimensional geometry in the construction of the upper half of the *Large Glass* alludes to what can be rationally understood, but not seen or imagined.

Hinges

The "hinge" is a term which Lyotard makes central in his book on Duchamp. A hinge is a fulcrum of transformation. Two things which pivot at a hinge are "mirrors" of each other; they are the same, but incongruent—the way that images are reversed in a mirror and not superimposable on each other. Duchamp names this curious quality of incongruents, joined at a hinge, "mirrorish."[24] Each of the incongruents is a transformation of the other. The hinge in Duchamp can be understood, via Lyotard, as a figure, in visual space, of the sophistical logic of retorsion: something is reproduced, but with a twist, which transforms it.

Lyotard proposes that we can view Duchamp's two major works, the *Large Glass* and *Given*, as similar but incongruent, a hinge between them. (The strong relationship between the two works is well noted in the literature on Duchamp, the full title of *Given* first appearing in the notes for the *Large Glass*.) Lyotard suggests that we can understand *Given* as a projection and transformation of all the elements of the *Large Glass*, and that they present the same object (the woman laid bare) but in very different ways.[25] There is a temporal paradox of the event here: the *Large Glass* presents the event of stripping-bare too early (the Bride is still a bride, not a wife), while *Given* presents it too late (she is already stripped, and perhaps, post-coital).[26] Lyotard also presents an extensive list of plastic hinges, consisting of analogous points of similitude between the two works, and operations of transformation which make these points incongruous.[27] For example, one point compares the two works in terms of the "mirrorish" and the "specular." This latter term indicates "homogenous" space, made for the habits of the eye and conforming to the conventions of perspective established in the Renaissance. While in the *Large Glass* there is the subversion of the specular, by emphasis of the incongruence of the upper and lower regions, in *Given* there is an identifying symmetry between the vanishing point—the vulva—and the viewing point, which allows Lyotard to make the provocative joke that in this work, "the one who sees is a cunt."[28] The result is a specular, and not a mirrorish, visual *dispositif*.

Appearance and apparition

Lyotard further elaborates the relation between the two works in terms of the distinction Duchamp makes between "appearance" and "apparition." Duchamp defines "appearance" as "the ensemble of usual sensory data permitting us to have an ordinary perception of this object."[29] The "apparition" is "the (formal) mold" of the appearance, for example, the 2-dim image in perspective of a 3-dim object or else its "(photographic) *negative*."[30] Lyotard proposes that the *Large Glass* presents an apparition, and *Given*, "merely" an appearance. This perhaps explains a fact which many found puzzling on the posthumous discovery of the last nude: Duchamp seemed to have abandoned all his previous radical innovations and returned to something more conventionally "retinal." Lyotard explains the difference between the two works as follows:

> What the viewer sees on the *Glass* is the eye and even the brain in the process of composing its objects, the images of these objects impressing the retina and the cortex according to laws of (de-)formation, which are their own and that organize the glass partition. But when the voyeur puts his eyes in the holes of the Spanish gate, he seems to have only an "ordinary perception" of the objects he sees.[31]

Rather remarkably, then, we could translate the difference into philosophical terms by suggesting that what *Given* presents is "the given," while the *Glass* presents what *gives* the given, the transcendental condition which constitutes (or deconstitutes) it. When Duchamp leaves *Given* as a final work, then, what it effects is a transformation of the way all his work can be perceived. It suggests not that Duchamp was content to leave the aesthetic or perceptual behind entirely, and pursue a rarefied and abstract conceptual art, but rather that these "intellectual" experiments are made to reflect back *on* "the given," the specular, the space of retinal art, and the body, the aesthetic, and sensation in general.

The works *Large Glass* and *Given* testify to a transformation which indicates an incongruence or incommensurabilty between the sensible and the intelligible, between perception and the thinkable conditions which make it possible; a transformation of one by the other in their mirroring difference. And Lyotard's work, which makes these themes apparent, itself transforms the understanding of Duchamp by making him a sophistical artist of retorsion, who employs conceptual strategies not in order to negate the body and sensation, but to transform it, to extend its capacities and invent new modes of perception. Dalia Judovitz gestures in this direction in her assessment of the significance of Lyotard's book:

> *Duchamp's TRANS/formers* reclaimed Duchamp from negation and the much trumpeted end of art by showing how he challenged the meaning of the aesthetic through an ironic strategy whose transformative potential restituted to art its capacity, not to be, but to happen, and make things happen ...[32]

20,000 Hz

One way of reading *Duchamp's TRANS/formers* is to see its place in Lyotard's complex *oeuvre* by looking back on it from the perspective of later works. In the 1980s, as we have seen above, he began to talk of a "crisis of perception" or "crisis of time and space," which he sees in the twentieth century, manifest through parallel and analogous developments in the sciences and the arts.[33] As noted above, these themes were displayed in the dramaturgy of *Les Immatériaux* with its exhibited "dematerialisation" of the body by new technologies and accompanying artistic works. Duchamp's work parallels this crisis of perception, but uses "rational" strategies to expand the possibilities of perception itself. It thus does not work to alienate, but to invent new modes of aesthetic meaning. This way of connecting points through Lyotard's disparate works thus challenges claims of his political enervation by emphasizing creative invention and the transformation of a potentially alienating reality.

The importance of Duchamp as responding to the crises that afflict modernity or postmodernity is indicated by Lyotard's evocation, in the first chapter of *Duchamp's TRANS/formers*, of the scandalous remarks he made in *Libidinal Economy* about how conditions of industrialization are not *only* destructive conditions of exploitation, but also conditions of inventive transformation. He refers here to the alteration of the human body, citing a case in which a worker was found to have adapted to tolerate intense noise (20,000 Hz), displaying no more loss of hearing than the neutralization of that specific frequency.[34] Duchamp may be seen as himself acting as a kind of transformer in relation to the conditions of modernity, of nihilism, which have cast doubt on the senses, on the intuitions of time and space. Unlike Husserl, Heidegger, or Merleau-Ponty, unlike many thinkers of the Frankfurt School, and indeed much of the continental philosophical tradition, Duchamp does not lament the advent of rationalization and industrial technology, but rather shows how these same conditions can be made to form a laboratory for profoundly transformative experimentation and invention. It is in transforming the mechanical and rationalized conditions of modernity, which many others can only critique, that Lyotard sees Duchamp as a paradigm case of a transformative artist: *affirmative*, rather than critical.

Ge-Stell and machination

All Duchamp's metaphors of machines work in this direction, and aim to divest art of its alliance with the natural human body and its sensual perceptions. Lyotard indicates that Duchamp continues the tradition of Cézanne's experiments, but "[i]n Duchamp, there is an abandonment of what is preserved in Cézanne, which is the idea of nature."[35] Bernard Stiegler believed that Lyotard remained beholden to Heidegger's notion of technology as *Ge-Stell*, and to some extent (especially in comparison with Stiegler's own profound revaluation of technology) this is true.[36] However, a point missed here is the way that, in Lyotard's work on Duchamp, the concept of "machination" works as a "*retorsion*" to the Heideggerian idea (a metaphysical one, according to Stiegler) of technology as *Ge-Stell*. And, although perhaps not clearly marked in its written documentation, it is also quite possible to see this manifest in *Les Immatériaux*, insofar as the whole exhibition can be seen as a retorsional *dispositif*, a transformer designed to reflect the feeling of the disorientation of the "natural" body by new technologies back onto itself, revealing not a simple negation or loss, but a new type of sensibility.

Machines, for Duchamp, are better named "machinations." Lyotard explains this latter term by referring to a definition of machines which describes them as "traps" for the forces of nature, and he associates these traps with sophistical ruses.[37] The important point here is the pluralization: this move turns away from the monolithic image of the industrial machine which, from the romantics to the phenomenologists and critical theorists of the twentieth century, loomed large as a threatening shadow over modernity. By contrast, the idea of machination makes the machine figure a multiplicity of singular strategies, rather than a homogenizing Heideggerian *Ge-Stell*, a single frame through which all beings are reduced to *Bestand*. This allows an affirmative, transformative relation to technology, one which has been specified and called for more recently by Yuk Hui—an important contemporary philosopher of technology influenced by Lyotard—in his notion of *technodiversity*. This idea fragments the single system which technology has often been thought to compose. It deconstructs the Heideggerian notion of *Ge-Stell* by recalling the diverse histories and meanings of technologies in different cultures, and advocating an experimental, exploratory pluralization of technologies.[38] This frees us from the devaluation of beings as *Bestand* and opens up plural, contingent, inventive, and transformable ideas of what technologies can be.

Affirming Lyotard

In contrast to the melancholy and politically impotent images of Lyotard constructed by the likes of Rancière and Stiegler, the image I have constructed here is of a thinker whose persistent importance can be affirmed. This Lyotard is a champion of arts of invention and transformation which have the essential task of helping us live with the fast-paced changes science and technology continue to effect in the contemporary world. Lyotard argues that these technoscientific changes affect us on an aesthetic level, that is, on the level of sensation, by untying and reconfiguring the relation between the faculties of sensibility and understanding. Art responds to this situation by exploring the same decoupling, but in and with sensibility. It thus reactivates, in a new way, that which postmodern nihilism seems to negate; it *affirms* this "new sensibility"[39] and invents new positive forms for it. In our quickly advancing (post)industrial world, with all the unprecedented transformations it brings about in (post)modern life, there are no solutions waiting there to be puzzled out on the basis of existing knowledges, facts, and experiences. They have to be *experimentally invented*, and that is why artistic practice is critical, in the double sense of being crucially important, and of intervening in and changing the conditions of existence.

Notes

1 See also Carole Talon-Hugon, "After Lyotard: Aesthetics in France Today," *Cités*, vol. 56, no. 4 (2013/14): 87–101.
2 See for example Jacques Rancière, *Aesthetics and Its Discontents*, tr. Steven Corcoran. (Cambridge UK and Malden MA: Polity, [2004] 2009), especially the chapters "Lyotard and the Aesthetics of the Sublime: A Counter-reading of Kant" and "The Ethical Turn of Aesthetics and Politics." A key Lyotard text in Rancière's argument is "The Other's Rights" (included in this volume).
3 On the many problems with Rancière's reading, see Peter W. Milne, "Sensibility and the Law: On Rancière's Reading of Lyotard," *Symposium*, vol. 15, no. 2 (2011): 95–119.
4 Jean-François Lyotard, "De la fonction critique à la transformation," interview with Jean Papineau, *Parachute*, 11 (1978): 5. See also Jean-François Lyotard, "Adrift" in *Driftworks*, ed. Roger McKeon (New York: Semiotext(e), 1984).
5 See Gilles Deleuze, *Nietzsche and Philosophy*, tr. Hugh Tomlinson (New York: Columbia University Press, [1962] 1983), 175–89.
6 See Bernard Stiegler, *States of Shock: Stupidity and Knowledge in the 21st Century*, tr. Daniel Ross (Cambridge UK and Malden MA: Polity, [2012] 2015), 98–102.
7 Ibid., 102.
8 See Daniel Birnbaum and Sven-Olov Wallenstein, "From Immaterials to Resistance: The Other Side of *Les Immatériaux*," in Andreas Broeckmann and Yuk Hui (eds), *30 Years after* Les Immatériaux, *Art, Science, Theory* (Lüneburg: Meson, 2015).
9 See Claire Nouvet, "Under Threat: Rights and 'The Thing,'" in this volume.

10 Jean-François Lyotard, "That Which Resists, After All," interview with Gilbert Larochelle, *Philosophy Today*, vol. 36, no. 4 (1992): 402–3.
11 See in particular "Gloss on Resistance" in Jean-François Lyotard, *The Postmodern Explained to Children: Correspondence 1982–1985*, tr. Julian Pefanis, Morgan Thomas et al. (London: Turnaround, [1986] 1992), 103–12.
12 I develop this argument in my article "System Failure (?)," tr. Zhou Jing, *Journal of the China Academy of Art*, vol. 41, no. 6 (2020): 88–100 [in Chinese].
13 Lyotard discusses this crisis in multiple places, but his most pithy statement is "Argumentation and Presentation: The Foundation Crisis" [1989], tr. Chris Turner, *Cultural Politics*, vol. 9, no. 2 (2013): 117–143.
14 Jean-François Lyotard, *The Inhuman: Reflections on Time*, tr. Geoffrey Bennington and Rachel Bowlby (Cambridge UK: Polity, [1988] 1991).
15 Lyotard was invited to act as *commissaire* or director/curator of the exhibition in 1983, working to develop a project instigated by a team from the Centre de Création Industrielle, including the design theorist Thierry Chaput, who continued as co-curator.
16 Jean-François Lyotard et al., *Les Immatériaux*, volume 2: *Album et Inventaire*, ed. Chantal Noël (Paris: Centre Georges Pompidou, 1985). Translation mine.
17 Ibid.
18 Sarah Wilson, "Lyotard/Monory: Postmodern Romantics" in *The Assassination of Experience by Painting: Monory*, tr. Rachel Bowlby (London: Black Dog, 2001), 21.
19 Charles Baudelaire, *The Painter of Modern Life and Other Essays*, ed. and tr. Jonathan Mayne (New York: Phaidon, [1863] 1995).
20 Jonathan Culler, "Introduction" in Charles Baudelaire, *The Flowers of Evil*, tr. James McGowan (Oxford: Oxford University Press, 1993), xxv–xxvi.
21 Jean-François Lyotard, "Marcel Duchamp ou le grand sophiste," *L'Art vivant*, no. 56 (1975): 34–5.
22 See Keith Crome, *Lyotard and Greek Thought: Sophistry* (Basingstoke UK and New York: Palgrave Macmillan, 2004).
23 In contrast to the US reception of Duchamp, which has focused largely on the ready-mades, Lyotard is in line with the French reception by focusing on the two great works, the *Large Glass* and *Given*. For some interesting comments on how the ready-mades—mostly neglected by Lyotard—might nevertheless be considered from the point of view of transformation (as a kind of limit case of minimal transformation), see Lyotard, "De la fonction critique à la transformation," 5.
24 See Jean-François Lyotard, *Duchamp's TRANS/formers*, ed. Herman Parret, tr. Ian McLeod. *Writings on Contemporary Art and Artists*, vol. 3 (Leuven: Leuven University Press, [1977] 2010), 127–33.
25 Ibid., 75.
26 This theme is also discussed in the "Art Présent" interview included in this volume.
27 Lyotard, *Duchamp's TRANS/formers*, 183–89.
28 Ibid., 185, trans. modified. Dalia Judovitz notes that this "phenomenological" issue of the specular and its critique has been the focus for most existing studies that have made reference to *Duchamp's TRANS/formers*. See her "Epilogue" in *Duchamp's TRANS/formers*, 239.
29 Marcel Duchamp, *Duchamp du signe, écrits*, ed. Michel Sanouillet with Elmer Peterson (Paris: Flammarion, 1975), 120; quoted in Lyotard, *Duchamp's TRANS/formers*, 181.
30 Quoted in Lyotard, *Duchamp's TRANS/formers*, 181.
31 Lyotard, *Duchamp's TRANS/formers*, 181.

32 Judovitz, "Epilogue," 255.
33 The most thorough development of this theme is in Lyotard, "Argumentation and Presentation: The Foundation Crisis."
34 Jean-François Lyotard, *Libidinal Economy*, tr. Iain Hamilton Grant (London and New York: Continuum, [1974] 2004), 110; Lyotard, *Duchamp's TRANS/formers*, 57–63.
35 Lyotard, "De la fonction critique à la transformation," 5. Translation mine.
36 Bernard Stiegler, "The Shadow of the Sublime: On *Les Immatériaux*" in Yuk Hui and Andreas Broekmann (eds), *30 Years since* Les Immatériaux (Lüneburg: Meson Press, 2015), 153.
37 Lyotard, *Duchamp's TRANS/formers*, 77–9.
38 Yuk Hui, *Recursivity and Contingency* (London: Rowman & Littlefield, 2019), §42.
39 Also a term taken from Hui, inspired by Lyotard. Hui, *Recursivity and Contingency*.

15

"hang on tight and spit on me": Lyotard and Contemporary Art

Stephen Zepke

> If the proletariat does not perceive that there is something absolutely analogous between what must be done today to social reality and what is done on a canvas or within sonorous space, not only will it not encounter the problem of art, it will never come upon revolution.[1]

Jean-François Lyotard not only enjoyed art, he was politically committed to it, making its "problem" nothing less than "revolution." Art's revolutionary power comes from its embodiment of an underlying "ontological rift" between primary libidinal forces and the rational *dispositifs* that represent and control them, a rift that for Lyotard defines both political economy and artistic production.[2] Art materializes this incommensurability in radical onto-political "gestures" that confront our supposed *a prioris* of time, space, and the organic body with forces that are "strangers to consciousness,"[3] their unbound energy of *aisthesis* creating "testimonies that represent nothing,"[4] pure intensities of "orgasmic death."[5] Although these unconscious forces are "ontologically located outside the system," they find expression in art works that "deconstruct" normal thoughts and feelings by revealing how "this 'order' conceals something else, that it represses."[6] While Lyotard's later work shifts from celebrating the deconstructive power of the aesthetic to mourning its loss and disappearance, his affirmation of art's constitutive incommensurability remains constant. This essay will focus on Lyotard's early libidinal work and its commitment to the political power of aesthetic experience, and compare it to recent theories of postconceptual contemporary artistic practices.

Lyotard's aesthetics of incommensurability is based upon Freud's economic perspective distinguishing between the primary and secondary processes of the psyche. Freud argues that the psyche reacts to excitation by releasing tension which causes pleasure, this pleasure principle maintaining the equilibrium and integrity of the organic body and the ego riding in it. The reality principle augments this process by making it consistent with the drive for self-preservation. Prior to these secondary drives, however, is a primary process that manifests in the death drive, a force that, Freud claims, is constantly seeking "to revert to the quiescence of the inorganic world."[7]

The death drive, he writes, is "a function of the mental apparatus which, though it does not contradict the pleasure principle, is nevertheless independent of it and seems to be more primitive."[8] As all the drives seek equilibrium, and the death drive is primary, Freud argues that "for *internal* reasons ... *the aim of all life is death*."[9] This ontological priority of the death drive is crucial for Lyotard, who follows Freud in giving greater importance to its "economic disturbances."[10] For Lyotard, the aesthetic intensities of art embody the death drive, and their violent and creative enjoyment (*jouissance*) cannot be sublimated by secondary mediations such as pleasure or consciousness. This aesthetic experience is an "unadulterated displacement" putting us "in direct contact with the unbound nature of the energy at work in the primary process."[11] Nevertheless—and it is an important point—"*Jouissance* is not death, but like death, at the same time that it discharges tension, it brings obscurity: the annihilation of representation, and the annihilation of words: silence."[12] Art qua *jouissance* allows us to experience the incommensurability of consciousness and libidinal force, an experience Lyotard often associates with the anti-representational strategies of modernism: "There is, in modern art," he writes, "a presence of desire, or rather, a presence in desire of the death drive," which is its immanent "revolutionary function."[13] Lyotard abandons his early Marxism in favor of this "political economy that would be nothing other than a libidinal economy,"[14] and a political art in which aesthetic experience negates the mediations and controls of representation and consciousness in favor of the anarchy of the unconscious. As Lyotard puts it,

> in the art work ... the space of dispossession—the space where energy flows freely in the primary process—refuses to be boxed back in, to be repressed by secondary-level bindings (linguistic and realistic) or by the complicity of Eros with Logos ... the art work offers the symptom its own space of dispossession in which to resonate.[15]

Art of this type is, to use a Kantian term central to Lyotard's later work on the sublime, a negative presentation, an aesthetic figure expressing the "*presence of absence*."[16] In the figure death drives are "recognizable as unrecognizable,"[17] disrupting spatio-temporal dimensions with the timeless.[18] "This 'presence,'" Lyotard insists, "cannot be a presentation,"[19] because the figural event is an aesthetic intensity incommensurable with all semantic and syntactic givens, it "presents itself like a fall, like a slippage and an error, exactly like the meaning of *lapsus* in Latin. The event clears a vertiginous space and time; untethered from its context or perceptual environment."[20] The aesthetic event erupts in the midst of its representation/repression, the *jouissance* of the death drive attacking "the order of thought" to produce "intellectually intolerable ... meaninglessness."[21] As we will see, Lyotard's affirmation of art's aesthetic intensities and meaninglessness is very different from more recent understandings of contemporary artistic practices.

Before considering this difference in more detail, however, it must be emphasized that aesthetic intensity always cohabits with its representation and repression, just as the unconscious and consciousness are necessarily co-implicated. The problem is not discovering another world, but of affirming and experiencing the dark and destructive intensities of this one. Art, for Lyotard, is a way of *unknowing* the world, of deconstructing theory or capital so that we can experience the *jouissance* of their immanent incommensurability. It is not, he says, "a matter of determining a new domain, another field, a *beyond representation*," because there is no "extra-semiotic order"; instead we must discover how signs "*can also* be, indissociably, singular and vain intensities in exodus."[22] Lyotard advocates an absolute immanence, "difference within identity … passion within reason,"[23] because, as he says in relation to capitalism, "Reproduction dissimulates destruction."[24] To be incommensurable means, for Lyotard, to be absolutely different from and yet absolutely immanent in the conditions of appearance, to be, and at once, Discourse/Figure. In the book *Discourse, Figure* Lyotard positions art and representation (in language and images) as incommensurables: "Art stands in alterity as plasticity and desire, a curved expanse against invariability and reason, diacritical space. Art covets the figure, and 'beauty' is figural, unbound, rhythmic."[25] But at the same time, the figure can only appear in and through (the disruption of) representation, "*within* discourse … of an 'order' that is never graspable except as disorder."[26] Art's ambition, at least in its literary form, "is to *signify* the other of signification."[27] Art qua other unleashes the pure variability of a free (i.e., non-dialectical) difference. For Lyotard, aesthetic experience qua *jouissance* is representation's own immanent revolutionary difference.

Peter Osborne has recently argued that the post-Kantian tradition of aesthetics, which obviously includes Lyotard, has "failed to achieve a convincing critical-theoretical purchase on *contemporary* art, because it has failed to come to terms with the decisive historical transformation in the ontology of the artwork that is constitutive of its very contemporaneity."[28] The contemporary, Osborne claims, is defined by its "derealised" distributed ontology, "the *distributive* unity of the relations between a materially embedded virtuality and an infinite multiplicity of possible visualizations."[29] This distributed ontology is shared by conceptual art, digital technologies and globalization, and gives contemporary art a "decisive difference from art of the past."[30] This difference is crucially located in the way conceptual art posits the concept and its discursive expression as the essential aspect of the art work, with aesthetic material merely conveying this content. Contemporary art is therefore distinguished from modernism's interest in ahistorical onto-aesthetic events that produce what Osborne nicely describes as a "ruptural futurity."[31] This future ended with conceptual art, and this historical shift means that "contemporary art *is* post-conceptual art."[32] The term "postconceptual art" therefore registers, Osborne claims, the "ontological mutation" that occurred with conceptual art, which "exposed the aesthetic misrecognition of the art work [by Lyotard and others] as an ideological fraud."[33] What is at stake here is much more than periodization, as Osborne puts it:

> In this construction postconceptual art is not a traditional art-historical or art-critical concept at the level of medium, aesthetic form, style or movement. It denotes an art premised on the complex historical experience and critical legacy of conceptual art, broadly construed in such a way as to register the fundamental mutation of the ontology of the art work carried by that legacy.[34]

What is interesting about Osborne's account is that like Lyotard's it concerns art's ontology, but for Osborne this ontology is entirely historically determined. Art's ontology changes along with the world, whereas for Lyotard, while the arts change, their ontology (i.e., their libidinal economy) remains constant. But while Osborne's claims for "postconceptual art" accurately describe art's recent move away from modernism's insistence on art's autonomy and its aesthetic essence, Lyotard's affirmation of the ahistorical and revolutionary aesthetic event projects the radicality of '68-thought into the present,[35] and there is an attractive vitality to its sublime violence. So bearing this in mind, let's see how confronting these positions plays out. Conceptual art, Osborne argues, established the "need for art actively to counter aesthetic misrecognition within the work,"[36] a shift that was subsequently solidified by the end of the avant-garde, the integration of "autonomous" art into the culture industry, and the globalization of the biennale that resulted from the post-1989 victory of capitalism. Conceptual art shared its "distributive unity" with digital technology, and both have now become integral to postconceptual art[37] within the frame of what Osborne calls "*photo-capitalism* ... a distinctly transnational and translinguistic cultural-economic form"[38] that marks "a strange convergence ... between the digital image and the commodity form" in globalized finance capital.[39] The derealization of art in the distributive unity of the concept and the data file, Osborne argues, "strangely 'corresponds' to the ontological status of the value-form ... In the infinite field of visualizations of the digital image, the infinity of exchange made possible by the abstraction of exchange value from use value finds its equivalent visual form."[40]

Insofar as its creation and circulation is "immaterial," Osborne claims that "postconceptual art articulates a post-aesthetic poetics,"[41] where what is experienced (art work, photo, commodity) merely provides "ontological support"[42] for its derealized and distributed essence (concept, data file, exchange value). While the aesthetically distributed form of conceptual practice famously formulated by Sol Le Witt and Lawrence Weiner is now clearly the norm in contemporary art,[43] Osborne argues that postconceptual art actually goes further, as its derealized and distributed ontology makes "medium" (and hence the aesthetic) irrelevant. In this sense, Osborne continues, it is the "strong programme of 'analytical' or 'pure' conceptual art" of Joseph Kosuth that is the model for postconceptual art.[44] Inspired by analytic philosophy, Kosuth's 1969 essay "Art After Philosophy" claimed Marcel Duchamp's readymade had transformed the art object into a question concerning its own conceptual conditions.[45] Duchamp, then, was the beginning of art as *philosophy* of art. Kosuth, often directly paraphrasing the logical positivist A. J. Ayer, argued that "works of art are analytic propositions" defining their conceptual "art condition."[46] This produced what Kosuth memorably called "*Art as Idea as Idea*,"[47] where: "The validity of artistic propositions is not dependent on any empirical, much less any aesthetic, presupposition about the nature of things." The artist, Kosuth continues, "is not directly concerned with the physical properties of things. He is concerned only with the way (1) in which art is capable of conceptual growth and (2) how his propositions are capable of logically following that growth."[48] For Kosuth, "the 'purest' definition of conceptual art would be that it is inquiry into the foundations of the concept 'art.'"[49] Although most postconceptual practices are not explicitly concerned with the meaning of "art," conceptual art's focus on the concept enabled contemporary art to escape its aesthetic conditions, to be able to engage all areas of life in the linguistic and conceptual terms they now shared. For Kosuth, "the propositions of art are not factual, but linguistic in *character*" and "accordingly, we can say that art operates on a logic."[50] Art's embrace of these shared modes of engagement with the world continue to drive the emergence of experimental art forms such as research-based practice, knowledge production and art/science collaborations. In this way contemporary art's aesthetic affects are increasingly limited to actualizing the work's conceptual conditions, which art constantly tests and tries to go beyond, as it seeks an ever more radical immanence in the world.

In 1991 Lyotard writes the foreword to Kosuth's book *Art After Philosophy and After*, clearly stating his objections to the conceptual and postconceptual artistic practices that had by that time become widespread. To do so, Lyotard returns to the arguments and vocabulary of *Discourse, Figure*, rejecting outright Kosuth's claims that art was linguistic and logical in nature. "Words are revealed as things," Lyotard writes, "signifiers are grasped as enigmas, writing is set down as a material thing. In other words, thought is art."[51] As we shall see, this argument echoes Lyotard's reading of Duchamp, which is quite opposed to Kosuth's. Thought is art, according to Lyotard, because both "yearn" to make the incommensurable excess of libidinal force present.[52] Art is a gesture that presents the "presence" of what cannot be presented and must remain silent.[53] This effectively denies the "after" in Kosuth's "Art After Philosophy," absorbing art and philosophy into an ahistorical gesture first made by the caveman and continued today by the contemporary artist. The first words of the essay draw the line: "After philosophy comes philosophy."[54] Later, Lyotard elaborates:

> After philosophy is before it. A man takes his finger, a stick, or a paintbrush, plunges it into an oxide paste or an ink, and draws some strokes on a support. Is he writing or painting? Neither one nor the other; this distinction will come later. He appeals by means of the visible-readable to a "presence" that is more than the calm acts of sight and reading. Today a man remakes this gesture with the typographic character of our informationalized world. He calls us to this other, near and far, that is the only motif of art.[55]

Lyotard grounds both conceptual art and philosophy in an atemporal aesthetic event that not only makes a mockery of Kosuth's attempts to usurp the latter with the former, but also rejects Kosuth's (and Osborne's) account of art's historical development. What makes art "art," according to Lyotard, is the aesthetic presence of the other, and whether this is in paint or type is a historical consideration of secondary importance. For Lyotard the history of art embodies this essential and incommensuarable otherness in so many variations of art's aesthetic pursuit of negative presentation. Language is certainly a possible mode of such a presentation, but negatively, "in rags," as a "cry" communicating "the gyratory madness into the domain of meaning."[56] But while this affirmation of aesthetic *jouissance* remained central to Lyotard's thinking about art, what clearly changed during this time was art's own understanding of its ontology, a shift Lyotard resists. Lyotard seems close to Deleuze and Guattari on this point, art cannot be philosophy because it is an aesthetic rather than a conceptual form of thought.⁵⁷ Osborne, on the other hand, argues that conceptual art marks a rethinking of art by art, which thereby becomes philosophically self-determining (in and as art), and makes art's ontology a matter of historical struggle. These developments seem undeniable from a historical perspective, which is precisely what makes Lyotard's rejection of them both uncomfortable, and seductive.

Lyotard's affirmation of contemporary art's political potential remains interesting because it rests on the same energetic economy as capitalism. Lyotard draws on Pierre Klossowski's insight that "economic norms … are *modes for the expression and representation of impulsive forces*,"⁵⁸ and combines it with Pierro Sraffa's mercantilist, neo-Ricardean theory of the commodity standard.⁵⁹ For Sraffa, an agreed commodity should play the role of currency in a theory of value that avoids the representational opposition of money and desire because it does not rest on the use-value/exchange-value distinction.⁶⁰ Instead a circular flow of production and consumption maintains the economy as a "homeostatically regulated whole,"⁶¹ modulating the violent and incommensurable irruptions of energy/wealth gained through annexation, looting, and speculation (as the death drives of the market). The consequences of this immanence of production and consumption are, Lyotard argues, that "price is combined and mixed in with the *exorbitant*," a "confusion" that "is at once impossible and inevitable," because in it "the singularity forces itself to be communicated."⁶² For Klossowski capitalism's industrial mode of production standardizes desire (turning it into "need"), commodities (producing "utensils" rather than "simulacrum") and affect, in what Lyotard calls a "libidinal neutralisation."⁶³ But Lyotard will also find the "*price of the irrational*"⁶⁴ charged by the artistic simulacrum in industrial production, a living currency paid by the industrial working class. In possibly his most controversial moment, Lyotard claims the workers in England's satanic mills "enjoyed the mad destruction of their organic body … the decomposition of their personal identity … the new monstrous *anonymity* of the suburbs and the pubs."⁶⁵ Through this agonizing *jouissance* capitalism liberated libidinal energy from its repression and representation in the production process, providing an "enjoyment" comparable to that of art. This means, Lyotard writes, "completely abandoning" the critique of capitalism in order to "exalt the incredible, unspeakable pulsional possibilities that it sets rolling,"⁶⁶ because it is never a matter of "*cleaving* the instances *in two*," it's about "rendering their confusion always possible and menacing, of rendering insoluble the question of knowing."⁶⁷ Politics, for Lyotard, is a struggle over primary process, and art and capitalism are (often complementary) means of producing intensities capable of overcoming their representation/repression in the human body and its consciousness.

To come back to Lyotard's reading of conceptual art, and by implication the postconceptual practices it gave rise to, art that ignores the primary process, or tries to represent/repress it in language or concepts, cannot produce real change because it remains on the level of knowing and refuses the *real* power of *un*knowing. This is why, Lyotard tells us, "we laugh at critique, since it is to maintain oneself in the field of the criticized thing."⁶⁸ Criticism, Lyotard spits, "is deeply rational, deeply consistent with the system. Deeply reformist: the critic remains in the sphere of the criticized, he belongs to it, he goes beyond one term of the position but doesn't alter the position of terms."⁶⁹ In the end, Lyotard sighs: "What does it matter what you say if the position of discourse remains the same?"[70] The critic is always already implicated in, always confirms what she criticizes because they share representation as a mode of communication. This is significant because of postconceptual art's embrace of what Tom Holert has called the "critical epistemological function" of artistic research, knowledge production and discursive practices.[71] Holert acknowledges that these employ processes essential to cognitive capitalism, and risk turning art into "a function of global knowledge industries"[72] and an "inevitable subset of the ideology that makes up general society's self-perception."[73] But rather than affirming unknowing (or as Lyotard will later call it, "stupidity"), Holert argues that contemporary art's epistemic engagements must strive to achieve "the dislocation and repurposing of knowledge itself."[74] This means doubling down on critique. What is needed, he argues, is a *self-critique* (or institutional critique) whereby art is able to purge itself of nefarious elements such as neoliberalism and its market forces, and "inhabit the supposedly unavoidable totality of the knowledge-based polis *differently*."[75] In this sense, Holert sees art's implication within the "knowledge economy" as its strength, giving it the chance to "become a driving element of the contemporary version of the general intellect."[76] Holert's revisionary optimism (which is shared by Osborne) seems unavoidable given his claim that "epistemology always precedes ontology," and that knowledge always precedes any "notion of being."[77]

This is a precise reversal of Lyotard's position, but it is also a sleight of hand, because saying that knowledge precedes *notions* of being is a tautology claiming knowledge precedes itself. For Lyotard the death drive is primary and unconscious, immanent but other, and our *experience* of it is incommensurable with any knowledge. If there is to be institutional critique it must be that practiced by Daniel Buren, whose work deploys, Lyotard argues, "strategies brought to bear on an aesthetic" that reveal the limits of the "rationality of the visible" and its "perceptual framework."[78] For Lyotard, "artists today are engaged not in the deconstruction of significations but in extending the limits of sense perception: making visible (or audible) what now goes unobserved, through the alteration of sense data, perception itself."[79] For Lyotard, "critique" means showing "what intensities are lodged in theoretical signs, what affects within serious discourse."[80] This is the point at which politics and artistic practice meet in and as libidinal economy, as aesthetic strategies that accelerate the libidinal intensities of capitalism (rather than critical strategies that try to purge it from rationality) beyond their human limits.

Significantly for our discussion of conceptual art, Lyotard finds these strategies in Marcel Duchamp's notes about *The Large Glass* (1915–23) and *Given* (1946–66). Duchamp's "commentary" is central to his artistic practice, but does not produce discursive or conceptual "knowledge," only "nonsense as the most precious treasure."[81] As Lyotard elsewhere sarcastically remarks, interpretation *as art* is "not only for Art & Language."[82] Duchamp's notes employ "mechanical techniques" and a "cold," "distant," "inhuman" logic that follows the *jouissance* of the English workers, and like it leads "to the demeasurement of what was held to be human."[83] For Lyotard, Duchamp's commentaries reflect the "new sensibility" of industrial workers, whose "different sensorium," Lyotard argues, "later spread through the arts and sciences, the jubilation and the pain of discovering that you can hold out (live, work, think, be affected) in a place where it had been judged senseless to do so."[84] In this way Lyotard repurposes

Duchamp's notes (and his work) as aesthetic rather than conceptual documents, cutting off at the pass Duchamp's conceptual post-history. This makes Duchamp a "model of political thought" whose works should be taken as "contributions not only to an aesthetics but to a topological politics."[85] The non-sensical geometry of Duchamp's machines "comment" on the perspectival and reproductive mechanisms of both democracy and capitalism, operating as a "hinge" opening each onto their incommensurable dimensions, and introducing "the possibility of representing unpresentable space."[86] In this way, Lyotard tells us, Duchamp invents "pointless" and "dissimulating" singularities that don't "belong to the things of power, to politicians, to technicians," they are celibate machines whose "non-power" negates (from the inside) capital's modes of (re)production.[87] Duchamp's nonsense machines deploy a "stupidity of the eye" against an optical "intelligence" that insists on seeing similarities and causality in everything.[88] As Lyotard puts it: "Duchamp wants colors that are unconsumable by the eyes, 'a certain inopticity, a certain cold consideration.'"[89] These unconsumable colors are perhaps consistent with Duchamp's attack on retinality, but they are more difficult to reconcile with his celebration of an artist's "grey matter." In any case, this color of thought invisible to human eyes, and unthinkable by human brains, requires, on Lyotard's reading, a new (cybernetic) sensibility, or non-sense.

This cybernetic dimension of Lyotard's "aesthetic" genealogy of contemporary art emerges from Duchamp's notes, passes to Warhol's desire to be a machine, before confronting what Lyotard calls, in an uncanny premonition of Osborne, "photographic capitalism."[90] Lyotard's 1972 essay on the work of his friend Jacques Monory argues that it both collaborates with and explodes the optical technologies of capitalist production through its use of photography. Monory's paintings are "both economical and libidinal," Lyotard tells us, their de-differentiating blue suspending them between the reproduction of value (representation) and an extravagant expenditure (profit qua *jouissance*), producing a simultaneous "fluidification and canalisation" of libidinal forces.[91] These ambivalent paintings borrow the glossy beauty of magazines and shopping catalogs, marking the absorption of "art" by the technological *dispositifs* of capitalism and "the 'politicisation' of the production of visual pleasure."[92] Lyotard sees this as a negative development because "photography has almost nothing to do with experience. It owes almost everything to the experimentation of industrial research laboratories."[93] Photography therefore delivers aesthetic experience to capital, which revalues it according to its (conceptual) imperatives of efficiency and innovation. Science thus provides the "a priori laws" of capitalist "beauty," and achieves a "meticulous programming, through optical, chemical and photo-electronic means" that unites a capitalist sensibility with scientific rationality in the disinterested pleasure of consumption.[94] But like the industrial worker Lyotard lionized in *Libidinal Economy*, Monory's paintings also embody the destruction implicit in capitalism's circulation of intensities, the artist enjoying the most perverse and dangerous of them like "a Dionysian with a bad conscience."[95] This "libidinal wandering" isn't blocked by photography (or as Lyotard elsewhere calls it "the industrial *ready-made*"[96]), quite the contrary, the consumption of photographic beauty is intensified and accelerated by Monory's paintings, producing a "*giddy* and *chancy* vagabonding of the libido" that offers a "generous *donation* of intensities" through an "erotic-financial potlatch."[97] Echoing Lyotard's interest in Mercantilist "vain expenditure," or "treasure squandered in *jouissance*,"[98] he argues that "the machine-body of the painter upsets the photo-optical machine by making it give more than it has received."[99] This is not, however, to suggest that painting takes us outside of capitalism, because its "expenditure" is simultaneously "arrested" by Monory's calculation, commodification, and circulation of this excess through its photographic framing.[100] But while this "reduces" painting to capital it also *intensifies* its libidinal energy: "The libidinal charge of the *motif* is ten times greater because of its position of *impower* in relation to the principle of exchange value, the only discharge *dispositif* admitted in the system."[101] Art's "*pictorial hysteria*" is therefore utterly ambivalent, Lyotard claims, both requiring and overcoming the technological prostheses of photography.[102] Monory, like Duchamp, affirms the technological *dispositifs* that enable capitalism to exploit libidinal force, but only in order to produce an excess (*jouissance*) that escapes them. In this way, libidinal "liberation" is always already inseparable from its commodification, circulation and "enjoyment" as profit. In this sense Monory's paintings affirm and embody the incommensurability and absolute immanence of libidinal forces and the capitalist technologies that circulate them, but, like Duchamp's nonsense, do so *against the human*. This is the assassination of experience by painting, an inhuman art whose *jouissance* both extends and exceeds the contemporary machinism of "photo-capitalism." This technologized libido driving our sensibility beyond its human limits will form the onto-aesthetic horizon of Lyotard's 1985 exhibition *Les Immatériaux*.

The exhibition focuses on a new "immaterialist materialism"[103] found in science and new technologies dealing with "complex agglomerates of tiny packets of energy,"[104] formless and imperceptible elements that are translated into machine languages and then recomposed into new objects. This interface marks, Lyotard claimed, the "continuity between mind and matter"[105] within the im-material digital realm, where virtual networks produce "signs" of their unrepresentable materiality. While human consciousness is a nodal point in these networks, new technologies clearly exceed our processing capacity, marking the next stage of a transcendental incommensurability. *Les Immatériaux* explored the potential of art to accelerate the dissolution of the visitor's "Human Being"[106] in this new world of circulating intensities. Once again, art does this through capitalism, as that part of its process that both accelerates and exceeds it. This requires, Lyotard claims, "a thought and a practice within the framework of the technoscience of interaction—one which, in short, would break from the thought and the practice of science, of technology, and of domination."[107] As such, the exhibition presented a cacophany of sounds, objects, and experiences organized into sixty "sites," all jumbled up and arranged without any obvious logic to the visitor. In this way, the exhibition exceeded "normal" experience and thought by producing an incommensurable "non-sense" of new technology. This cybernetic "skin" is no less libidinal for being partly detached from organic life, and Lyotard embraces it as a contemporary materialization of the death drive produced by capitalism's creative nihilism. The exhibition thereby extends the genealogy of *non-sense* artistic practices into the digital realm, where capitalism's fate is increasingly bound to science and rationality. Lyotard is "critical" of how new communication and calculation technologies standardize capitalist valuations and their reproduction, reflecting how Lyotard's work after *The Postmodern Condition* (1979) increasingly detaches the "bad" immaterial of techno-scientific capitalism from the "good" immaterial of experimental art. In this sense *Les Immatériaux* is part of Lyotard's shift away from his earlier attempts at accelerating the incommensurable aspects of our political/libidinal economy, and towards a more "critical" ethics of the Other.

Lyotard's commitment to Freud's libidinal economy, and his understanding of its implications for both political economy and contemporary art, are a provocative expression of '68-thought. But the question remains as to its relevance to contemporary artistic practices today. From Lyotard's perspective, the transcendental and ahistorical ontology of the death drive and its various representations and repressions are as relevant today as they ever were, and as we have seen, he provides a fascinating genealogy of cybernetic practices that trace the interface of capitalist and artistic production in its terms. There is, however, a case to be made, as Osborne does, that contemporary art's own understanding of itself has significantly deviated from this way of thinking. Postconceptual art marks a shift in contemporary art's ontology from a primarily aesthetic practice to a conceptual one, reflecting wider shifts in contemporary life towards distributed ontologies of production (art, digital technology, capital). This not only marks an insistence on the historical specificity of art's current ontology, but also the necessity of historical engagement if art is to be political. There is something to be said for both positions, it seems to me, even while admitting that they are clearly hostile to each other. Finally, however, the incandescent anger and fierce exaltation of Lyotard's early work brings a level of commitment to aesthetics *as* politics that gives art an extraordinary power. A power, perhaps, that philosophers find easier to affirm than artists.

Notes

1   Jean-François Lyotard, "Notes on the Critical Function of the Work of Art" [1970], in *Driftworks*, ed. Roger McKeon (New York: Semiotext(e), 1984), 79. The quotation in the essay's title comes from Jean-François Lyotard, *Libidinal Economy*, tr. Iain Hamilton Grant (London and New York: Continuum, [1974] 2004), 109.
2   Jean-François Lyotard, *Discourse, Figure*, tr. Antony Hudek and Mary Lydon (Minneapolis MN: University of Minnesota Press, [1971] 2011), 205.
3   Jean-François Lyotard, *The Inhuman, Reflections on Time*, tr. Geoffrey Bennington and Rachel Bowlby (Cambridge UK: Polity, [1988] 1991), 90.
4   Jean-François Lyotard, "The Affect-phrase," in this volume, 68.
5   Jean-François Lyotard, "Adrift," in *Driftworks*, 16.
6   Ibid., 29.
7   Sigmund Freud, "Beyond the Pleasure Principle" [1920], *The Standard Edition of the Complete Psychological Works of Sigmund Freud*, tr. and ed. James Strachey, XVIII (London: Hogarth, 1955; London: Vintage, 2001), 62.
8   Ibid., 32.
9   Ibid., 38.
10 Ibid., 34.
11 Lyotard, *Discourse, Figure*, 315.

12 Ibid., 352.
13 Lyotard, "Notes on the Critical Function," 72–3.
14 Jean-François Lyotard, "The 'intensities' are what imports, not the meaning" [1975], in *The Interviews and Debates*, ed. Kiff Bamford (London and New York: Bloomsbury, 2020), 36.
15 Lyotard, *Discourse, Figure*, 383.
16 Ibid., 196.
17 Ibid., 282.
18 Freud, "Beyond the Pleasure Principle," 67. Freud remarks that Kant's claims for time and space in the Transcendental Aesthetic are "open to debate" because the unconscious is "timeless." (Ibid.)
19 Jean-François Lyotard, "Foreword: After the Words" [1991], in *Textes dispersés II: artistes contemporains/ Miscellaneous Texts II: Contemporary Artists*, ed. Herman Parret, tr. Vlad Ionescu, Erica Harris and Peter W. Milne (Leuven: Leuven University Press, 2012), 519.
20 Lyotard, *Discourse, Figure*, 129–30.
21 Lyotard, *Libidinal Economy*, 171.
22 Ibid., 49.
23 Ibid., 51, see also 66.
24 Ibid., 212.
25 Lyotard, *Discourse, Figure*, 7.
26 Jean-François Lyotard, "Doing Away with the Illusion of Politics" [1972], in Lyotard, *The Interviews and Debates*, 29.
27 Lyotard, *Discourse, Figure*, 13.
28 Peter Osborne, *Anywhere or Not at All, Philosophy of Contemporary Art* (London and New York, Verso, 2013), 8.
29 Peter Osborne, *The Postconceptual Condition* (London and New York, Verso, 2018), 139.
30 Osborne, *Anywhere or Not at All*, 8.
31 Ibid., 16.
32 Ibid., 19.
33 Ibid., 50.
34 Osborne, *The Postconceptual Condition*, 20.
35 [The phrase "'68-thought" or *la pensée soixante-huit* refers to the thinkers who became associated with the period around the May 1968 student and worker uprising and strikes. Whilst constructed in retrospect, the phrase might refer to the work of French philosophers such as Michel Foucault, Jacques Derrida, or Jacques Lacan, but also writers from the United States who were being published in France, such as Herbert Marcuse's *One Dimensional Man*, which appeared in French in 1968.—Eds]
36 Osborne, *Anywhere or Not at All*, 50.
37 Ibid., 124.
38 Ibid., 118.
39 Ibid., 129.
40 Ibid., 131.
41 Ibid., 33.
42 Ibid., 49.
43 Sol Le Witt's famous definition of conceptual art is: "In conceptual art the idea or concept is the most important aspect of the work. When an artist uses a conceptual form of art, it means that all of the planning and decisions are made beforehand and

the execution is a perfunctory affair. The idea becomes a machine that makes the art." (Sol LeWitt, "Paragraphs on Conceptual Art" [1967], in Alexander Alberro and Blake Stimson (eds), *Conceptual Art: A Critical Anthology* (Cambridge MA: MIT Press, 1999). 12) Osborne also mentions Lawrence Wiener's slightly stricter rules (*Anywhere or Not at All*, 54, 61):

"1. The artist may construct the piece
2. The piece may be fabricated
3. The piece need not be built

Each being equal and consistent with the intent of the artist the decision as to condition rests with the receiver upon the condition of receivership" (quoted in Alberto Alberro, *Conceptual Art and the Politics of Publicity* (Cambridge MA: MIT Press, 2003), 97).

44 Osborne, *Anywhere or Not at All*, 49.
45 Joseph Kosuth, "Art After Philosophy" [1969], in *Art After Philosophy and After: Collected Writings 1966–90*, ed. Gabriele Guercio (Cambridge MA: MIT Press, 1991), 18.
46 Ibid., 20.
47 Ibid., 30.
48 Ibid., 20.
49 Ibid., 25.
50 Ibid., 20–1.
51 Lyotard, "Foreword: After the Words," 519.
52 Ibid., 521.
53 Ibid., 519–21.
54 Ibid., 519.
55 Ibid., 527.
56 Lyotard, *Libidinal Economy*, 79.
57 A claim that keeps ontology in the realm of philosophy. Deleuze and Guattari explicitly reject conceptual art, and reference Kosuth in doing so, in *What Is Philosophy?*, tr. Graham Burchell and Hugh Tomlinson (New York: Columbia University Press, [1991] 1994), 198–9.
58 Pierre Klossowski, *Living Currency*, ed. Vernon W. Cisney, tr. Nicolae Morar and Daniel W. Smith (London and New York: Bloomsbury, [1970] 2017), 47.
59 Lyotard, *Libidinal Economy*, 212–3.
60 Ibid., 145–50.
61 Ibid., 167.
62 Ibid., 79.
63 Ibid., 84.
64 Klossowski, *Living Currency*, 66.
65 Lyotard, *Libidinal Economy*, 109–10.
66 Ibid., 136.
67 Ibid., 26.
68 Ibid., 94.
69 Lyotard, "Adrift," 13.
70 Lyotard, *Libidinal Economy*, 117.
71 Tom Holert, *Knowledge Beside Itself, Contemporary Art's Epistemic Politics* (Berlin: Sternberg Press, 2020), 58.
72 Ibid., 14.
73 Ibid., 19.

74 Ibid., 18.
75 Ibid., 31.
76 Ibid., 34.
77 Ibid., 11.
78 Jean-François Lyotard [1978] (1979), "Preliminary Notes on the Pragmatic of Works: Daniel Buren," tr. Thomas Repensek, *October*, no. 10, 66.
79 Ibid., 67.
80 Lyotard, *Libidinal Economy*, 102.
81 Jean-François Lyotard, *Duchamp's TRANS/formers*, ed. Herman Parret, tr. Ian McLeod. *Writings on Contemporary Art and Artists*, vol. 3 (Leuven: Leuven University Press, [1977] 2010), 49.
82 Lyotard, "Preliminary Notes . . .," 62.
83 Lyotard, *Duchamp's TRANS/formers*, 57, 59.
84 Ibid., 16. Lyotard is quoting himself from *Libidinal Economy*, 110.
85 Ibid., 25, 26.
86 Ibid., 90.
87 Ibid., 101, 69.
88 Ibid., 76.
89 Ibid., 135.
90 Jean-François Lyotard, "Sketch of an Economy of Hyperrealism" [1973], in *Textes dispersés I: esthétique et théorie de l'art/ Miscellaneous Texts I: Aesthetics and Theory of Art*, ed. Herman Parret, tr. Vlad Ionescu, Erica Harris and Peter W. Milne (Leuven: Leuven University Press, 2012), 111.
91 Jean-François Lyotard, "Libidinal Economy of the Dandy" [1972], in *The Assassination of Experience by Painting Monory*, tr. Rachel Bowlby (London: Black Dog Publishing, 1998), 120.
92 Ibid., 133.
93 Lyotard, *The Inhuman*, 122.
94 Ibid.
95 Lyotard, "Libidinal Economy of the Dandy," 140.
96 Lyotard, *The Inhuman*, 121.
97 Lyotard, "Libidinal Economy of the Dandy," 146.
98 Lyotard, *Libidinal Economy*, 192.
99 Lyotard, "Sketch of an Economy of Hyperrealism," 113.
100 Lyotard, "Libidinal Economy of the Dandy," 146.
101 Ibid., 153, trans. modified.
102 Ibid., 177.
103 Lyotard, *The Inhuman*, 45.
104 Jean-François Lyotard, "Les Immatériaux: A Conversation with Bernard Blistène" [1985], in Lyotard, *The Interviews and Debates*, 80.
105 Jean-François Lyotard, "Complexity and the Sublime," in Lisa Appignanesi (ed.), *Postmodernism: ICA Documents* (London: Free Association Books, 1989), 20.
106 Lyotard, "Les Immatériaux," 79.
107 Jean-François Lyotard, "After Six Months of Work . . ." [1984], in Yuk Hui and Andreas Broeckman (eds), *30 Years after Les Immatériaux, Art, Science, Theory* (Lüneburg: Meson Press, 2015), 34. This point—and much else in my account—has been influenced by Maria Aroni's fascinating doctoral thesis *The Aesthetics of Curating: Exhibition Making After the Conceptual Turn* (London: Kingston University, 2016), which takes *Les Immatériaux* as one of its case studies.

16

Uncertain? For sure. Limping? Certainly: Limp Thoughts on Performance Practice

Kiff Bamford

Restricted blood flow to the limbs results in claudication.[1] Claudication makes one limp. Such limping is used by Lyotard, both as a physical manifestation and as a metaphor for thinking without certainty, in the two texts, "Apathy in Theory" and "Interview with *Art Présent*," presented in this volume for the first time in English translation. They don't present a theory of "limping" but encourage rather a multiplicity of theories which trade on the inherent excitement of the unknown, the as yet undetermined. This is the same "manner" which appealed to Lyotard in Kant's third *Critique*; the same wandering attention that appealed in Freud and an openness to the sometimes uncertain encounters in art practice. In this chapter these themes from the two "new" texts will be drawn out through specific examples of performance art practice, their dissemination and attempts at a limping commentary. The vibration of inner organs fired by a sound installation, the smell of recently cut marine ply, the odd encounter of Lyotard with Augustine of Hippo via cassette recorders which should be obsolete, lay bare the body's limits.

"Apathy in Theory" was first published in the journal *Critique* in January 1975 and subsequently included as the first chapter of the 1977 collection *Rudiments païens* (Pagan Rudiments). This process of publishing articles then incorporating them into subsequent works was commonplace for Lyotard—even the virulent *Libidinal Economy* absorbed a review of *La Vie sexuelle dans la Chine ancienne* (*Sexual Life in Ancient China*) by Robert van Gulik, also published previously in *Critique*. Such fragmentary beginnings mirror the present fate of *Rudiments païens*, having never been published in its entirety in English. Pagan rudiments were soon occluded by the shiny postmodern and the debates that raced off elsewhere, largely away from politics. Yet our publication of "Apathy in Theory" finally completes the set: all elements of the volume now exist in English translation, though they make a motley crew dispersed across five different publications and seemingly isolated from one another. The lack of desire to maintain the collection in English is no surprise given the range of figures and topics dealt with by Lyotard. It would certainly challenge an editor to conjure a guiding thread through the proper names of Blaise Pascal; Louis Marin; Ernst Bloch and Michel Butor, and the themed chapters on the struggle of women, minorities, revolutionary theater, and the hesitancy of Freud's writing in the chapter translated here. Yet it is a similar diversity across different fields which motivates this present collection and its participants, to argue for and to explore a decompartmentalization of study and a reexploration of Lyotard's potential for critical practice.

The pagan is taken as a figure for Lyotard because of its multiplicity; not the worship of a single all-powerful deity but the commonplace pagan gods who dwelt alongside everyday activities: even the acts of coitus or pissing was attended by a god, a goddess, or several gods, Lyotard recalls.[2] In this pagan multiplicity the grand other of theory is dissembled and the presumption of an all-seeing, all-embracing "master" is brought down. The gendering is significant: as Lyotard asks in the opening to the chapter "*Féminité dans la métalangue*," "It may be that, from the moment you write, you are compelled to be a man."[3] This opening is itself placed under the subheading "*Écriture mâle*" (male writing). It is a subheading that is absent in the English translation, as is the subtlety implied in the chapter's title, given in English as "One of the Things at Stake in Women's Struggles," a left-over from its first publication in Italian. The essay has been one of the more frequently referenced elements from *Rudiments païens*, being also a key touchstone for contributors to the 2007 collection *Gender after Lyotard*. However, the given English title implies that this is Lyotard preaching "on" women's struggles and therefore risks ignoring the nuanced discussions of what a feminine writing might be, discussions which were never fully developed or answered directly by Lyotard but which return at least in the penultimate remark of the Gertrude Stein notice in *The Differend*: "'Feminine writing': inscribe that this cannot be filled in, from one sentence to the next? Would it be a genre?"[4] The "this" to which the sentence refers is characteristically left unclear, unfilled: refusing to give pre-prepared answers to the reader.

Paganism also infers the roman *pagus* which signifies the physical and legal border zone, where dwellers are not members of the *polis*, not citizens with full rights: foreigners, slaves, women, children. Lyotard also uses the Greek equivalent *métèque* as indicative of the pejorative label given to those from elsewhere in xenophobic French slang. "Greasy foreigner" is the translation used in the 1975 work of "fiction theory" *Pacific Wall*, written in the context of southern California where white skin is seen as a signifier of "blankness" or unquestioned belonging among the pungent eucalyptus trees in the utopian campus of the University of California at San Diego. Ashley Woodward has recently reconsidered *Pacific Wall* in the context of a postcolonial libidinal economy, indicating how Lyotard's writings consider the subtle distinctions of an impiety that does not acquiesce to the imperial dominance which thrives on the blankness of acceptance and political quietude.[5] As Achille Mbembe declares in *Necropolitics*: "Every gesture of writing is intended to engage a force, or even a *différend*."[6]

"Apathy in Theory" details an aligned struggle: a struggle with thoughts that refuse to sit within the accepted notions of knowledge, that sit without the *polis* of what should be thought. This rudimentary aspect of paganism is complex and self-contradictory, following the twists and turns of impious thoughts which provoke and demand judgment, whilst refusing to supply a ready guide. Instead, the role of affect is introduced. Introduced, not as a guide to judgment but as the signal of a demand, the presence of something that requires judgment without prejudgments. Affect, present not only in psychoanalytic theory or more specifically the writings of Freud, but in art practice, practices that are taken up as the subject of the *Art Présent* interview and which link to the questions taken up again in the exciting late essay "The Affect-phrase."

Incertitude

For Lyotard there is a particular moment discernible in Freud's work that correlates to the manner of working he describes as apathetic. It is a mode of writing and thinking which allows lines of thought to be followed regardless of the need and pressures to prove according to usual conventions, through demonstrable evidential claims. Rather, it is a mode based on an affective instinctual "hunch" which, because it is uncertain in its very method, cannot subscribe to accepted conventions of thinking. Lyotard suggests that such an approach occurs in the work of Freud at the time of *Beyond the Pleasure Principle* because of the uncertain nature of the drives about which he is speculating: the proposal of a "third" regime of the drives characterized not as oppositional to one another but as aligned, correlated, inter-related. The uncertainty inherent in the drive dualism and its dissimulating effects parallels the "hesitation in the discourse of knowledge"[7] when confronted by this indeterminacy, or to put it otherwise the proposals do not lend themselves to the established characteristics of thinking that Lyotard lampoons under the nomination of the theoretical.

Theoretical terror is Lyotard's target in "Apathy in Theory," thus reminding us of the context of its writing. It came in the wake of *Libidinal Economy* (1974) which had drawn the ire of many readers for its ethical indeterminacy, for its parodic approach to Marxist theory, for its scandalously untheoretical style: Lyotard would later denounce it as "my evil book." In some ways we could argue that the presence of this essay in *Rudiments païens*, lightly adapted from its first presentation in the journal *Critique* in 1975, puts paid to the simplistic compartmentalization of Lyotard's writing as having an identifiable before and after the so-called libidinal period. For is this essay not echoing the challenge of *Libidinal Economy* and with it the highly charged writing style which strikes a chord with aficionados of Deleuze and Guattari? The section of "Apathy in Theory" titled *Advocatus Diaboli* (Devil's Advocate) shows Lyotard at work in the process of retranslating Freud (hence the multiple explanatory translator's notes,) whilst acting also as the nominated contestant, or witness to Freud's own "critical reflection [*Besinnung*: reverting to the sense]."[8] As a popular title given to the adversary in the Roman Catholic process of assessing candidature for canonization, the *Advocatus Diaboli* seeks to undermine and challenge. The refusal to accept the claims of a dominant genre, even and especially within the same voice, emerges within the pagan work and demonstrates a bridge to both *The Postmodern Condition* and *The Differend*. In the pagan work the triad of addressor, addressee and reference, are used as the basis for a pragmatic analysis of the relation between nodes and modes of address whilst in *The Differend* the pole of referent is further subdivided into sense and referent: four instances to ascertain how claims are established, dismissed and silenced. Investigating the operational modes that form the basis for a discourse weighted to an already established schema, which gives voice to some whilst silencing others, is already very present in Lyotard's work on paganism. So too is the refusal to accept the "intimidation" to remain silent about that which does not conform to the prescription of truth accepted by the dominant theoretical genre, as dictated by the dominant *Imperium*.[9]

The possibility of a connection between the most stylistically outrageous of Lyotard's books—*Libidinal Economy*—and his seemingly most restrained—*The Differend*—is significant. It forces us to undermine the assumption that we should or could simply take Lyotard's own word for the moves he makes; how we should judge what has been published and what should be disregarded, passed on or passed over. Often he reflects the attitude of many artists whose concern is only for their current work, consequently resisting attempts by a curator, interviewer, or art historian to return them to earlier work in discussion, unless that work is part of the current project. In the art world this fear comes perhaps from the convention of the retrospective which is traditionally both the apogee and death knell of an active practice. The desire of others to turn always to the work which made them established is a refusal of that which engages them now, it dissimulates the new for the already acknowledged. Likewise, when the "evil book" quotation is used to dismiss the *Libidinal Economy* (spoken over a decade after its publication): "I used to say that it was my evil book, the book of evilness that everyone writing and thinking is tempted to do,"[10] we might counter such an easy refutation with another, similar quotation (also spoken over a decade since its publication) about *The Differend*: "which is a terrible book, a horrible book."[11] In the light of "Apathy in Theory" we should be more cautious about both these declarations—they are not simple dismissals within the context of success or failure but rather express the need to pursue the new and to play with the discourse of knowledge in order to destabilize that which he terms theoretical terror. For if Lyotard was to agree that one or other of these books was his "master" work it would suggest he had succeeded, arrived, and through such arrogance stymy the wandering trails of thought. When he did come close to self-aggrandizement in declaring *The Differend* his "book of philosophy" it was firmly tongue in cheek. The declaration itself is a parody—"my book of philosophy"—which prompted protestations from Jacques Derrida that he was not perhaps the best judge: exactly![12] Marcel Duchamp made a similar point, concretized through a self-portrait *With my tongue in my cheek* (1959) which incorporates a cast of his cheek pushed out by the tongue hidden inside, benefiting also from an additional pun in French where *la langue* conveys both tongue and language. With one's tongue in one's cheek, however, speech is impeded. As Lyotard declares in the *Art Présent* interview: with Duchamp there are only paradoxes, it is his task to multiply paradoxes and "to defy all commentary." "All the wordplay, all the puns, all the linguistic research, it's the same thing. They are linguistic paradoxes."[13]

Parody is the strategy offered by Lyotard at the end of "Apathy in Theory" to overturn the theoretical as the dominant genre of discourse. Within this context there is another self-referential remark worth revisiting, to demonstrate the extent to which Lyotard can be said to have pursued his own exhortation to destroy theory by rendering it one genre among others, to lay bare its limitations through fiction-theories. When interviewed by the artist and concrete poet Alain Arias-Misson for the art and poetry journal *Lotta Poetica* in 1987 Lyotard explains the context for the commissioning of

The Postmodern Condition. Following the insistence of the director of the Council of Universities of the government of Quebec to write a report on the "problems of knowledge in industrially developed societies" Lyotard was made to consider the possibilities of exploring the report as a genre. It was not without interesting precedents, Lyotard reflects, citing *The Georgics* by Claude Simon for its fragmentary use of historical reports within a multivocal fictional context.

> So I said, all right, something could be done in report style, why not, it's interesting, brief. Like a communiqué, so I'll try to write on this question of the changing state of knowledge. I told stories in the book, I referred to a quantity of books I'd never read, apparently it impressed people, it's all a bit of a parody.[14]

This confession is used by Perry Anderson in *The Origins of the Postmodern* to cast aspersions on the false crowning of *The Postmodern Condition* as a bible to the postmodern while at the same time making the nuanced observation that this was already undertaken in Fredric Jameson's introduction to the English translation, which destroyed it from within.[15] Yes, the footnotes proliferate as with all "weighty" tomes and is all the more marked in contrast to the svelte appearance of *The Differend*, then in preparation, which was published without footnotes. In the Lyotard archive I read correspondence from an American friend explaining, with regret, the poor reception of an article solicited from Lyotard for a US journal—without the required number of footnotes it apparently doesn't deserve a proper reading. This is Lyotard's point, and one from which we might still learn. In his 2018 book *New Dark Age* the artist James Bridle recounts the increased percentage of scientific journal articles that are retracted, of which a significant proportion are the result of researcher misconduct, not through deliberate attempts at parody but because of the reliance on automated data collection and pressure to publish that has resulted in a seemingly exponential rise in articles themselves, thus rendering the peer review process invalid.[16] The destruction of theory for which Lyotard calls is an undermining of the presumptions to truth which might shelter mere axiomatic assumptions. In the *Art présent* interview the rhetorical call to destroy theory is qualified: not to destroy like a terrorist but to multiply theories, to dissemble its claims to dominance. It is a challenge echoed in Donna Haraway's embrace of "speculative fabulation," not to abandon facts but to show there must be other ways of thinking besides the constraints of accepted narratives: "It matters what matters we use to think other matters with; it matters what stories we tell to tell other stories with."[17]

For Lyotard theoretical terror is the dominance of a model that constrains, whether the dominant model of Western philosophy from Plato to Jacques Lacan, or the unachievable ideals of Karl Marx, especially when strangled by bureaucracy as exemplified by the French Communist Party. The theoretical is the realm of the unattainable idealized objects paraded outside the cave's opening to which Plato emboldened his student to cleave, neglecting the "imitations" of the everyday which included their own bodies, desires and passions. A revocation of all passions except that of conviction: true over false, good over bad, or the ultimate resolution of revolution above all else. When Lyotard proclaims his adoption of a "degree zero" approach to language in *The Differend* he parodies the abstracted search for neutrality of so-called "ordinary language" philosophers who take inspiration from the Wittgenstein of the *Tractatus*. In "Apathy in Theory" Lyotard quotes Wittgenstein's call to silence as that which Freud refused in his speculative writings, dismissing the limitations of the unsayable and the terror of silence.[18] Where then does the parody end for Lyotard, does it have any seriousness? Yes, of course in that the "serious" is the playful rearticulation of possibilities for thought. The playful model he identifies in the wanderings of the Freud text he follows with care and in the artistic tendency not to shoulder the weight of the world's woes on one's shoulder but to experiment regardless of the pressure to prove, to make useful, to monetize or, in the words of the present UK government, to pursue a "high-value" course of study. This is the apathy that Lyotard exhorts us to and its potentially misleading usage needs some clarification.

"This wanderer is apathetic" because they do not know, they are not certain and are not turned or tuned to the conventions of theoretical discourse: they do not seek to be convinced. Conviction closes enquiry, it requires and follows a set of logical moves internal to its system (what Lyotard later calls "phrase regimens") in order to achieve the desired (and predictable) outcome. What Freud does not do—as the wanderer, writing *Beyond the Pleasure Principle*—is dismiss the effects of uncertainty: the writing does not signal Freud's conviction regarding the workings of the drives but indicates "at least its *existence* as a theoretical hypothesis subject to discussion."[19] This is in spite of Freud's acknowledgment that he is not convinced, that he cannot believe it: contravening as it does the basis of knowledge production as reliant on the "decidability of causes."[20] Through the analysis of Freud's hesitation within the text Lyotard jumps on the decisive presence of undecidability within his thinking: his desire to ascertain the absence of determinacy. Lyotard concludes that what Freud experiences is in fact not a lack of conviction but the undecidability of affect, a common function inherent to the drives which are his concern. Rather than being founded on the opposition of life / death; need / desire; pain / pleasure as posited in the previous theory of the drives, Freud finds the symptoms of the cases he follows to be indiscernible from one another. The drives themselves operate in the same manner: without stable guiding principles. Lyotard leads us to Freud's account of the case of Dora. Her multiple physical, bodily symptoms are seen as pronouncements that are rendered undecidable because they are blocked together, signifying not life or death but life and death, whether the life of the symptom or the threatened death of the organic body. The respiratory system signifies that it is being killed at one and the same time that the symptom declares that it lives.

Opening Uncertainty

Thank you.
Thank you for watching that with me.
Thank you for watching the screen filled with a mouth trying to keep open.
Struggling to stay open, "to stay open for you;" verbalizing the simultaneous physical struggle of the programmed conceit.

It is 2017 in the cinema of the Institute of Contemporary Art (ICA) off the Mall in London. Outside there is a protest to "save our NHS." Inside we have just watched a visual display of the state of dentistry in the United States circa 1974, courtesy of the performance artist Vito Acconci and his ten-minute video *Open Book*.[21] Projected on the cinema screen rather than presented on a monitor, this work is transformed from a strange, intimate gesture into something more macabre. The soundtrack is rendered literally cinematic, the protagonist's—the artist's—voice inescapable as its pleading becomes more threatening: "I stay open for you!" How can he remain open for us? What might that mean? Of course it is metaphorical as well as literal but what does it mean, this opening of which the mouth speaks? I am reminded of this challenge when reading Lyotard's interview for *Art Présent* where he draws on Beckett's *Watt* and the strange description of his movements. But I didn't know the interview then: it hadn't found me, though I wanted to remain open to allow it to limp to me stuck in a bound cycle of repetition.

The symposium I have begun to describe was entitled *Performance and Uncertainty*, co-programed with artist and colleague Harold Offeh at two venues in Leeds and London. *Open Book* was shown at both iterations. Working together because of our shared interest in reperformance, repetition, the *re*- of performance, it was initially our intention that the idea of reperformance would be our theme, but it felt too staid, ground already well-trodden. Uncertainty was proposed instead, proposed by chance on the same day that news came through of the fatal assault on a Member of Parliament in the north of England, not far from my home; the brutal assault on a young, optimistic, MP whilst walking in public in her constituency. We were eating noodles, Harold and I, when the news came through. A couple of hours before our planning meeting at the ICA.

Uncertainty became the moniker that accompanied the aftermath both of the murder and the result of the Brexit campaign which had likely contributed to her death, accompanied as it was by the words "Britain First." In Brazil, in the same summer of 2016, the Sao Paulo Biennale was accompanied by a declaration of uncertainty, following the removal of the president and the political ramifications which have continued to play out as a result over subsequent years. Yet the curators issued a statement which encapsulated the positive need to ensure that uncertainty was not a cloak of fear which would simply allow conservative retrograde politics to flourish but, rather, that uncertainty of thought is necessary.

The destabilization of thought fixed within known parameters is what concerns Lyotard in his essays presented here; the theory against which he rails is that which responds only to the yes and no of conviction. The Apathy in theory of which he writes is not indifference in the sense of political quietude, of political indifference, but rather the indifference to those affects of conviction operating within theory that enable a binary response of true or false, yes or no. It is this refusal of bivalence that is termed "apathy." An apathy toward the one passion—conviction—which the theoretical understands; apathy refuses to be blinded by conviction in order to remain open to complexity. The promised "I can stay open" of Acconci's mouth similarly draws on this apathy—we do not know how to react—we are rendered uncertain. This menacing, pleading voice. The husky Italian-American accent, well known to those who have encountered Vito Hannibal Acconci in any spoken form. This same voice whose live presence was removed through death, in the same year as the symposia. As I declared in the presentation that followed the screening of *Open Book*, I was unsure what I was doing. And this was not a conceit. For me "Apathy in Theory" and its accompanying interview begin to echo some of what had led me to that point and now, after the event, I can perhaps uncover some of the feelings which drove them.

Limping

The interview with *Art Présent* was published in Spring 1979, the same year as *The Postmodern Condition*, the work which would significantly alter Lyotard's reception and reputation. However, the interview itself predates this: dated Late 1978 it opens with a quotation from "Apathy in Theory" and ends with another quotation from the same collection—*Rudiments païens*—in a joyful leap of continuity. The interview has been hidden not only from English-speaking eyes, this being its first English translation, but also to some extent from the French it would seem. It was published in a small-circulation art magazine which ceased to exist after only nine issues; the interview between Lyotard and Alain Pomarède, its editor, was in the penultimate issue. It has not escaped the attention of scholars seeking to recognize Lyotard's limited but important writings on cinema, however, for this interview revolves round experimental cinema. It is seen as one of the remedies to the vulgarity he writes of in "Apathy in Theory," the vulgarity to pretend to speak the truth through that theoretical mode of mastery, to continually venerate the theoretical genre above others. In contrast Lyotard turns to the forces of lightness in "painting, music, experimental cinema as well, obviously, as those of the sciences" : a lightness he takes up limping ...[22]

> '*Was man nicht erfliegen kann, muss man erhinken ... Die Schrift sagt, es ist keine Sünde zu hinken*' (What we cannot reach flying we must reach limping ... The book tells us that limping is no sin.)

Freud chose to close *Beyond the Pleasure Principle* with this quotation, the last line of Friedrich Rückert's "*Die beiden Gulden*" (The Two Coins); a version of one of the short stories—*maqāmah*—of Al-Hariri, the Arab poet also known as Al-Hariri of Basra (1054–1122). The Arabic *maqāmah*, combines rhymed prose (*saj*) and poetry echoing the name of the form, literally settings or assemblies, and the gatherings at which they were traditionally delivered. The lines incorporate rhetorical flourishes, wordplay and other such complexities, while the narrator of the *maqāmah* recounts the stories of a wanderer, their encounters and exploits, with both comic and serious—ethical and religious—content. The first phrase of this quotation was also used as the title to Lyotard's interview when reprinted in German, in 1986.[23]

Claudication

"The Old Blind School" is an empty series of adjoining buildings appropriated for use as a temporary exhibition space. Formerly the home of a Trade Union's social support center there are faded, peeling murals in some communal spaces: the interior surface of a cupula pictures a glorious socialist future. Downstairs, a warren of installations with no attempt to render the spaces gallery-like. The concrete floor is dusty or partially covered in worn linoleum tiles, one's feet scuffs against the edge, the lip of the lino or the raised surface of residual rubber adhesive. Several hours spent moving between the labyrinth of rooms on the ground floor, the first floor, across linking corridors between the buildings. Brick, early twentieth-century school architecture. Following the exhibition plan to explore every corridor, room, stairwell; second floor: projections, very few visitors now and cut off from the daily life of the city outside. I am tired and, glancing at my watch, mount the stairs to the additional room in the attic, a small room according to the plan which represents it as an extension beyond the drawn projection of the building's footprint. I emerge to find a room within a room and the smell of freshly cut marine ply. Crossing the threshold I am hit by a wall of enveloping sound; red LED display-readers punch out words scrolling from left to right: pausing, flashing. A central, large bass speaker makes the whole structure vibrate whilst hidden speakers bring additional, distanced sounds into the space. The clarity of an intoned voice is interrupted by a cheap horned speaker—invoking political rallies or a mosque's call to prayer—that crackles into life. I remember it as dark, yet there were lights, enough to read the texts provided: booklets of the script I presumed, yet the clearly laid out voices of the text don't match the words that are broadcast, sounds which alternate between single voices and crowds chanting, or overlap to create a cacophony that is felt on the body, through the body as the skin, the organs vibrate to the deep oscillations of the subwoofer. All the time the smell of sawn wood composite—the stuff of temporary installations and shelters. Inside there is one other visitor, I smile weakly but otherwise we ignore one another to face the confusion alone.

Two years later I have read more about the piece.[24] I have read of its evocation of the Shiite festival of Ashura with the breast-beating crowd who reenact the assassination of Imam Al Hussein, the grandson of the Prophet Mohammed. I know that the multiple voices narrate not only the events of the story and its theatrical, ritual reenactment but also stranger, more familiar additions—a snippet from Lewis Carroll which feels culturally more familiar yet not straightforward, except for the invocation of judgment in absurdity. I know of the connection to resistance in Lebanon, to the artist's own personal history; the shift from oppressed to oppressor, the role of theater as a means of representation: "is it possible to script justice" asks the artist in an attending publication. Having read about this, but feeling no clearer in relation to the experience I had in the Old Blind School, I contacted the artist to ask if she might contribute to the symposium being planned, now under the title *Performance and Uncertainty*. We arrange a video call. I feel uncertain as to what I am asking but try to convey to the artist Rana Hamadeh the effect that the piece had on me, although it had no clarity, neither in my reaction, attempted analysis, nor retelling. I look away from the eye of the camera to grope for an explanation. I had visited the piece, it had affected me in a way that I couldn't account for but I was sure it offered something that was in keeping with our ambitions for the symposium. "Do you know what I mean?" I ask, hopefully. "No," she replies, "but I am getting a feeling of what you might mean."

We agreed that the piece would be incorporated into the symposium at Leeds, not as a sound installation but as a performance through which the visitors would wander.[25] The technical set-up was complex. It is an eight-channel sound play which requires four full-range corner speakers, two full-range middle speakers, two large subwoofers, a horn speaker, a cheap speaker, two microphones, a sound engineer, some lengths of chain, an office plant and a full day of technical set-up and sound checking before the performance. It also required me to sing a song from Lewis Carroll and to hold an interview with the artist as part of the performance. Later, following the first projection of Acconci's *Open Book* and my accompanying remarks, I gave two short readings. In comparison to Rana's sound play they were simple. I read into a microphone then moved around the now-seated audience, still reading: first a section from the *Confessions* of St. Augustine on time, "How can I measure time...?" then a section from Lyotard's *The Confession of Augustine*, "Witness," read once straight and then read again but backwards in sections, phrases, which made new, jumbled sense.

By the time of the London event, the reading of *The Confession of Augustine* had become more theatrical. It was a month later to the day with a new program, only the Acconci video and my poor joke about the state of dentistry in the United States remained the same. The audience were in fixed seats and presenters spoke from the small stage of the ICA cinema. This time I read into two microphones, one amplified for the present audience and an old recording microphone attached to a cassette tape recorder. I knelt on the stage, spotlit from below by a single lamp and, before I read, pressed "record" and "play" on the tape recorder:

Witness

Not memory, then, but the said inner human, who is neither man nor inner, woman and man, an outside inside. This is the only witness of the presence of the Other, of the other of presence, A singular witness, the poem. The inner human does not bear witness to a fact, to a violent event that it would have seen, that it would have heard, tasted, or touched. It does not give testimony, it is the testimony. It is the vision, the scent, the listening, the taste, the contact, each violated and metamorphosed. A wound, an ecchymosis, a scar attests to the fact that a blow has been received, they are its mechanical effect. Signs all the more trustworthy since they do not issue from any intention or any arbitrary inscription: they vouch for the event since they remain after it. Augustine's *Treatises* abound in these analyses of semiotic value: the present object evokes the absent one, in its place.

The inner human does not evoke an absence. It

is not there for the other; it is the Other of the there, who is there, there where light takes place without place, there where sound resounds without duration, and so forth. Explosive and implosive, it is the *plosum*, the plosion cancelling the *a priori* forms of inscription and hence of possible testimony. A witness in proportion to there being none, and there can be no witness of this blow that, we repeat, abolishes the periods, the surfaces of the archive. The tables of memory fall to dust, the blow has not passed. The inner human attests *ab intestat*.[26]

Blinded by the light, I fumbled to press "stop" on the cassette recorder, to feel my way across the buttons to press "rewind," then to "play" again as the recorded sound of what I had read was replayed, and over which I read the text again but in reverse: single words, grouped words or phrases, to reread the text again; duetting with my own recorded voice. This was rehearsed in part, but never before an audience had I read in this way the odd recreation of Lyotard's own duet with Augustine, itself a dialogue with his interior self, or with his imagined voice of God.

Gerald L. Burns comments that Lyotard's own writing in this his last, unfinished, text becomes indecipherable from that of Augustine: the voices of commentary melt into the commentated-on and in the fragments of the unfinished text in particular, the two merge.[27] Lyotard notes that Augustine had lifted "whole verses from the psalmists," together with the use of a meter or rhythm comprised of two unequal parts—the *qinah*, identified in the late nineteenth century through analysis of Hebrew laments—which "move the body in minimal choreographic figures; one limps in jerks so as to deplore the infirmity of being unable to walk straight."[28] I don't know the extent to which my body moved on the stage of the ICA but I know that inside I danced, limping because the ground was unclear.

At one moment my recorded and voiced readings met and crossed one another—the point of the wound, the scar: "they vouch for the event since they remain after it"; "since they remain after it, they vouch for the event." This is what I gained from Rana Hamadeh's sound play, led by Lyotard's limping incertitude.

Notes

1   A somewhat unfamiliar medical term, claudication or intermittent claudication causes limping; the reader is asked to put up with the awkward unfamiliarity of this term, to limp on in the knowledge that Lyotard's metaphorical reference to this medical condition is unrelenting in the interview with *Art Présent*, published in this volume, extending its singular appearance in "Apathy in Theory." To aid the reader the following note is added to the translated *Art Présent* interview: "Intermittent claudication is a cramping pain that limits walking ability. It may be neurogenic or vascular . . . Claudication most commonly affects the calf muscle." Michael Kent, *The*

Oxford Dictionary of Sports Science & Medicine, 3rd ed. (Oxford: Oxford University Press, 2006), 116.
2. Jean-François Lyotard, *Libidinal Economy*, tr. Iain Hamilton Grant (London and New York: Continuum, [1974] 2004), 6.
3. Jean-François Lyotard, "Féminité dans la métalangue" in *Rudiments païens* (Paris: Klincksieck, [1977] 2011), 145–56. Translated as "One of the Things at Stake in Women's Trouble," by Deborah J. Cherry in *The Lyotard Reader*, ed. Andrew Benjamin (Oxford, UK and Cambridge MA: Blackwell, 1989), 111, trans. modified.
4. Jean-François Lyotard, *The Differend: Phrases in Dispute*, tr. Georges Van Den Abbeele (Minneapolis MN: University of Minnesota Press, [1983] 1988), 68. "*L' « écriture féminine »: inscrire que ça ne peut pas être comblé, d'une phrase à l'autre? Serait-ce un genre?*" *Le Différend* (Paris: Les Éditions de Minuit, 1983), 105.
5. Ashley Woodward "'White Skin': Lyotard's Sketch of a Postcolonial Libidinal Economy," *Journal of the British Society for Phenomenology*, vol. 51, no. 4 (2020): 337–51.
6. Achille Mbembe, *Necropolitics*, tr. Steven Corcoran (Durham NC: Duke University Press, [2016] 2019), 1.
7. Jean-François Lyotard, "Apathy in Theory" in this volume, 146.
8. Ibid., 141.
9. Jean-François Lyotard, "Art Présent Interview" in this volume, 149.
10. Jean-François Lyotard, *Peregrinations: Law, Form, Event* (New York: Columbia University Press, 1988), 13.
11. Jean-François Lyotard, "Resisting a Discourse of Mastery: A Conversation with Jean-François Lyotard" with Gary A. Olson, *JAC* 15, no. 3 (1995), 408.
12. "« *Mon livre de philosophie* » *dit-il*," Blurb on the back cover of the French edition of *The Differend*; for Derrida's comment see "Philosophy: The case for the defence" [1984], in Kiff Bamford (ed.), *Jean-François Lyotard: The Interviews and Debates* (London and New York: Bloomsbury, 2020), 67.
13. Lyotard, "Art Présent Interview" in this volume, 157; 156.
14. Jean-François Lyotard, "Interview with Arias-Mission," *Eyeline* (November 1987), 17.
15. Perry Anderson, *The Origins of the Postmodern* (London and New York: Verso, 1998), 25.
16. James Bridle, *New Dark Age* (London and New York: Verso, 2018), 86–93.
17. Donna J. Haraway, *Staying with the Trouble: Making Kin in the Chthulucene* (Durham NC: Duke University Press, 2016), 12. Haraway is paraphrasing the social anthropologist Marilyn Strathern.
18. Lyotard, "Apathy in Theory" in this volume, 149.
19. Ibid., 145.
20. Ibid., 146.
21. Vito Acconci, *Open Book* (1974), Video, 10:09 min, color and sound.
22. "Apathy in Theory" in this volume, 141.
23. Jean-François Lyotard, *Philosophie und Malerei im Zeitalter ihres Experimentierens*, tr. Marianne Karbe (Berlin: Merve Verlag, 1986), 51.
24. Rana Hamadeh, *Can you Pull in an Actor With a Fishook or Tie Down His Tongue With a Rope?* 2014, installed at The Old Blind School, Liverpool, UK, as part of the exhibition *A Needle Walks into a Haystack* curated by Mai Abu ElDahab and Anthony Huberman, the 8th Liverpool Biennial, July 5–October 4, 2014.

25 Rana Hamadeh, *Can you Make a Pet of Him Like a Bird or Put Him on a Leash For your Girls?* 8-channel live sound-play/performance, commissioned and produced by Western Front, Vancouver, 2015. Performed at The Tetley, Leeds, February 4, 2017.
26 Jean-François Lyotard, *The Confession of Augustine*, tr. Richard Beardsworth (Stanford CA: Stanford University Press, [1998] 2000), 7–8.
27 Gerald L. Burns, "The Senses of Augustine," *Religion & Literature*, vol. 33 no. 3 (Autumn 2001): 1–23.
28 Lyotard, *The Confession of Augustine*, 85.

"Afterward": Lyotard's Prescience

Peter Gratton

> *Complete information means neutralizing more events. What is already known cannot, in principle, be experienced as an event. Consequently, if one wants to control a process, the best way of so doing is to subordinate the present to what is (still) called the "future," since in these conditions the "future" will be completely predetermined and the present itself will cease opening onto an uncertain and contingent "afterwards." Better: what comes "after" the "now" will have to come "before" it.*
>
> —Lyotard, "Time Today"[1]

A leitmotif of this book, from the editors' introduction through each of its chapters, has been Lyotard's supposed "prescience," his seemingly uncanny ability to describe what will have been the case if his various reflections on the modern and postmodern were correct. *The Postmodern Condition* describes, just on the cusp of the Reagan/Thatcher era, the neoliberal era to come, with its diminution of knowledge to points of data, and historical and cultural fragmentation after the loss of metanarratives. The 1985 exhibition *Les Immatériaux*—something of an exhibition for what can't be exhibited—spoke to a virtual future in which material needs are ignored and nations clash over rivalries in information technologies. Even his sly parable of scientists dreaming of uploading minds into satellites, all to save the human archive before the explosion of the sun, seems less far-fetched than the various idiotic pronouncements of the supposed impact of barely off-world missions by whatever billionaire holds the business press spellbound this week. *The Differend* and *Just Gaming* rightly spoke of the loss of all metanarratives and the coming cultural collapse from it, and we, as the heirs of Lyotard's thought, struggle in his shadow to do all we can to build links in and between incommensurate phrasings, even as others still deny that such obvious incommensurabilities exist. Sure, critics misunderstood his descriptions as prescriptions for what should come—his celebration of fragmentation was more a Nietzschean form of affirmation of reality than a callous disregard for all that dissensus has wrought—and yet they still blithely repeat decades-old cliches about Lyotardian postmodernism leading to a post-truth world as if Lyotard's work was less a response than the cause of what was already underway. Nevertheless, critics and the critical practitioners of this book agree as to his prescience, a foreknowledge required of all works of the past to be readable or even legible in the present.

Lyotard could speak to the *now*, which makes him relevant and marketable, and there isn't a volume on any dead philosopher—and darned if I haven't been known to write it myself—that doesn't testify to their powers of divination, their *prescience*. It's not enough that philosophers speak to *their* time, or indeed to the times before their times, in a manner that allows us to gain the only possible distance we can get from our milieus, since we have no access for the vaunted god's eye or eternal point of view, and so all we have to go on is the reality of worlds that were never like ours. There is hope in that: reading and translating discourses from the past is all we have left some days, in the utter nihilism of the present, to give voice to the part of us craving to see the pastness of the past, its utter foreignness to our own time, as a reminder that this too shall pass. No doubt, much of what's called "critical theory" in all its senses does just this and has been of necessity backward-looking—after all, to know where we are, we must have some sense of how we got here—from Nietzschean/Foucauldian genealogies to Heideggerian and Derridean moves to "deconstruct" the Western metaphysical tradition, to feminist writings valorizing moments of difference in the canon, to postcolonial works bearing witnesses to the horrors of a past long denied by the colonial powers and their latter-day apologists.

However, Lyotard's writings are striking not only for refusing any linear temporal ordering between past/present/future, but also for aligning justice and what is called "critical practice" in these pages with thinking the future. That's not to say that he ever really gave up the study of history, as he says he did as a child due to a lack of memory, or that his rewritings of modernity and works of anamnesis don't continue to inform his readers of the legacies of Augustine, Kant, Freud, and countless others. Nevertheless, Lyotard's writings always seemed to aim to be on the cusp on what was coming such that he could offer a glance at a future to come—what he dubbed the "still secret"[2]—and could intimate what was in the offing that others had missed. In short, Lyotard was, despite himself and all that he wrote challenging Hegel, a *speculative* philosopher, though not one given to "reconciliatory speculation."[3] If Lyotard rejected philosophical realisms as alibis for the status quo, he nevertheless attempted a critical practice of witnessing the reality of the future (*l'à-venir*).[4] One just needs to open the first pages of all of his major works to see how many provide speculative genealogies of the future and offered, perhaps more than any philosopher of his era, propositions given in the future tense. And testing his speculative theses would be one way, if not *the* way, modernity employs history and thus would engage his work. Books, Lyotard foretold in *The Differend* in one of his seemingly many prescient moments, would cease to exist in this century, replaced by objects communicating what we already know anyway, which is why the market rewards foresight above all else, deeming anything else "dated" and all but illegible. The modern, Lyotard often noted, is best defined not by its emphasis on the "now," as it is often said, but on its relation to the future. As Jürgen Habermas, Lyotard's sometime *bête noire*, put it, "because the new, modern world is distinguished from the old by the fact that it opens itself to the future, the epochal new beginning is rendered constant each moment that gives birth to the new."[5] In sum, the modern is the "epoch that lives for the future, that opens itself to the novelty of the future." For Habermas, this meant that modernity is imbued with the norm of self-critique, beholden to no past or tradition, and is beset by a call for progress that Lyotard thought was part of a metanarrative no longer convincing by the 1970s, if not earlier, and which certainly has grown no more convincing since. An ever-impending sense of collapse is the only constant in the capitalistic flux of the neoliberal era, and whether something adheres to the task of infinite accumulation is the only criterion left for humanity to judge—aesthetically, politically, ethically, economically, or otherwise. Even if progress were still a given societal norm, there is nevertheless a hiatus or disjuncture in Habermas's formulations above: the constant arrival of each "epochal new beginning" that marks modernity (whenever and wherever it historically and geographically occurs) is not "open to the novelty of the future" since it can only think the future as indebted to the past (present), that is, as paying yields on investment. (Even as the enlightened and messianic expectation described by Habermas in the 1980s has since given way to catastrophic apocalypticism, both share a similar ADHD temporality.)

Prescience is not just rewarded but is at the heart of neoliberal capitalism, since industrial economies depend on a given material moving from past (raw materials) to present (commodities) to future (reinvestment) in a manner avoided in post-Fordist economies. The task of metaphysics has been speculative in a similar sense. The special sciences are left to determine or provide an encyclopedia of what is; metaphysics concerns the determination of the possibility of anything being what it is. This modal difference, fleshed out in works ranging from Aristotle's *Metaphysics* to Hegel's *Science of Logic*, between actuality (*Wirlichkeit*) and existence (*Dasein*), defines thinking as projecting or having prescience of what may be, thus linking the metaphysical with economic or "futurist" speculation or the metaphysics of divinity (predeterminism) with the present-day efforts of predictive metrics to curate the future. As Lyotard writes,

> In the time set out by concept and will, the project is only the "projection" of present consequences on the future (as in "futurology"). This kind of projection forbids the event; it prepares, preconceives, controls it in advance. This is the time of the Pentagon, the FBI, Security, the time of Empire.[6]

Resisting this governance of time, critics have often devolved into nostalgia for a past that never was (e.g., valorizing the Keynesian period as a high point, even as it survived on racial and colonial subsidies) while exhibiting a tragic temporality of a civilizational being-towards-death. Others, often within Continental philosophy and building on Martin Heidegger, Jacques Derrida, Alain Badiou, and Emmanuel Levinas, are left with nothing but an utter affirmation of the event to come. The early twenty-first-century devolution of Continental theoretical acumen into hands-thrown-up repetitive calls for the to-come (what may) surely led to a better understanding of French and German vocabulary relating to tense and the event, but more often than not evoked nothing less than a negative theology of an indescribable *Ereignis* of a God who would save us because we couldn't. Badiou's all-too-long period of prominence—his misogyny and heterosexism being but a hint of the metaphysical rot of his system—testifies to what was lost with Lyotard's death. The state of things was to await a miracle of an event beyond anything within this state of things, all else being political reformism or "democratic materialism" irrelevant once the logic of the world changes. Full presence will be restored in the coming Cultural Revolution.

But critical practice cannot wait, it does not wait, for all that. For Lyotard, as in Derrida, the future is a metonymy for absolute difference or the *differend* as such, and each chapter in this book serves to illustrate how one might, without any surety of success, bear witness to the unpresentable while following up on all of the figures, such as the child, Lyotard used to evoke or convoke performatively what he infamously called the postmodern. Lyotard wrote:

> [I]t must never be forgotten that if thinking indeed consists in receiving the event, it follows that no-one can claim to think without being *ipso facto* in a position of resistance to the procedures for controlling time.
>
> To think is to question everything, including thought, and question, and the process. To question requires that something happen that reason has not yet known. In thinking, one accepts the occurrence for what it is: "not yet" determined.[7]

But Lyotard did not leave us without anything determined or demanded of us. Critical practice, as shown here, is, to use an old word that has long fallen into dis- or misuse: "justice," which is not a concept and, as no one doubts, not a (present) thing. To think, for Lyotard, meant devising phrases beyond the *déjà dit* to testify to the abyss always before us and deconceal *differends* and silences that haven't been or can't be phrased, which he thought was the practice of justice. Inventing impossible idioms, whether materially or linguistically, is left to us as bearing witness to what is impossible in the metanarratives mourned today. This practice—critical in all senses—is an affirmation or yes to the multiple temporalities across which we live. There is no wishing away the loss of metanarratives, which Hannah Arendt dubbed to oddly far less controversy the "loss of authority," and there is only terror that awaits those nostalgic for another to arrive and end our mourning. The tasks of critical practice await constant (re)invention, but critical practice is necessary to witness the heterogeneous while devising new figures of the unpresentable in presentation itself beyond Lyotard's Thing, infancy, or debt. This critical practice, as in these pages, is multifarious, affirmative, and at times galling, if not outrageously out of date, with nothing left afterward to sum up or give as a moral for what is to be done, prescient only in its formal opening to the surprises left to be thought.

Notes

1 Jean-François Lyotard, *The Inhuman: Reflections on Time*, tr. Geoffrey Bennington and Rachel Bowlby (Cambridge UK: Polity, [1988] 1991), 65.
2 Jean-François Lyotard and Jacques Derrida, "Philosophy: The case for the defence" in *Jean-François Lyotard: The Interviews and Debates*, ed. Kiff Bamford (London and New York: Bloomsbury, 2020), 70.
3 Lyotard, *Inhuman*, 4.

4 Lyotard and Richard Kearney, "'What is just?' (*Ou Justesse*)" in Lyotard, *The Interviews and Debates*, 157.
5 Jürgen Habermas, *The Philosophical Discourse of Modernity: Twelve Lectures*, tr. Frederick Lawrence (Cambridge UK and Malden MA: Polity, [1985] 1987), 5.
6 Lyotard and Kearney, "What is just?," 157.
7 Lyotard, *Inhuman*, 74.

Bibliography

Alberro, Alexander and Blake Stimson. Eds. *Conceptual Art: A Critical Anthology*. Cambridge MA: MIT Press, 1999.
Amair, Jean et al. *Socialisme ou barbarie An Anthology,* Translated by David Ames Curtis et al. London: Eris, 2018.
Anderson, Perry. *The Origins of Postmodernity*. London and New York: Verso, 1998.
Arendt, Hannah. *The Origins of Totalitarianism* [1951]. London: Harcourt Brace, 1967.
Aristotle, *The Complete Works of Aristotle*. Edited by Jonathan Barnes. Princeton NJ: Princeton University Press, 1984.
Bamford, Kiff. *Jean-François Lyotard*. London: Reaktion, 2017.
Badiou, Alain. *Logics of Worlds. Being and Event, 2* [2006]. Translated by Alberto Toscano. London and New York: Continuum, 2009.
Baudelaire, Charles. *The Painter of Modern Life and Other Essays*. Edited and Translated by Jonathan Mayne. New York: Phaidon, 1995.
Baudelaire, Charles. *The Flowers of Evil* [1857]. Translated by James McGowan. Oxford: Oxford University Press, 1993.
Beckett, Samuel. *Watt*. New York: Grove, 1953.
Bennington, Geoffrey. *Late Lyotard*. CreateSpace, 2008.
Berger, John. *Hold Everything Dear: Dispatches on Survival*. London and New York: Verso, 2016.
Berlant, Lauren. *Cruel Optimism*. Durham NC: Duke University Press: 2011.
Best, Steven and Douglas Kellner. *Postmodern Theory: Critical Interrogations*. New York: The Guilford Press, 1991.
Blake, William. *Collected Poems*. London and New York: Routledge, 2002.
Branche, Raphaëlle. *Papa, qu'as-tu fait en Algérie? – Enquête sur un silence familial*. Paris: La Découverte, 2020.
Bridle, James. *New Dark Age*. London and New York: Verso, 2018.
Broeckmann, Andreas and Yuk Hui. Eds. *30 Years after* Les Imm*atériaux, Art, Science, Theory*. Lüneburg: Meson, 2015.
Burns, Gerald L. "The Senses of Augustine." *Religion & Literature* 33, no. 3 (Autumn, 2001): 1–23.
Césaire, Aimé. "Culture and Colonization." Translated by Brent Edwards. *Social Text* 103, vol. 28, no. 2 (Summer 2010): 127–44.
Cetacean Rights: Fostering Moral and Legal Change. Available online: https://www.cetaceanrights.org/ (accessed January 31, 2021).
Chamayou, Grégoire. *Drone Theory* [2013]. Translated by Janet Lloyd. London: Penguin, 2015.
Chamoiseau, Patrick. *Chronicle of the Seven Sorrows* [1986]. Translated by Linda Coverdale. Lincoln NE: University of Nebraska, 2003.
Crome, Keith. *Lyotard and Greek Thought: Sophistry*. Basingstoke, UK and New York: Palgrave Macmillan, 2004.

Deleuze, Gilles. *Nietzsche and Philosophy* [1962]. Translated by Hugh Tomlinson. New York: Columbia University Press, 1983.

Deleuze, Gilles and Félix Guattari. *What Is Philosophy?* [1991]. Translated by Hugh Tomlinson and Graham Burchell. New York: Columbia University Press, 1994.

Drabinski, John E. *Glissant and the Middle Passage: Philosophy, Beginning, Abyss.* Minneapolis MN: University of Minnesota Press, 2019.

Drabinski, John E. "Césaire's Apocalyptic Word." *South Atlantic Quarterly* 115, no. 3 (2016): 567–584.

Dussel, Enrique. *Beyond Philosophy: Ethics, History, Marxism and Liberation Theology.* Edited by Eduardo Mendieta. Lanham MD: Rowman & Littlefield, 2003.

Dunayesvkaya, Raya. *Marxism and Freedom: From 1776 Until Today.* New York: Humanity Books, 2000.

Fanon, Frantz. *Toward the African Revolution* [1964]. Translated by Haakon Chevalier. New York: Grove Press, 1994.

Fanon, Frantz. *The Wretched of the Earth* [1961]. Translated by Constance Farrington. Penguin: London, 2001.

Freud, Sigmund. *The Standard Edition of the Complete Psychological Works of Sigmund Freud*, vol. 18. Translated and Edited by James Strachey, London: Hogarth, 1955; London: Vintage, 2001.

Gaillard, Julie; Claire Nouvet and Mark Stoholski. Eds. *Traversals of Affect: On Jean-François Lyotard.* London and New York: Bloomsbury, 2016.

Glissant, Édouard. *Poetics of Relation* [1990]. Translated by Betsy Wing. Ann Arbor MI: University of Michigan Press, 1999.

Grebowicz, Margret (ed.). *Gender After Lyotard.* Stanford CA: Stanford University Press, 2007.

Grebowicz, Margret and Zach Reyna. "The Animality of Simone Weil: I Love Dick and a Nonhuman Politics of the Impersonal," *the minnesota review* 97 (2021): 77–94.

Haraway, Donna J. *Staying with the Trouble: Making Kin in the Chthulucene.* Durham NC: Duke University Press, 2016.

Holert, Tom. *Knowledge Beside Itself, Contemporary Art's Epistemic Politics.* Berlin: Sternberg Press, 2020.

Hui, Yuk. *Recursivity and Contingency.* London: Rowman & Littlefield, 2019.

Hui, Yuk. *The Question Concerning Technology in China. An Essay in Cosmotechnics.* Falmouth UK: Urbanomic, 2016; Cambridge MA: MIT Press, 2019.

Hui, Yuk. *Art and Cosmotechnics.* Minneapolis MN: University of Minnesota Press, 2021.

Jameson, Fredric. *Postmodernism, or the Cultural Logic of Capitalism.* Durham NC: Duke University Press, 1991.

Jameson, Fredric. *Archaeologies of the Future: The Desire Called Utopia and Other Science Fictions.* London and New York: Verso, 2007.

Kaliszewska, Zofia A and Jon Seger et al. "Population histories of right whales (Cetacea: Eubalaena) inferred from mitochondrial sequence diversities and divergences of their whale lice (Amphipoda: Cyamus)," *Mol Ecol*, vol. 14, no. 11 (2005): 3439–56. doi:10.1111/j.1365-294X.2005.02664.x

Kent, Michael *The Oxford Dictionary of Sports Science & Medicine*, 3rd ed. Oxford: Oxford University Press, 2006.

Klossowski, Pierre. *Living Currency* [1970]. Edited by Vernon W. Cisney. Translated by Nicolae Morar and Daniel W. Smith. London and New York: Bloomsbury, 2017.

Kosuth, Joseph. *Art After Philosophy and After: Collected Writings 1966–90.* Edited by Gabriele Guercio. Cambridge MA: MIT Press, 1991.

Land, Nick. "Machinic desire." *Textual Practice*, vol. 7, no. 3 (1993).
Langlois, Krista. "When Whales and Humans Talk," *Hakai Magazine*, April 3, 2018. Available online: https://www.hakaimagazine.com/features/when-whales-and-humans-talk/ (accessed January 31, 2021).
Latour, Bruno and Paolo Fabbri. "The Rhetoric of Science: Authority and Duty in an Article from the Exact Sciences." Translated by Sarah Cummins. *Technostyle*, vol. 16, no. 1 (Winter 2000): 115–34.
Lyotard, Jean-François. *La Phénoménologie*. Paris: Presses Universitaires de France, 1954.
Lyotard, Jean-François. *Discourse, Figure* [1971]. Translated by Antony Hudek and Mary Lydon. Minneapolis MN: University of Minnesota Press, 2011.
Lyotard, Jean-François. *Dérive à partir de Marx et Freud*. UGE, 10/18: Paris, 1973.
Lyotard, Jean-François. *Rudiments païens,* Genre dissertatif. Paris: UGE, 10/18, 1977; republished Paris: Klincksieck, 2011.
Lyotard, Jean-François. *Duchamp's TRANS/formers* [1977]. Edited by Herman Parret. Translated by Ian McLeod. *Writings on Contemporary Art and Artists*, vol. 3. Leuven: Leuven University Press, 2010.
Lyotard, Jean-François. "Notes on the Return and Kapital." Translated by Roger McKeon, *Semiotexte(e),* vol. 3, no. 1 (1978): 44–53.
Lyotard, Jean-François. "Preliminary Notes on the Pragmatic of Works: Daniel Buren" [1978]. Translated by Thomas Repensek, *October*, no. 10 (1979): 59–67.
Lyotard, Jean-François. "De la fonction critique à la transformation." interview with Jean Papineau, *Parachute*, no. 11 (1978): 4–9.
Lyotard, Jean-François. *The Postmodern Condition* [1979]. Translated by Geoff Bennington and Brian Massumi. Minneapolis MN: University of Minnesota Press, 1984.
Lyotard, Jean-François et al. *Les Immatériaux*, volume 2: *Album et Inventaire*. Edited by Chantal Noël. Paris: Centre Georges Pompidou, 1985.
Lyotard, Jean-François. *Driftworks*. Edited by Roger McKeon. Semiotext(e): New York, 1984.
Lyotard, Jean-François. *Philosophie und Malerei im Zeitalter iheres Experimentierens*. Translated by Marianne Karbe. Berlin: Merve Verlag, 1986.
Lyotard, Jean-François. "Interview with Arias-Mission." *Eyeline* (November 1987): 17–19.
Lyotard, Jean-François. *The Differend* [1983]. Translated by Georges Van Den Abbeele. Minneapolis MN: University of Minnesota Press: 1988.
Lyotard, Jean-François. *Peregrinations: Law, Form, Event*. New York: Columbia University Press, 1988.
Lyotard, Jean-François. *Heidegger and "the jews"* [1988]. Translated by Andreas Michel and Mark Roberts. Minneapolis MN: University of Minnesota Press, 1990.
Lyotard, Jean-François. *La Guerre des Algériens: Écrits 1956–1963*. Paris: Galilée, 1989.
Lyotard, Jean-François. *The Lyotard Reader*. Edited by Andrew Benjamin. Oxford, UK and Cambridge MA: Blackwell, 1989.
Lyotard, Jean-François. "Argumentation and Presentation: The Foundation Crisis" [1989]. Translated by Chris Turner. *Cultural Politics* 9, no. 2 (2013): 117–143.
Lyotard, Jean-François. "Complexity and the Sublime." in *Postmodernism: ICA Documents*. Edited by Lisa Appignanesi. London: Free Association Books, 1989.
Lyotard, Jean-François. *The Inhuman: Reflections on Time* [1988]. Translated by Geoffrey Bennington and Rachel Bowlby. Stanford CA: Stanford University Press, 1991.
Lyotard, Jean-François. *Phenomenology* [1954]. Translated by Brian Beakley, Minneapolis MN: University of Minnesota Press, 1991.

Lyotard, Jean-François. "Voices of a voice" [1990]. Translated by Georges Van Den Abbeele, *Discourse* 14, no. 1 (1992): 126–145.

Lyotard, Jean-François. "That Which Resists, After All." interview with Gilbert Larochelle, *Philosophy Today* 36, no. 4 (1992): 402–17.

Lyotard, Jean-François. *The Postmodern Explained: Correspondence 1982–1985* [1988]. Translated by Julian Pefanis and Morgan Thomas et al. Minneapolis MN: University of Minnesota Press, 1993.

Lyotard, Jean-François. *Toward the Postmodern*. Edited by Robert Harvey and Mark S. Roberts. New York: Humanity Books, 1993.

Lyotard, Jean-François. *Political Writings*. Translated by Bill Readings and Kevin Paul Geiman. Minneapolis MN: University of Minnesota Press, 1993, 85–89.

Lyotard, Jean-François. *Libidinal Economy* [1974]. Translated by Iain Hamilton Grant. Bloomington and Indianapolis IN: Indiana University Press; London: Athlone 1993; London and New York: Continuum, 2004.

Lyotard, Jean-François. "Resisting a Discourse of Mastery: A Conversation with Jean-François Lyotard" with Gary A. Olson, *JAC* 15, no. 3 (1995): 391–410.

Lyotard, Jean-François. *Postmodern Fables* [1993]. Translated by Georges Van Den Abbeele. Minneapolis MN: University of Minnesota Press, 1997.

Lyotard, Jean-François. *Signed, Malraux* [1996]. Translated by Robert Harvey. Minneapolis MN: University of Minnesota Press, 1999.

Lyotard, Jean-François. *Misère de la philosophie.* Paris: Galilée, 2000.

Lyotard, Jean-François. "Resistances. A Conversation," with Sergio Benvenuto. Translated by Gianmaria Senia, *European Journal of Psychoanalysis*, no. 2 (Fall 1995–Winter 1996) Available online: https://www.journal-psychoanalysis.eu/resistances-a-conversation/ (accessed January 31, 2021)

Lyotard, Jean-François. *The Confession of Augustine* [1998]. Translated by Richard Beardsworth, Stanford CA: Stanford University Press, 2000.

Lyotard, Jean-François. *Soundproof Room: Malraux's Anti-Aesthetics* [1998]. Translated by Robert Harvey. Stanford CA: Stanford University Press, 2001.

Lyotard, Jean-François. "Emma: Between Philosophy and Psychoanalysis" [1989]. Translated by Michael Sanders, in *Lyotard. Philosophy, Politics, and the Sublime*. Edited by Hugh J. Silverman. New York and London: Routledge, 2002, 23–45.

Lyotard, Jean-François. *The Lyotard Reader and Guide*, Edited by James Williams and Keith Crome. Edinburgh University Press: Edinburgh, 2006.

Lyotard, Jean-François. *Enthusiasm: The Kantian Critique of History* [1986], Translated by Georges Van Den Abbeele. Stanford CA: Stanford University Press, 2009.

Lyotard, Jean-François. *Textes dispersés I: esthétique et théorie de l'art / Miscellaneous Texts I: Aesthetics and Theory of Art*. Edited by Herman Parret, Translated by Vlad Ionescu, Erica Harris and Peter W. Milne. Leuven: Leuven University Press, 2012.

Lyotard, Jean-François. *Textes dispersés II: artistes contemporains / Miscellaneous Texts II: Contemporary Artists*, Edited by Herman Parret. Translated by Vlad Ionescu, Erica Harris and Peter W. Milne. Leuven: Leuven University Press, 2012.

Lyotard, Jean-François, *The Interviews and Debates*, ed. Kiff Bamford. London and New York: Bloomsbury, 2020.

Lyotard, Jean-François. *Readings in Infancy* [1991]. Edited by Robert Harvey and Kiff Bamford, London and New York: Bloomsbury, 2023.

Marx, Karl. *Capital* [1867]. Translated by Ben Fowkes. New York: New Left Review, 1976.

Mbembe, Achille. *Necropolitics* [2016]. Translated by Steven Corcoran. Durham NC: Duke University Press, 2019.

Merleau-Ponty, Maurice. *Sense and Non-sense* [1948]. Translated by Hubert L. Dreyfus and Patricia Allen Dreyfus. Evanston, IL: Northwestern University Press.

Milne, Peter W. "Sensibility and the Law: On Rancière's Reading of Lyotard," *Symposium* 15, no. 2 (2011): 95–119.

Milne, Peter W. "Temporality and the Lyotardian Sublime: Kant between Husserl and Freud," *Journal of the British Society for Phenomenology*, vol. 51, no. 3 (2020): 201–14.

Nancy, Jean-Luc and Philippe Lacoue-Labarthe. *Le retrait du politique*. Paris: Galilée, 1983.

Nelson, Maggie. *The Argonauts*. London: Melville House, 2015.

Nelson, Robert H. *Reaching for Heaven on Earth: The Theological Meaning of Economics*. Lanham MD: Rowman & Littlefield, 1991.

Osborne, Peter. *Anywhere or Not at All, Philosophy of Contemporary Art*. London and New York, Verso, 2013.

Osborne, Peter. *The Postconceptual Condition*. London and New York: Verso, 2018.

Pagès, Claire. Ed. *Lyotard à Nanterre*. Paris: Klincksieck, 2010.

Pagès, Claire "To begin with," *Journal of the CIPH*, 96, 2 (2019), 1–15. DOI: 10.3917/rdes.096.0001. Available online: https://www.cairn-int.info/journal-of-the-ciph-2019-2-page-1.htm

Rancière, Jacques. *Aesthetics and Its Discontents*. Translated by Steven Corcoran, Cambridge UK and Malden MA: Polity, 2009.

Socialisme ou Barbarie. *Socialisme ou barbarie: Anthologie : grèves ouvrières en France*. La Bussière, France: Acratie, 2007. Translated as *Socialisme ou Barbarie: An Anthology*, translations Anon. London: Eris, 2018.

Standing, Guy. *Basic Income, and How We Can Make It Happen*. Harmondsworth: Penguin, 2017.

Stiegler, Bernard. *States of Shock: Stupidity and Knowledge in the 21st Century* [2012]. Translated by Daniel Ross. Cambridge UK and Malden MA: Polity, 2015.

Talon-Hugon, Carole. "After Lyotard: Aesthetics in France Today," *Cités* 56, no. 4 (2013/14): 87–101.

Tan, Andrew T. H. ed. *The Global Arms Trade Handbook*. London and New York: Routledge, 2010.

Van Den Abbeele, Georges. "Algérie l'intraitable: Lyotard's National Front," *L'Esprit Créateur* XXXI (Spring 1991): 144–57.

Vega, Amparo. "Socialisme ou Barbarie et le militantisme de Lyotard," *Cités* 45 (2011): 31–43.

Vega, Amparo. *Le premier Lyotard: philosophie critique et politique*. Paris: L'Harmattan, 2010.

Van Parijs, Philippe and Yannick Vanderborght. *Basic Income: A Radical Proposal for a Free Society and a Sane Economy*. Cambridge MA: Harvard University Press, 2017.

Walcott, Derek. *What the Twilight Says*. New York: FSG, 1999.

Wilson, Sarah. "Lyotard/Monory: Postmodern Romantics" in *The Assassination of Experience by Painting: Monory*. Translated by Rachel Bowlby. London: Black Dog, 2001.

Woodward, Ashley, "The End of Time," *Parrhesia*, no. 15 (2012): 87–105

Woodward, Ashley, "'White Skin': Lyotard's Sketch of a Postcolonial Libidinal Economy," *Journal of the British Society for Phenomenology*, vol. 51, no. 4 (2020): 337–51.

Notes on Contributors

Editors

Kiff Bamford is an artist and academic, currently Reader in Contemporary Art in the Leeds School of Arts at Leeds Beckett University, UK. Publications on the work of Jean-François Lyotard include the monographs *Lyotard and the "figural" in Performance, Art and Writing* (2012) and the short biography *Jean-François Lyotard: Critical Lives* (2017). Editorial work includes collating, introducing, and editing *Jean-François Lyotard: The Interviews and Debates* (2020) and, with Robert Harvey, the first complete English translation of Lyotard's *Lectures d'enfance* (1991) published in 2023 by Bloomsbury as *Readings in Infancy*.

Margret Grebowicz is Associate Professor at the University of Silesia in Katowice, Poland. She has held professorships at University of Houston-Downtown, Goucher College, and the University of Tyumen, Russia. She is the author of *Mountains and Desire: Climbing vs. The End of the World, Whale Song, The National Park to Come, Why Internet Porn Matters*, and co-author of *Beyond the Cyborg: Adventures with Donna Haraway*. Her articles about Lyotard have appeared in such places as *Philosophy Today, Hypatia*, and *Rereading Jean-François Lyotard: Essays on His Later Works*. She is editor of *Gender after Lyotard*, as well as series editor of Practices for Duke University Press.

Contributors

Georges Van Den Abbeele is Professor of French, English, and Comparative Literature, University of California, Irvine, USA, formerly Dean of Humanities (2013–2018). He is translator of several books and articles by Lyotard, including *The Differend: Phrases in Dispute* (1988); *Postmodern Fables* (1993) and *Enthusiasm: the Kantian Critique of History* (2009) and written contributions to many collections including "The Work of Jean-François Lyotard" (*Diacritics* 1984), "Passages, Genres, Differends: J-F Lyotard" (L'Esprit Créateur, 1991), "Community at Loose Ends" (Minnesota 1991), and *A Lyotard Dictionary* (2011).

Keith Crome is Principal Lecturer in Philosophy, and Education Lead for the Department of History, Politics and Philosophy, Manchester Metropolitan University; as well as President of the British Society for Phenomenology. He is author of *Lyotard and Greek Thought* (2004) and editor, with James Williams, of *The Lyotard Reader and Guide* (2006).

John E. Drabinski is Professor of African American Studies and Comparative Literature at the University of Maryland. He is the author of four books, most recently *Glissant and the Middle Passage: Philosophy, Beginning, Abyss* (2019) and *Levinas and the Postcolonial: Race, Nation, Other* (2012). In addition to dozens of essays on Africana and European philosophy, he has edited books and journal issues on Édouard Glissant, Frantz Fanon, Jean-Luc Godard, James Baldwin, and Emmanuel Levinas and Martin Heidegger. He is currently finishing a book-length study of Baldwin's non-fiction entitled *"So Unimaginable a Price": Baldwin and the Black Atlantic* to be published by Northwestern University Press.

Derek R. Ford is an Assistant Professor of Education Studies at DePauw University, Indiana, USA. Published in a variety of journals, he has also written and edited many books, including *Inhuman Educations: Jean-François Lyotard, Pedagogy, Thought* (2021), *Communist Study* (2016), *Education and the Production of Space* (2017), *Politics and Pedagogy in the "Post-Truth" Era: Insurgent Philosophy and Praxis* (2018), and edited *Keywords in Radical Philosophy and Education* (2019). Articles on Lyotard include "A figural education with Lyotard" (*Studies in Philosophy and Education*, 2015) and, with Tyson Lewis, "Lyotard and the sublime unconscious of education: Communicative capitalism and aesthetics" (*Philosophy of Education*, Urbana, 2017).

Jill Gibbon is an artist and Reader in the School of Arts, Leeds Beckett University, UK. A politically engaged artist, she is working on a long-term project documenting the secretive world of the international arms trade by drawing undercover at arms fairs. In 2018 she was the recipient of a Social Research Foundation Grant which resulted in a major solo exhibition and catalog, *The Etiquette of the Arms Trade*. Articles have been published in *Millennium: Journal of International Studies* and *Journal of War and Culture Studies* and chapters in *Experiencing War* (2011) and *Masquerades of War* (2015).

Peter Gratton is Professor of Philosophy in the Department of History and Political Science at Southeastern Louisiana University. He is author of *Speculative Realism: Problems and Prospects* (2014), *The State of Sovereignty: Lessons from Political Fictions of Modernity* (2012), and the editor of seven books, including two on Jean-Luc Nancy. He has also published articles in journals such as *Angelaki*, *Philosophy Today*, and *Telos* and authored the Lyotard entry of the *Stanford Encyclopedia of Philosophy* (2018).

Yuk Hui is a philosopher and currently teaches at the City University of Hong Kong. He is the author of several monographs including *On the Existence of Digital Objects* (2016), *The Question Concerning Technology in China: An Essay in Cosmotechnics* (2016, 2019), *Recursivity and Contingency* (2019), and *Art and Cosmotechnics* (2021). He organized two symposiums respectively dedicated to the fortieth anniversary of *The Postmodern Condition* in 2019 at the China Academy of Art and the thirtieth anniversary of *Les Immatériaux* in 2014 at the

Leuphana University, the latter resulting in an anthology *30 years after* Les Immatériaux (2015).

Bartosz Kuźniarz is Associate Professor in the Institute of Philosophy at the University of Białystok in Poland. His books include *Pieniądz i system: O diable w gospodarce* (*Money and System: On the Devil in the Economy*, 2006), *Farewell to Postmodernism: Social Theories of the Late Left* (2015), and *Król liczb: Szkice z metafizyki kapitalizmu* (*The Lord of Numbers: Essays in the Metaphysics of Capitalism*, 2020). Since 2006 he has been a regular contributor to the Polish press, most notably its premier newspaper, *Gazeta Wyborcza*.

Jean-François Lyotard (1924–98) was one of the most important French philosophers of the twentieth century. He was the author of classic philosophical texts such as *Discourse, Figure* ([1971] 2011), *Libidinal Economy* ([1974] 1993), *The Differend* ([1983] 1988), and *The Postmodern Condition: A Report on Knowledge* ([1979] 1984).

Roger McKeon is a translator. Born in Paris, he studied philosophy under Jean-François Lyotard at the University of Paris, Nanterre, moving to New York in 1974 where he worked as a translator for the United Nations for twenty-seven years. He edited the first book of Lyotard's writings in English, published as *Driftworks* in 1984. He led the translation desk for Lyotard's contribution to the infamous 1975 *Schizo-Culture* conference, republished by Semiotext(e) in 2014. He has undertaken other translations for Semiotext(e) and contributed many translations to the publication *Jean-François Lyotard: The Interviews and Debates*, edited by Kiff Bamford (2020).

Claire Nouvet is Associate Professor in the Department of French and Italian at Emory University, Atlanta, USA. She is the co-editor of *Minima Memoria: In the Wake of Jean-François Lyotard* (2007), *Traversals of Affect: On Jean-François Lyotard* (2016) and author of books including *Abélard et Héloïse: la passion de la maîtrise* (2009) and articles on Lyotard, including 'Nothing to say: the Negative Phrase of Affect (*Paragraph*, 2017).

Claire Pagès is maître de conférences in German and Political Philosophy at the Université de Tours and a former program director at the Collège international de philosophie (2013–2019). Her work covers the philosophy of human sciences, particularly modern and contemporary German philosophy and psychoanalysis, together with a special interest in the work of Jean-François Lyotard. Publications relating to Lyotard include the monograph *Lyotard et l'aliénation* (2011), editor of *Lyotard à Nanterre* (2010) and a special issue of the online journal *Rue Descartes* titled "Socialisme ou barbarie" (no. 96, 2019/2).

Ashley Woodward is Senior Lecturer in Philosophy, University of Dundee. He is author and editor of a number of books including *Lyotard and the Inhuman*

Condition: Reflections on Nihilism, Information and Art (2016), *Acinemas: Lyotard's Philosophy of Film* (co-edited with Graham Jones, 2017), and *Lyotard's Philosophy of Art* (forthcoming). He is an editor of *Parrhesia: A Journal of Critical Philosophy* and of the translation series Groundworks (Rowman & Littlefield).

Stephen Zepke is an independent researcher living in Vienna, Austria. He has published widely on philosophy, art, and cinema. He is the author of several books including *Art as Abstract Machine, Ontology and Aesthetics in Deleuze and Guattari* (2005) and *Sublime Art: Towards an Aesthetic of the future* (2017); also co-editor of *Deleuze and Contemporary Art* (2010), *Deleuze, Guattari and the Production of the New* (2008), and *Art History after Deleuze and Guattari* (2017).

Marina Zurkow is a media artist and a full-time faculty member at Tisch School of the Arts, New York University. She has used life science, bio materials, animation, dinners, and software technologies to foster intimate connections between people and nonhuman agents. Her work spans gallery installations and unconventional public participatory projects. Recent solo shows include Chronus Art Center, Shanghai, bitforms gallery, NY, Montclair Museum of Art, and Diverseworks, Houston. She is a 2011 Guggenheim Fellow, and received grants from NYFA, NYSCA, the Rockefeller Foundation, and Creative Capital. She is represented by bitforms gallery.

Index

Acconci, Vito 211, 214, 216 n.21
Adorno, Theodor W. 41, 111, 134
   and Horkheimer, Max 94, 100
aesthetics 4, 44, 59, 92, 154–9, 171, 191, 193, 198–200
   affirmative aesthetics 9–10, 177, 180, 187
affect 4, 21, 43, 42, 89, 93, 206–7
   affective state 75, 81, 197
   of conviction 144–6, 211
   debt of 23,
   inarticulation 48, 57
   unconscious (Freud) 40, 61 n.13
   undecidable affect 147, 210
affect-phrase 4, 5, 59, 172
   inarticulation 7, 22, 24, 67–73
   see also Lyotard, "The Affect-phrase"
afropostmodern 15, 85–6, 89–97
Algeria
   Algerian War 5, 8, 11 n.16, 56, 99–108
   FLN (Front de libération nationale) 56, 104–5, 107
   Lyotard's experience in 4, 7–8, 99–108, 112, 126
Althusser, Louis 106, 110 n.45
anamnesis 6, 51, 55–6, 58–60, 22
apathy 210–11
   see also Lyotard, "Apathy in Theory"
animal 4, 6, 29–30, 33–7, 70–3, 76, 127
   human animal 59, 70–3, 75–6, 78, 112
Aristotle 51–2, 54, 57, 157, 221
   and the affect-phrase 67, 70–2, 75, 78
Arendt, Hannah 75, 222
arms industry, 169–73
Amnesty International 6, 47, 78, 173 n.1
Anderson, Perry 112, 119, 20
Augustine of Hippo 10, 46, 102, 205, 215, 220
   see also Lyotard, *The Confession of Augustine*
Auschwitz 114, 118

Bataille, Georges 153
Beckett, Samuel 78, 151, 152, 162 n.5, 211
body, the 27–9, 87, 89, 116–18, 145, 152–4, 159
   sensations of 4, 172–3, 181–2, 185, 213–15
Butor, Michel 24, 156, 163 n.13, 205

capitalism 1, 8, 40, 51, 58, 61 n.13, 111–20, 193–200, 221
   late capitalism 126, 129
   and Socialisme ou Barbarie 101–2
Castoriadis, Cornelius 99–101
   see also Socialisme ou Barbarie
cetaceans 4, 27–37
Césaire, Aimé 86–8, 90, 92, 97 n.11
Cézanne, Paul 159, 178, 186
childhood 18–22, 58
   infans, infantia (without speech) 16, 40, 48, 72, 81
cinema 141, 152–5, 211–12
   acinema 135
class struggle 100, 103, 107
colonialism 7–8, 87–9, 92, 102, 104–6, 108, 220–1
community 39, 45–9, 75–81, 107
   exclusion from speech community 78–81
critique 1–4, 58, 85, 94, 96, 112, 149, 161
   against critique (affirmation) 177–9, 186, 196–7
   marxist critique 99–101, 103, 111

Defence and Security Equipment International (DSEI) 169–72
Deleuze, Gilles 30, 96, 178
   and Guattari, Félix 195, 202 n.57, 207,
Derrida, Jacques 85, 201 n.35, 208, 216 n.12, 221–2
desire 111, 119, 143, 145, 148, 192–3, 196, 210

development 16–20, 39–42, 55–9, 94, 112–17, 131–2, 179, 183
    see also system, the
differend, the 2, 7–8, 59, 67, 85, 89, 91, 93, 95, 222
    see also Lyotard, *The Differend*
domus, the 16–18
Duchamp, Marcel 5, 9, 153, 156–8, 180–6, 194–8
    The Bride Stripped Bare by Her Bachelors, Even (The Large Glass) 7, 156–7, 184–5
    Étant Donnés (Given) 158, 184–5

enlightenment, the 94, 100, 113–14, 127, 131, 133
epistemology 92, 113–14, 197
    episteme 126–7, 129, 131, 134, 135 n.3

Fanon, Frantz 4, 7, 85–90, 92, 97 n.3, 108
feeling
    aesthetic 68, 70, 183
    "is feeling a phrase?" 4, 67, 69–72, 172
    and passibility 49 n.1
    of uncertainty 2–3, 10, 47, 68, 120, 181, 186
    unspeakable 71; see also affect-phrase
figural, the 58, 192–3
    see also Lyotard, *Discourse, Figure*
forgetting 43, 45, 47, 58, 69, 179
    see also anamnesis
FLN, see Algeria
Foucault, Michel 85, 126, 135 n.3 and 4, 201 n.35
French Communist Party 104, 112, 209
Freud, Sigmund 9–10, 21–3, 39–40, 68–72, 141–50, 191–2, 205–7
    Beyond the Pleasure Principle 4, 141–3, 147, 149, 151, 162 n.1, 207, 210, 212
    the case of Dora 145, 210
    Civilization and its Discontents 4, 6, 149
    death drive 143–8, 191–2, 196–7, 199–200
    Project for a Scientific Psychology 39
    temporality of the unconscious 51–2, 56–7
    working through (*Durcharbeitung*) 6, 23, 44, 59–60, 115, 13
    see also affect, unconscious

Glissant, Édouard 88–90, 92–3, 96, 97 n.4

Habermas, Jürgen 131, 133–4, 220–1
Hamadeh, Rana 10, 213, 216 n.24, 217 n.25
Haraway, Donna 29, 209, 216 n.17
Hegel, Georg W. F. 126–30, 132–5, 220, 221
Heidegger, Martin 51–2, 88, 93–4, 97, 129, 180–1, 186, 220–1
Husserl, Edmund 51–3, 57, 61 n.4, 144, 186

infancy, see childhood, *infans*
inhuman, the 2, 4, 8–9, 11, 30, 33, 37, 53
    and childhood 19, 22
    and the "system" 6, 56–7, 112–13, 116–17, 119–20, 197
    and the work of art, 60, 199
    see also Lyotard, *The Inhuman*
intensities 154, 191–3, 196–9
intractable, the 2, 4–5, 45, 56
Islam 8, 102

Jameson, Fredric 55–6, 125–6, 209
jouissance 70, 192–3, 195–9
justice 17, 35, 55, 60, 77, 170, 170, 213, 220, 222
    injustice 4–5, 30, 78, 101, 113, 179

Kant, Immanuel 56, 59, 68, 70, 126, 133, 192
    Critique of Judgement 127–9, 133–4, 205
    sublime 61 n.4, 129
Klee, Paul 158
Klossowski, Pierre 148, 196
Kosuth, Joseph 194–5

Lacan, Jacques 4, 39, 201 n.35, 209
Laplanche, Jean 39–40
law, the 35, 42, 46–8, 60, 78, 80–1
Lefort, Claude 19, 54, 99
Les Immatériaux [exhibition] 2–3, 9, 125, 134, 150–3, 185–6, 199–200, 219
Levinas, Emmanuel 78, 85, 221
libidinal 8, 111–12, 148, 171, 191–2, 194–200, 206

Luhmann, Niklas 129–31, 136 n.17
Lyotard, Jean-François
  "The Affect-phrase" 5–7, 34, 67–73, 207
  "Apathy in Theory" 4–5, 9–10, 141–9, 151, 205–8, 210, 212
  Confession of Augustine, The 214
  Differend, The 6–8, 30, 53, 56, 67–8, 72, 96, 133, 169, 173, 206–10, 219–20
  Discourse, Figure 162 n.6, 193, 195
  Duchamp's TRANS/formers 183, 185
  Heidegger and "the jews" 40–3, 94
  Inhuman, The 6, 8, 61 n.5, 112, 131
  Just Gaming 53, 219
  Libidinal Economy 9, 111, 119, 185, 198, 205, 207–8
  Misère de la Philosophie 7, 52, 55, 73 n.1
  "The Other's Rights" 5–7, 33, 39, 75–81, 187 n.2
  Phenomenology 51–2, 99, 108 n.6, 162 n.6
  Political Writings / La Guerre de Algériens 99–108, 131
  Postmodern Condition, The 1, 6, 8, 125–33, 200, 207, 209, 212, 219
  Postmodern Explained, The 20, 114
  Postmodern Fables, The 4, 21, 27, 34, 62 n.17, 172; *see also* zone, the
  Rudiments païens (Pagan Rudiments) 9, 205–7, 212, 216 n.3

Malraux, André 24
Marin, Louis 8, 56, 205
Marx, Karl 58–9, 99, 111–12, 126, 128, 209
Marxism 8, 51, 55, 59, 100–5, 112–14, 120, 125, 131–2
  Lyotard's approach to 3–4, 62 n.34, 99–103, 106–7, 111, 127, 192, 207
may 1968 56, 93–4, 161, 163 n.17, 201 n.35
Mbembe, Achille 206
memory, *see* anamnesis, forgetting
Merleau-Ponty, Maurice 102, 106, 151–2, 162 n.6, 186
metanarrative 1, 5, 7–8, 86–93, 96, 111, 113–15, 118, 127–9, 219, 221–2
Monory, Jacques 9, 182, 198–9

négritude 87, 91–2
Nelson, Maggie 9
Newman, Barnett 52, 60, 61 n.5, 63 n.45, 134
Nietzsche, Friedrich 112, 178, 181, 219–20
North Atlantic right whale, the 4, 6, 27–32, 34–6

Offeh, Harold 1, 211
Orwell, Georges, *Nineteen-Eighty-Four* 19, 179
Osborne, Peter 193–200
  postconceptual art 191, 193–7, 200

paganism (Lyotard) 111, 206, 208
paralogy 8–9, 127–8, 132–5, 135 n.7
pedagogy 5–6, 15, 17–19, 25, 160
performativity 6, 17, 43–4, 112, 120, 129–30
phenomenology 52–3, 86, 99–100
phōnē (voice) 22–4, 59, 70–3
phrases 5, 24, 53–4, 57, 61 n.4, 67–9, 71–3
  see also Lyotard, *The Differend*; Lyotard, "The Affect-phrase"
Pomarède, Alain (*Art Présent*) 4, 151–62, 212
postmodern, the
  and the afropostmodern 85–6, 93–6
  postmodern condition 55, 58, 115, 118, 120, 129–33, 187
  postmodernity 118, 180, 182
  and the "thing" 45
  understandings of 7–8, 56, 80, 88, 93–7, 125–6, 134–5, 209
  see also Lyotard, *The Postmodern Condition*
Pouvoir Ouvrier 99–100, 107, 111

Rancière, Jacques 9, 134, 177, 179, 187
resistance
  aesthetic 18–19, 44–5, 179, 181
  political 48, 58–9, 96, 102–3, 117, 126–7, 178–9
  psychological 6, 18–19, 56, 58, 179, 222
rights 6, 10 n.2, 29–30, 33–7, 39, 45–7, 206
  see also Lyotard, "The Other's Rights"

Sade, D.A.F. de 148–9, 153, 159
Sartre, Jean-Paul 87, 107

Snow, Michael, *Wavelength* 154
Socialisme ou Barbarie (SouB) 4, 8, 59, 62 n.17, 99–105, 111–12, 127
sophists 183–6
Souyri, Pierre 99–102
Stiegler, Bernard 9, 133 n.1, 178–9, 186–7
sublime, the
   in Burke 80
   in Kant 129, 133–4
   for Lyotard 133–4, 19
   negative 93
   of technoscience 119–20
system, the
   inhumanity of 6, 42, 57, 112
   in Luhmann 130; *see also* Luhmann
   resistance to 5, 8, 19, 42, 44–5, 58, 132–4, 191
   totalizing development of 17, 40–1, 43, 59, 112, 127–9, 131

technology 1–2, 9, 88, 118, 126–30, 135, 171, 179–80, 186–7, 199–200
"thing," the 2, 4, 6, 39–49, 56, 59–60, 72, 179
time (temporalities)
   in cinematic practice 5, 152–4
   in Duchamp 157–8
   in Freud 6, 57, 144, 147
   Husserl's approach 52–3
   Lyotard's approach 51–60, 69–70, 72, 180–2, 222; *see also* anamnesis
   parachronicity 6, 56–9

Vega, Amparo 2, 10 n.6
Vincennes (University of Paris VIII) 160, 163 n.16

Walcott, Derek 88–92, 96, 97 n.9
Writing
   against history 90–1; *see also* Walcott
   Freud's speculative 4, 9, 207, 210; *see also* Lyotard "Apathy in Theory"
   Lyotard on 19–21, 58,
      hearing and listening 21–4
      male and "feminine" 206
      and materiality 195
      and resistance 19, 179
      as re-writing 23
      and the "thing" 45, 59–60
   Lyotard's 1, 5, 15, 207–8, 214–15, 220
Wittgenstein, Ludwig 53, 61 n.4, 133, 160, 210

Yemen, the war in 169–71, 173 n.1

Zeno of Elea 152
zone, the 5–6, 16–19, 23–5, 206

www.ingramcontent.com/pod-product-compliance
Lightning Source LLC
Chambersburg PA
CBHW062142300426
44115CB00012BA/2008